CALIFORNIA SLAVIC STUDIES

CALIFORNIA SLAVIC STUDIES

Volume VI

GUEST EDITORS

ROBERT P. HUGHES
SIMON KARLINSKY
VLADIMIR MARKOV

UNIVERSITY OF CALIFORNIA PRESS
BERKELEY · LOS ANGELES · LONDON   1971

CALIFORNIA SLAVIC STUDIES
Volume 6

UNIVERSITY OF CALIFORNIA PRESS
BERKELEY AND LOS ANGELES, CALIFORNIA
UNIVERSITY OF CALIFORNIA PRESS, LTD.
LONDON, ENGLAND

ISBN: 0-520-09358-5
LIBRARY OF CONGRESS CATALOG CARD No.: 61-1041
© 1971 BY THE REGENTS OF THE UNIVERSITY OF CALIFORNIA

CONTENTS

Introduction vii

I. NINETEENTH-CENTURY AUTHORS AND WORKS

The Tone(s) of *Evgenij Onegin* 3
    HUGH MCLEAN

The Architecture of Love in Gogol''s "Rome" 17
    LOUIS PEDROTTI

The Ludicrous Man-of-the-Family: A Recurrent Type in Dostoevskij   29
    OLEG A. MASLENIKOV

II. TWENTIETH-CENTURY AUTHORS AND WORKS

POETRY

The Drum Lines in Majakovskij's "150 000 000" 39
    ROMAN JAKOBSON

Mandel'štam's Monument Not Wrought by Hands 43
    KIRIL TARANOVSKY

Nothung, the Cassia Flower, and a "Spirit of Music" in the Poetry of
   Aleksandr Blok 49
    ROBERT P. HUGHES

Symphonic Structure in Andrej Belyj's "Pervoe svidanie" . . . 61
    SIMON KARLINSKY

PROSE

Remizov's *Prud*: From Symbolism to Neo-Realism 71
    ALEX M. SHANE

Mixail Zoščenko and the Problem of *Skaz* 83
    I. R. TITUNIK

The Role of Nature in *The Quiet Don* 97
    HERMAN ERMOLAEV

Solženicyn and the Legacy of Tolstoj 113
    KATHRYN B. FEUER

III. GENERAL STUDIES

Toward a Normative Definition of Russian Realism 131
    JOHN MERSEREAU, JR.

Expressionism in Russia 145
    VLADIMIR MARKOV

Nieborów, the *Kuźnica* Program, and the Role of the Young in the Stalinization of Polish Literature 161
    LAWRENCE L. THOMAS

On Modern Russian Literature and the West 171
    CZESŁAW MIŁOSZ

INTRODUCTION

THIS SPECIAL issue of *California Slavic Studies* contains essays by American Slavic scholars from several generations. In a way the group of contributors to this volume suggests at least a partial outline of the growth of Russian literary studies as it occurred in the last quarter of a century in the United States. A major impetus to this development was provided by the arrival in this country of Russian-born scholars who were trained in Europe and who brought into Slavic studies on this continent their imagination, knowledge, and experience.

These outstanding teachers from abroad, men like Gleb Struve, Roman Jakobson, and, later, Kiril Taranovsky, joined American colleagues like Oleg Maslenikov in instructing and inspiring succeeding generations of literary scholars now active in institutions of higher learning. Hugh McLean, Louis Pedrotti, John Mersereau, Jr., and Kathryn Feuer, to continue to mention only those who are participating in this volume, were among the first beneficiaries of their training and guidance. At the University of California since 1947, Professor Gleb Struve has had a distinguished teaching career and has directed, among others, the dissertations of the following contributors to the present collection: Herman Ermolaev, Irwin Titunik, Alex M. Shane, and the three editors. The strong tradition of combined Polish and Russian literary studies that Gleb Struve and the late Wacław Lednicki upheld at Berkeley is continued and represented here by the papers of Czesław Miłosz and Lawrence L. Thomas.

Not only the list of contributors, but the topics of the studies included in this volume reflect the manifold interests and scholarly pursuits of Professor Struve. Papers on acknowledged classics of Russian nineteenth-century literature, such as Puškin, Gogol', and Dostoevskij, are supplemented by an even greater number on twentieth-century poetry and prose. There are articles on writers recognized and studied in the Soviet Union—Blok, Majakovskij, Šoloxov—but, characteristically, writers and trends not given their due in their own country are also represented: Russian Expressionism, Belyj, Mandel'štam, Remizov, Zoščenko, and Solženicyn.

The inclusion of important but neglected writers reflects the particular merit of Gleb Struve's work in redressing literary inequities and reaffirming literary reputations. This concern permeates both his highly regarded books and essays on Soviet and émigré literature and his much-admired editions of major twentieth-century Russian poets: Mandel'štam, Pasternak, Cvetaeva, Axmatova, and Gumilev, among others.

It is therefore fitting that this volume be dedicated to our illustrious colleague and friend, Gleb Struve, distinguished teacher, scholar, and editor, and one of the founders of *California Slavic Studies*.

NINETEENTH-CENTURY AUTHORS AND WORKS

THE TONE(S) OF *EVGENIJ ONEGIN*

BY

HUGH McLEAN

IN 1832 EVGENIJ BARATYNSKIJ, furtively and with many admonitions concerning the necessity of secrecy, delivered himself of the following diatribe in a letter to Ivan Kireevskij. The reasons for the furtiveness were probably both emotional and tactical: fear of offending Puškin, if he should somehow get wind of his friend's unexpected "treachery"; feelings of guilt or shame about what might appear an all too obvious display of literary cattiness, jealousy, and disloyalty; and unwillingness to provide any ammunition for the Bulgarin camp, which was then engaged in a vicious and bitter campaign against Puškin and the whole circle of "aristocratic" poets. In any case, the judgment was a harsh one:

Have you read the eighth chapter of *Onegin*, and what do you think about it and in general about *Onegin*, which Puškin has now finished? I have felt differently about it at different times. Sometimes *Onegin* has seemed to me Puškin's best work, sometimes the opposite. If everything in *Onegin* were Puškin's own, it would undoubtedly vouch for the writer's genius. But the form belongs to Byron, *the tone too*. Many poetic details are borrowed from somebody or other. The only things in *Onegin* that are Puškin's own are the personalities of his characters and the local descriptions of Russia. The characters are pale. Onegin is not profoundly developed. Tat'jana has nothing special about her. Lenskij is insignificant. The local descriptions are beautiful, but only where there is pure plasticity. There is nothing that would decisively characterize our Russian way of life. In general, this work bears the mark of a first attempt, although of a man of great talent.[1]

We need not, of course, agree with Baratynskij's invidious judgment (actually, as the letter itself indicates, not all of Baratynskij's assessments of Puškin's novel were so categorically negative as this one). It may, however, be salutary for us, in approaching on tiptoe (as we usually do) the hallowed precincts of the classics, to be reminded that in their own day these classics were by no means instantly recognized as such or viewed with the automatic reverence we now feel obliged to bestow on such a towering, unassailable monument of Russian literature as *Evgenij Onegin*. Baratynskij's letter shows that at the time of its publication, judgments very unenthusiastic, to say the least, concerning Puškin's masterpiece could be pronounced not only by philistines, but by a man of unimpeachable literary sophistication and taste, who was himself a first-rate poet.

This paper is based on a lecture delivered at the University of Texas in March, 1968.
[1] Quoted from A. S. Dolinin, ed., *Russkie pisateli XIX veka o Puškine* (Leningrad, 1938), pp. 64–65. Italics mine.

Baratynskij's opinion may be utterly mistaken—I think it is—but it may nevertheless have a kind of therapeutic value for us: it may help to freshen our own response to the work, to liberate us from the clichés of thought and attitude loaded onto *Evgenij Onegin* during the past hundred and forty-odd years. There is nothing more tiresome, or more likely to kill a work of art for any naturally independent and rebellious person, than to be told in solemn tones that he must dutifully genuflect before it as an established classic.

I would like to focus attention here on a single word from Baratynskij's heretical pronouncement, the word *ton* ("tone"), not, at least initially, with the aim of defending Puškin against Baratynskij's charge that the "tone" of *Evgenij Onegin* is wholly derivative from Byron, nor of concurring in it, but simply in an effort to define and specify this rather elusive critical category. What is "tone" in literature, and what is the specific "tone" of *Evgenij Onegin*?

Used in this sense, as a category of literary criticism, the word "tone" is, of course, essentially a metaphor. The literal meaning, applicable only to music, is metaphorically extended to other forms of art and beyond art into life itself. Not only may a work of literature have "tone": so may a way of life. *Evgenij Onegin* itself contains examples of this latter usage, for instance in stanza 42 of chapter 1, where Puškin, inveighing against the stuffiness of virtuous society ladies, exclaims, *Dovol'no skučen vysšij ton* ("The high-society tone is pretty tiresome"). Here "tone" indicates a whole style of life, a stance, a posture, an outward "image" one seeks to create which does not necessarily correspond to the inner world of feeling (perhaps it is this artificiality that makes it "tiresome").

In his critical writings, although not in *Evgenij Onegin* itself, Puškin also uses the word *ton* in its specifically literary sense, meaning, according to the *Slovar' jazyka Puškina*, "emotional shading, expressivity of diction" (*èmocional'nyj ottenok, vyrazitel'nost' rěči*). One of the most illuminating examples of Puškin's use of the word *ton* in this literary sense occurs, by a neat coincidence, in one of his several unfinished articles on Baratynskij himself. Speaking of Baratynskij's poem *Bal*, Puškin says: "Poèt s udivitel'nym iskusstvom soedinil v bystrom rasskaze *ton* šutlivyj i strastnyj, metafiziku i poèziju" ("With amazing art the poet has combined in a swift-moving narrative a jocular and a passionate *tone*, metaphysics and poetry").[2] However accurate or inaccurate they may be concerning their ostensible subject, the remarks poets make about other poets often

---

[2] Quoted from *Puškin o literature*, ed. N. V. Bogoslovskij (Moscow, 1934), p. 154. Italics mine.

provide revealing clues to their own aspirations for their own poems; and surely this statement about *Bal* could be applied, with perhaps even greater appropriateness, to *Evgenij Onegin* itself. *Šutlivyj i strastnyj*, jocular and passionate: certainly these adjectives would be acceptable as qualifiers of *Evgenij Onegin's* "tone," and perhaps we could add some others as well—"lyrical," a sticky, but indispensable word; perhaps "epic"; and, most crucial and most elusive of all, "ironic."

What is particularly notable about this sequence of adjectives modifying the substantive "tone"—both Puškin's own and those I have added—is their disharmony, their contradictoriness. The emotions they denote seem to be incompatible. How can you be at once jocular and passionate, lyrical and ironic? Would not such an unlikely combination of chemical opposites mixed together in a single literary vessel produce either an explosion or a tasteless fizzle? How can such antagonistic ingredients be held in dynamic suspension without neutralizing one another?

These questions are difficult ones, and perhaps in the last analysis unanswerable: they point toward the ultimate riddle of the magic integrity of a great work of art; and no amount of analysis, literary, chemical, or otherwise, can ever provide us with its exact formula. But we have to try! Otherwise there would be little sense in talking *about* literature at all. Even if we cannot arrive at any precise and reproducible formula, we can perhaps help to explain some aspects of that mysterious integrity.

First, I would like to dispose of an ancillary question, the one raised by Baratynskij with his charge that the tone of *Evgenij Onegin* was wholly derivative from Byron. This is the characteristically nineteenth-century genealogical or "diachronic" question, so much beloved by literary historians, Ph.D. examiners, and, as we see, even by poets: not "What is it?", but "Where did it come from?" Fascinating as this question is, it is in some sense an evasion of the central issue here, the synchronic and descriptive problem of defining what the term "tone" means as applied to literature in general and to *Evgenij Onegin* in particular. It is a side-track, and I shall try to avoid being switched off onto it for long. If Puškin (or Baratynskij) was not the first poet so ostentatiously to juxtapose utterly disharmonious "tones" in a single work of art, where did they get the idea of doing such a thing? Was it indeed from Byron, who, in *Don Juan* especially (and Baratynskij was undoubtedly referring to this work) does combine, or at least alternate, a jocular with a passionate, a lyrical with an ironic, tone? Or, as Viktor Šklovskij has suggested, does it go back, perhaps via Byron or perhaps directly, to Laurence Sterne, whose *Sentimental Journey* is surely one of the most extraordinary mixes in all world literature of intense feeling, lyric and passionate par excellence, with the most irreverent and anti-lyrical clowning?[3] Or perhaps from a host of other models?

Certainly Baratynskij's accusation of wholesale dependence on Byron could be disputed, if only by the fact that *Ruslan i Ljudmila*, which Puškin wrote before he knew anything of Byron at all, can also be said to combine, in a manner not unlike that of *Evgenij Onegin*, a jocular and a passionate tone. And the ancestors of *Ruslan i Ljudmila* have been traced back through a long tradition of eighteenth-century mock epics, including Voltaire's *Pucelle d'Orléans*, Gresset's *Vert-Vert*, Pope's *Rape of the Lock*, Bogdanovič's *Dušen'ka*, and many others, all the way back to antiquity and the *Battle of the Mice and the Frogs*.

These questions of genealogy, however, have already been studied in detail by pleiads of scholars. I prefer instead to deal with the more intrinsic problems of *how* a poet (or, in this case, a poet-novelist) can combine such seemingly incompatible tonal ingredients as jocularity and passion, lyricism and irony; and *why* he should choose to do so.

To answer at all fully the question of *how* Puškin accomplishes this combination in *Evgenij Onegin* would require an exhaustive analysis of such elements of the novel as point of view, structure, and style, which would fill a large volume. Here I can only suggest a few basic features.

First of all, it appears that one of the determinants of tone is the "point of view," the angle of vision from which we perceive the action and characters of the novel. In *Evgenij Onegin* we do not see the characters "directly," as we would see them in a classic novel from the epoch of high realism, for instance *Anna Karenina* (a novel which, incidentally, might be taken as an attempt to explore, from a very different "point of view" and in a very different "tone," an alternative ending for *Evgenij Onegin*: what would have happened if Tat'jana had made the opposite decision, disdained her marriage vows, and ventured upon an adulterous love affair with her Byronic adorer?). In Tolstoj's novel, the characters stand immediately before us, endowed with the illusion of "reality," of being live people who "really" existed and whose experiences "really" occurred. The essence of Tolstoj's realistic art is to give us the illusion as we read that we are experiencing life directly, to make us forget the very printed page before us. When Anna dies beneath the train, we feel that she dies because she really died in this way: this was her fate, the outcome of her character and her tragic circumstances. Her death does not strike us as

---

[3] Viktor Šklovskij, "*Evgenij Onegin* (Puškin i Stern)," *Očerki po poètike Puškina* (Berlin, 1923).

one of several possible alternative endings selected by Tolstoj for an artificial construct called a novel.

In *Evgenij Onegin*, on the other hand, we see the characters only through the eyes of a narrator interposed between us and them. This narrator, however, is not of the kind familiar in realistic fiction, where narrators, though they may fulfill other important functions as well, ordinarily serve to limit the angle of vision to the narrative plane itself. In Turgenev's *Sportsman's Sketches*, for instance, or in *David Copperfield*, the illusion of reality is enhanced by the fact that we always see the action only through the eyes of a participant in it. Furthermore, the "discovery" by a narrator either of the events themselves or of their meaning can be used to "motivate" the implementation of the plot, to provide a logical explanation for the *sjužet*, the sequence in which events are recounted. In realistic fiction narrators may range from the maximum participation of an "autobiographical" novel like *David Copperfield* to the totally self-abnegating voyeurism of the nameless narrator of *The Brothers Karamazov*; but in any case they clearly belong to the same order of being, exist on the same plane of reality, as the characters about whom they speak. In brief, they are themselves characters.

The narrator of *Evgenij Onegin*, however, does not quite fit this pattern. For one thing, he is not very securely anchored to the novel's plane of fictional reality: he keeps escaping into the real world. He is a somewhat stylized figure, to be sure; but at certain crucial points in his factual biography and in his personality he is demonstrably identifiable with the author himself, with Aleksandr Sergeevič Puškin. Moreover, this identification is not merely one to be demonstrated by scholars, guessed at by astute readers, or assumed by naïve ones; it belongs to the texture of the novel itself. After noting the vital fact of Evgenij's birth in Petersburg and observing that his readers may likewise have "shone" in that illustrious capital, Puškin's narrator adds on his own account:

> Там некогда гулял и я
> Но вреден север для меня.

And at this point the author appends a footnote, "Written in Bessarabia," which was in fact quite true and for Puškin's contemporaries immediately evoked the whole story of his prolonged "southern exile." Thus from the very outset an intentional crossing of strands is made part of the very fabric of the poem—a deliberate confusion of Dichtung with Wahrheit, of a fictional narrator, a friend of the novel's fictional heroes, with the real author.

This author-narrator not only continually interposes his own associations, reflections, reminiscences, and comments between us and the characters—the famous digressions, many of which are "real" in a sense that no fictional character, however "realistic," can ever be—but he periodically reminds us that the characters in the novel are after all only his inventions. He may playfully cause the planes of reality and fiction to intersect by claiming a "real" friendship with his fictional creature, Evgenij Onegin, or by having his real friend Vjazemskij, at a Moscow ball, encounter and entertain his imaginary offspring, Tat'jana. Yet this very game only underscores the fact—a fact Tolstoj used every means at his command to conceal—that he, Puškin, is a real man, while Evgenij and Tat'jana are his imaginary creations.[4]

---

[4] See the brilliant and discerning discussion of this question by Leon Stilman, "Problemy literaturnyx žanrov i tradicij v *Evgenii Onegine* Puškina: k voprosu perexoda ot romantizma k realizmu," *American Contributions to the Fourth International Congress of Slavicists* (The Hague, 1958), pp. 321–366. F. D. Reeve, in *The Russian Novel* (New York, 1966), p. 22, has attacked Stilman (without naming him) for separating *Evgenij Onegin* from "realism" on the grounds that Puškin repeatedly and ostentatiously breaks the illusion of fictional reality, aggressively asserting the literariness of his novel. Reeve flatly denies Stilman's statement that "the method of realism ... precludes anything that might remind the reader that he is dealing with a poetic invention" (Stilman, p. 330), arguing that there is "quick agreement among readers that *Don Quixote*, *The Karamazov Brothers*, and *War and Peace* are realistic novels" (Reeve, p. 22), even though Cervantes's narrative is interrupted by poems and stories, *War and Peace* by historico-philosophical argument, and *The Brothers Karamazov* by Ivan's "poem."

It is not very rewarding to try to thread one's way through all of Reeve's confusions and mistakes, but the last example alone is sufficient to demonstrate that Reeve has not grasped Stilman's point at all. To take the case of Dostoevskij alone: the "Legend of the Grand Inquisitor" is solidly and firmly grounded on the plane of fictional reality, in no sense destroying its illusion: on that plane, it is a perfectly plausible product of the character who "wrote" it, with no suggestion that it is the author's invention. Its introduction is adequately motivated as Ivan's self-revelation to Alëša; and this revelation not only epitomizes the fundamental philosophical issues at stake in the novel, but is admirably integrated into the plot, since it helps explain Ivan's complicity in his father's murder. It would be unthinkable (i.e., unrealistic) for Dostoevskij, speaking qua author after the termination of Ivan's "poem," to insert, for instance, a discussion of his own real models and antecedents for the fictitious Ivan's legend—to include in the novel, for example, something like Dmitrij Čiževskij's famous articles on Schiller in *The Brothers Karamazov*. Or for Dostoevskij to discuss with the reader what alternative fates he might have assigned his characters: he is indeed a realist.

Reeve's argument consists of setting his own quite arbitrary definition of "realism" and then showing that *Evgenij Onegin* fits this definition. The question is too involved to be argued further here. I would only suggest that at the bottom of Reeve's confusion is the common misunderstanding that only "realistic" art can deal meaningfully with reality, with real life; thus non-realists become either phantasts or simply liars—a misunderstanding that Reeve has the honor of sharing with Tolstoj and many others, as Tolstoj's denunciations of Shakespeare and Wagner demonstrate. Soviet scholars have helped perpetuate this mistake by their insistence that realism

He, Puškin, is the god who not only gave them life, but by divine fiat determined every step in their fates. Before the visions in his "magic crystal" became clarified in the course of his work on his "free novel," he, the author, was free to alter their destinies at will. Thus it was he, the author, who killed Vladimir Lenskij, and not Evgenij Onegin, as the author indirectly confesses by presenting to us a series of alternative destinies that might have been assigned to Lenskij had the author not condemned him to perish in the snow on that fateful morning. Lenskij's poetic talent, snuffed out so prematurely, might have resounded down the ages, bringing to his name the adulation of posterity, the gratitude of future generations; or, more prosaically, "realistically," and doubtless more probably, he might have laid aside his lyre with his youth, settled down on a country estate, and lived out the life of an ordinary Russian gentleman—cuckolded by his wife, suffering from gout at forty, and finally dying in his bed, surrounded by children, weepy women, and doctors.

The paradox here, of course, is that despite the fact that Puškin so ostentatiously murders his characters, not only fictionally, as in Lenskij's case, by causing him to die on the duelling-ground, but literarily, by denying the illusion of their reality—despite this fact, the characters refuse to die. The illusion created is so powerful that they have continued to live despite their creator's efforts to destroy them. They have lived in the minds and hearts of millions of readers for nearly a century and a half now, and they show no signs of decrepitude. Indeed, they seem to have attained, insofar as any human artifact can claim to have attained it, a state of immortality. Even Lenskij refuses to lie there in the snow. Again and again he rises up before us to sing his Schillerian (or Žukovskian) songs, to adore his adorable Ol'ga, and to defend her honor, or rather his own, by calling out his cynical and frivolous friend and insisting that he pay the price for his irresponsible flirtation with another man's sweetheart.

By denying his characters' reality, however, Puškin achieves an important artistic effect: he marks off and enforces an emotional distance between his readers and his characters. We cannot, to use the current barbarism, wholeheartedly identify with characters presented in the way Puškin presents them. We must keep our distance. We are constantly being reminded, either directly or indirectly, of the fictionality of these characters, and after all, it's rather silly to get excited about the lives of people who never existed. Moreover, these very reminders are an important

---

is a kind of ultimate stage in the "progress" of art. It is time to be more realistic about realism.

formative ingredient of the novel's "tone"; and the characters must live in an atmosphere dominated by this tone. It is not a lethal or even a particularly hostile atmosphere: at times the author (narrator) may be affectionate and even admiring in his remarks about his characters. But just as often he is jocular or ironic; and surely the most ironic of ironies an author can inflict upon his characters is to remind them constantly of their nonexistence.

This epistemological irony, so to speak, is only the most devastating of the many ironies the author inflicts on his hapless creatures. Even on the fictional plane, the atmosphere is heavily charged with irony and mockery, and in it the characters' pretensions, their pomposities, their self-inflating fantasies cannot survive. Their masks are dissolved, and we are forced to see the "natural humanity" that lies beneath them, sometimes attractive, sometimes even noble, but more often weak, shallow, thoughtless, or deluded.

Some characters withstand this irony better than others. The hero, Evgenij Onegin, probably fares worst of all. The first words he utters in the novel—in fact, the first words anyone utters—are that famous first stanza which everyone knows by heart. Its wit and verbal elegance are so captivating that some readers perhaps do not notice that the emotional content is really rather unpleasant: a young man is callously and sneeringly complaining about how tedious it will be for him to have to sit by the bedside and "adjust the pillows" of the dying uncle whose fortune he looks forward to inheriting. Not only does he regard this prospect with weary and petulant disdain; but by an adroit manipulation of a quotation from Krylov, he manages, without actually naming the animal at all, to associate his relative and benefactor with an ass.

In the following stanza the author labels the hero of his novel a *molodoj povesa*, a "young rake"—a term also fraught with emotional as well as moral ambiguities. He then proceeds to a flashback summary of Evgenij's origins and education and from there to a detailed account of "one day" in his life as a Petersburg dandy, after which both he and the milieu he represents are considerably the worse for wear.

Correspondingly, our last view of Evgenij Onegin is at that especially "evil minute" in his life: Tat'jana has announced that although she loves him still, she will remain true to her husband forever; she has just swept out of the room, leaving Evgenij in tears, morally and spiritually demolished. At this point the jingling of spurs heralds the appearance of Tat'jana's husband. It is indeed an "evil minute" for Evgenij, to say the least, and to take leave of him at such a moment, as Puškin does, is almost an act of cruelty or *Schadenfreude* on the author's part. This leave-taking is in fact a kind of built-in structural irony, which Puškin immediately underscores by pointing it out, "laying it bare," to use the Formalists' vivid phrase. Evgenij Onegin is not only abandoned forever in this most unpleasant predicament, but he is, so to speak, forcibly pushed back into non-being, into fictionality, when the author takes leave of him *as a character*, as his creature, and then of the work itself, in that final brilliant digression. (It is true that in the novel as now printed Evgenij is in fact allowed to escape from his discomfiture and take off on, if not complete, his "Journey," finally disappearing in a cloud of Odessa dust. But the escape is illusory, since it is clear, if only from the author's preface to the "Journey," that Onegin's travels, according to the original fictional calendar, the *fabula*, preceded the final encounter with Tat'jana in Petersburg.)

Tat'jana, it is true, fares somewhat better at the author's ironic hands than her male counterpart. The author is not only chivalrous toward her, he loves her:

... Я так люблю
Татьяну милую мою!

The epithet *milaja*, "dear, sweet," is applied to her repeatedly. Yet even Tat'jana is not wholly spared the author's irony. Her sentimental education had been made up of the "seductive deceptions," as Puškin calls them, of Richardson, Rousseau, Goethe's *Werther*, not to mention their female imitators, Mme Cottin, Mme de Krüdener, and Mme de Staël. The result of this education, in Tat'jana, was a disastrously unrealistic view of the human condition, a fatal naïveté. Her mind filled with these souped-up fantasies and her heart yearning for a prince charming more charming than any of the provincial bucks she was exposed to, Tat'jana is disproportionately dazzled by the elegance, the hauteur, and the world-weariness of Onegin. She immediately jumps to the conclusion that his is the heart destined by Heaven, in its loftiest councils, to be joined with hers. Being a bold and passionate girl, she takes the bold, but very unwise step—even bolder and unwiser in that day than it would be in this—of announcing this discovery in a secret letter to Onegin himself, that famous letter, so beautiful and yet so silly. (Tat'jana had seen Evgenij only once before, and that in a very conventional social gathering; she really had no idea what sort of man he was.)

Perhaps the most remarkable thing about Tat'jana's letter is that Puškin manages to convey so clearly both its beauty and its silliness: this young heart aching for love, touchingly pouring out its passion and yearning in a letter to a man who for her is at this point not a real person at all, but a screen on which she projects her composite literary and erotic fantasies. But in the letter itself, just as in Onegin's callous complaint about his uncle's fatal illness, the beauty and elegance of the style—in this case, of Puškin's translation from Tat'jana's French[5]—have perhaps blinded some readers to the fact that in content, for all its touching sincerity, the letter is a tissue of clichés from beginning to end, like most love letters, alas. Thus a kind of structural irony—Tat'jana's later misery is brought on by her own foolishness—is echoed by an irony of style, a collection of inflated literary commonplaces hiding behind the brilliance of Puškin's iambics.

In the course of the action, it is true, Tat'jana is allowed to grow and to reach a higher level of maturity than her male opposite ever achieves. In her final appearances as a Petersburg grande dame she seems to escape from the author's irony altogether. He seems to be as dazzled by her as Onegin himself. In any case, Tat'jana's counter-rejection of Evgenij's proffered love not only satisfies the multiple demands of poetic justice, structural balance and symmetry, and also conventional morality; it is a mark of Tat'jana's maturity, of her hard-won wisdom. During her solitary research project in Onegin's library she had gained considerable insight into his character, enough to convince her that a love affair with such a man was not likely to bring her much happiness.

Furthermore, by the time she has reached chapter 8, Tat'jana understands, as Puškin does and Onegin does not, that we must face our life as it is in the present, that the past is over and done with and cannot be recaptured (except, perhaps, in art). As is shown by the symbolic progression of the seasons in the novel, nature, and our human species with it, may undergo eternal renewal, the winter's death being followed by the spring's resurrection, the rising generation crowding out the old. But the individual man is not eternally renewed: he is born, lives, and dies but once. This is, no doubt, an unpleasant fact—indeed, the most unpleasant fact of all, the one we would most of all like to deny or wish away. But it is a fact nonetheless. If we accept it as gracefully as we can, living in the full consciousness that we shall never live this moment again, and approaching each season of life with the spirit, the feelings, and the expectations appropriate to it, we will get more satisfaction out of it. This, I suppose, is the "message," the moral of *Evgenij Onegin*, if we care to look for one, the true "wisdom of Puškin."

---

[5] Professor Stilman's article has reminded me that Puškin's claim to have translated Tat'jana's letter is more than simply another example of Puškinian anti-illusionistic (non-realistic) playfulness. As Sipovskij showed long ago, it actually does resemble one of Julie's letters in *La nouvelle Héloïse*. Cf. V. V. Sipovskij, *Puškin; žizn' i tvorčestvo* (St. Petersburg, 1907), p. 584.

Such wisdom, however, can be swallowed only in small doses. Furthermore, the delicate structure of the novel might crack if overloaded with ponderous philosophizing. Therefore, when he articulates the point directly, as he does in stanza 10 of chapter 8, Puškin masks even his own wisdom with irony. He affects to eulogize not the mature acceptance of passing years, but rather the acquisition of worldly wisdom in its worst sense— the shedding of youthful passion and idealism in favor of a cold and conventional careerism:

> Блажен, кто с молоду был молод,
> Блажен, кто во-время созрел,
> Кто постепенно жизни холод
> С летами вытерпеть умел;
> [So far so good; but now the irony creeps in.]
> Кто странным снам не предавался,
> Кто черни светской не чуждался,
> Кто в двадцать лет был франт иль хват,
> А в тридцать выгодно женат;
> Кто в пятьдесят освободился
> От частных и других долгов,
> Кто славы, денег и чинов
> Спокойно в очередь добился,
> О ком твердили целый век:
> N.N. прекрасный человек.

To summarize our conclusions thus far. By means of a variety of techniques, both structural and stylistic, Puškin has imposed upon us a complex attitude toward his characters, including not only empathy with their emotions, sharing of their joys and sorrows, but an acute awareness of their weaknesses, their folly, their self-delusions, and even of their fictionality. This complex attitude is the intellectual counterpart, in both author and reader, of the complexity of tone, that mixture of jocularity and lyricism, that is such a striking feature of the novel itself.

I turn now to the second question posed earlier, *why* does Puškin choose to tune his novel to this particular key, to give it a tone at once "jocular and passionate," lyrical and ironic? The answer, I think, is that no matter what literary conventions he may have been following and no matter what his models may have been, this combination of contradictory tonalities suited him. In some way it harmonized with his own nature, and he made it very much his own. It suited him because it expressed a vision of life, a philosophy, an attitude toward the world and toward human experience that appealed to him. It was his own existential stance, one he maintained to a remarkable degree in his own life.

To put it very mechanically, the essence of the Puškinian ethos is to operate both the mind and the heart at maximum capacity and maintain them in perfect balance. It is the commitment and the willingness to live intensely, fully, passionately, feeling your pulse throb every time you hold a girl's foot in your hands as you help her mount a horse. The Puškinian irony leads to no repudiation of life, no cynical disengagement, no "alienation," to use the currently popular term, no mocking from a safe distance (as Gogol' did) at the absurdities and follies of one's fellow men. On the contrary, one of the principal functions of the lyric digressions in *Evgenij Onegin*, it seems to me, is precisely to set us straight on this point. The author may expose his characters to some pretty corrosive irony, but he wants to make it clear that he—and we—are in the same soup, or, to use his figure, the same pond:

> В сем омуте, где с вами я
> Купаюсь, милые друзья.

For the author, as for his characters, the seasons are passing, and life with them:

> Ужель и впрям, и в самом деле,
> Без элегических затей,
> Весна моих промчалась дней
> (Что я шутя твердил доселе)?
> И ей ужель возврата нет?
> Ужель мне скоро тридцать лет?

The author, too, must try to face manfully the loss of his youth and the onset of middle age. There is no use pretending he is happy about it. His youth was fun, and he is sad to see it pass. But pass it must, and he is ready:

> Я насладился, и вполне;
> Довольно! С ясною душой
> Пускаюсь ныне в новый путь
> От жизни прошлой отдохнуть.

Thus the lyric dimension of *Evgenij Onegin*, on which Professor Lo Gatto has laid so much stress[6], is certainly a crucial one; it is an emblem of the

---

[6] Ettore Lo Gatto, "L'*Onegin* come 'diario lirico' di Puškin," in *Analecta Slavica: A Slavonic Miscellany* (Amsterdam, 1955); "Sull' elemento lirico-autobiografico nell'*Evgenij Onegin* di Puškin," *Studies in Russian and Polish Literature in Honor of Wacław Lednicki* (The Hague, 1962), pp. 105–113; *Puškin: storia di un poeta e del suo eroe* (Milan, 1959). I also found very stimulating the discussion of Professor Lo Gatto's position by Stanley Mitchell: "The Digressions of *Yevgeny Onegin*: Apropos of Some Essays by Ettore Lo Gatto," *Slavonic and East European Review* (January, 1966), pp. 51–65.

author's common humanity both with us and with his characters. For Puškin it would have seemed pompous to pretend, as the realistic novelists did later in the century, that his characters really existed and the author not at all, so that the author could hide, like God, behind the scenes, omniscient and omnipotent, rewarding, punishing, and judging as he pleased. Puškin's sense of relativity required him to inject into the work itself his constant awareness that literature is, after all, only a game of make-believe through which we express and articulate our thoughts and feelings about life. It is not life itself.

On the other hand, one of the functions of the author-narrator in the novel, as noted earlier, is to force us to keep our distance from the characters and to judge them intellectually and rationally. In this the author himself is our model. His heart may be hot, but he keeps a cool head. And his irony, the jocular, mocking aspect of the novel's "tone," is the literary expression of that cool head. Irony is a kind of spiritual air conditioner.

Čajkovskij's opera, incidentally, shows what happens to the story of Onegin and Tat'jana, Ol'ga and Lenskij, if you turn off this machine. The atmosphere becomes sticky, the underpinnings of the wonderfully delicate, intricate, balanced structure rot, and it collapses. You are left with a banal, trite, and sentimental bore—which may nevertheless be a vehicle for some delightful music. But Puškin, in his magnificent novel in verse, succeeded in fulfilling the program he had set for himself in his famous dedication to Pletnëv, in maintaining a perfect balance between *uma xolodnyx nabljudenij / i serdca gorestnyx zamet* ("the cold observations of the mind and the mournful notations of the heart").

THE ARCHITECTURE OF LOVE IN GOGOL''S "ROME"

BY

LOUIS PEDROTTI

> Я люблю купол . . .
> (Gogol': "Architecture Today")
>
> Ай! ай! ай! ничего, ничего . . . молчание.
> (Gogol': "Diary of a Madman")

"WHAT IS LOVE? It is the homeland of the soul, the beautiful yearning of a man for those bygone days where his life had its unblemished beginning, where the innocence of the baby has left its inexpressible and indelible mark everywhere, where a man feels that he is in his own native land." Such is Gogol''s definition of love given in an early sketch called "Woman," completed in 1830.[1] Indeed, one may say that this distillation of an abstraction is the closest Gogol' comes to the fundamentals of love in any of his works.

Credibly treated love scenes are notably absent from his fiction. All the more odd is this absence of passion for a man of such high passions as Gogol'. His high-blown romantic yearnings seemed incapable of consummation. It is as if he felt compelled to stop short this side of the threshold of love, just as Popriščin in his imagination recoils in quavering timidity outside Sophie's boudoir, in the story called "The Diary of a Madman." A shy reticence to become intimately engaged in love scenes marks the bulk of Gogol''s work. Moreover, his heroines are for the most part caricatures, extremes of a sort, often unapproachable ideals of beauty and purity, sometimes flat, banal, one-dimensional creatures without character and personality, and at other times grotesque models of ugliness and vulgarity. With Gogol', women do not occupy the middle ground of human reality. A wife's soul, he writes in an article contained in his *Selected Passages from Correspondence with Friends*, serves either as a lucky charm for her husband, preserving him from moral infection, or else it is a thing of evil, destined to bring about his ruin.[2] The Madonna and the Magdalene join hands with the painted puppet in Gogol''s strange world of women.

Gogol''s Ukrainian stories present idealized country girls, one-dimensional and stereotyped. The romance, if it may be so termed,

---

[1] "Ženščina," N. V. Gogol', *Sobranie sočinenij v semi tomax* (Moscow, 1966-1967), VI, 10.
[2] "Ženščina v svete," ibid., p. 211.

between Andrij and the Polish girl in *Taras Bul'ba* is highly stylized, devoid of human qualities. Ivan Špon'ka's brief "courtship" scene with Mar'ja Grigor'jevna is grounded from the beginning by the curse of aphasia: the two "lovers" remain silent for fifteen minutes, until Špon'ka finally brings the symbolism in this parody of love to its full apogee with his inane observation about the multitude of flies in summertime. The beautiful ideal whom Piskarev pursues in "Nevsky Prospect" represents an additional grotesque of love for Gogol': love is an illusion; the woman of his dreams is in reality a prostitute. In the second part of the same story, Pirogov woos a vacuous and vapid German Hausfrau, conveniently married. Popriščin becomes convinced that women can fall in love only with the devil. Even Čertokuckij's wife in the story "The Coach" is nothing more than a doll, voluptuous and languorous, but for all that, unable to arouse her sleeping husband. Xlestakov's "love" for the mayor's daughter (in *The Inspector General*) is exposed in all its ridiculous infantilism when the sentimentally undirected hero turns immediately to the girl's mother and, with no change of pace or breath, proposes to her as well.[3] Čičikov (in *Dead Souls*), for all his professed concern for producing a set of little Čičikovs, is unconvincing, if not aimless, in his amorous adventures. The symbolism of the lover's dilemma, and perhaps also Gogol''s, is brought to its exquisite and inevitable reduction in the farce called *Marriage*, during Podkolesin's leap to liberty from the window, just before his wedding. Gogol''s flight from menacing reality is nowhere so poignantly told as here.[4]

There is, of course, evidence in Gogol''s personal correspondence of examples of his own tendency to show caution before the labyrinth of love. On July 24, 1829, when he was only twenty years old, he wrote his mother from St. Petersburg that he was forced to flee abroad to Lübeck in order to escape the torments of "love." "Who," he writes, "could have expected such weakness in me? But I saw her—no, I won't mention her name—she is too lofty for anyone, not just for me. I'd call her an angel, but this term is out of place for her.... She is a deity, only invested somewhat with human passions." "No, this is not love," he continues. "At

---

[3] Osip Senkovskij, editor and factotum of *The Library for Reading*, expressed annoyance over the lack of love interest in the comedy and recommended that Gogol' add another female role to attract Xlestakov's eye. See *Biblioteka dlja Čtenija* (St. Petersburg, 1836), XVI, part V: "Kritika," 30–34.

[4] For an absorbing interpretation of the Freudian implications of the treatment of love in Gogol''s works see: Hugh McLean, "Gogol''s Retreat from Love: Toward an Interpretation of *Mirgorod*," *American Contributions to the Fourth International Congress of Slavicists, Moscow, September 1958* ('s Gravenhage: Mouton, 1958), pp. 225–244.

least I haven't heard of a love like this. In a burst of madness and the most terrible spiritual torments I thirsted, I seethed just to stare, I hungered for just one glance .... To look upon her once more—this was my one and only desire, growing stronger and stronger, with an inexpressibly burning anguish." The pitch of his fervor reaches such proportions that he can think only of leaving:

> I saw that I had to run away from myself if I wanted to save my life and provide even the shadow of peace for my tormented soul .... No, this being that He had sent to take away my peace of mind and to unsettle my shakily created world was not a woman. If she had been a woman, she could not with all the power of her charms have produced such terrible, indescribable impressions. She was a deity created by Him, a part of Him Himself. But for God's sake, don't ask me her name! She is too lofty, too lofty![5]

The Popriščins and the Podkolesins were indeed chips off the old block.

Throughout Gogol''s motley world of fantasy this "homeland of the soul," the irrevocable commitment of spirit and the total, the joyous abandonment of self to the senses may be found in only two extant works, both so-called fragments of novels. They were begun in 1839, while the author was in Rome. The first of the fragments is no more than a brief series of cameo scenes collected under the title *Nights at a Villa*. Yet nowhere in Gogol''s artistic work do his outbursts of devotion and love achieve the credibility of this feverish account of his relationship with Count Iosif Viel'gorskij, the young man dying of tuberculosis before his eyes. The second of the pieces, "Rome," was apparently intended by Gogol' as a novella to be called *Annunziata*. The work under its present title appeared in print in 1842.

Gogol''s infatuation with Italy and especially with Rome is evident from the testimony of his correspondence. Of particular pertinence to the present subject is his remarkable letter to Marija Balabina, one of his former pupils in St. Petersburg, written in Rome during April, 1838.[6] Excerpts from this letter read like a prologue to his story and help to establish the atmosphere in which the work was conceived. Writing about the effect upon him of seeing the Eternal City, Gogol' exclaims, "I felt as if I had seen my homeland, where I hadn't been for several years, and where my thoughts alone had lived. But no, that's not it at all: it wasn't my homeland that I had seen, but the homeland of my soul, where my soul had lived before I was born into this world." Then follows a catalogue

---

[5] P. A. Kuliš, *Zapiski o žizni N. V. Gogolja* (St. Petersburg: Aleksandr Jakobson, 1856), I, 76.

[6] Citations from this letter are taken from N. V. Gogol', op. cit., VII, 182–190.

of the esthetic delights of Rome, wherein is manifest Gogol'' s preference for the plastic and the architectural forms of art.

> Again the same sky, sometimes all silvery, decked out in a kind of glittery satin, at other times a deep blue, as it likes to show itself through the arches of the Colosseum. Again the same cypresses, those green obelisks, the tips of the domelike pines that sometimes seem to be floating in the air. The same pure air, the same clear expanse of view, the same eternal dome so majestically rounded in the air.

In the ensuing passage from this letter Gogol' uses that effective artistic device whereby inanimate objects are endowed with human attributes and people are dehumanized by being compared with things. Again, it is the architectural form here that is the vehicle for the author's anthropopathy. Gogol' writes,

> I visited the Colosseum, and I felt that it recognized me, because, as is its custom, it was magnificently gracious and on this occasion particularly loquacious. I felt such beautiful sentiments being born within me that it just had to be talking to me. Then I made off for St. Peter's and all the other places, and I felt that this time they had all become more talkative with me. I think that when I first met them they were more shy and reserved and considered me a *forestiere*.

The final excerpt cited below shows no less Gogol''s rapture for Rome and contains his famous "rhinomaniac" wish, to turn himself into a single portion of the human body, his own symbolic trademark:

> What air! It seems that when you inhale through your nose at least 700 angels will fly into your nasal nostrils [sic]. An amazing spring! I look, and I never get tired of looking. Roses have now covered all Rome. But my senses are even more captivated by the flowers that have just burst into bloom and whose name I must confess I have for the moment forgotten. We don't have them at home. You know, there often comes over me the raging desire to turn myself into one nose, so that there would be nothing more of me—no eyes, no arms, no legs, nothing but one stupendous nose, whose nostrils would be the size of big buckets, so that I might inhale as much as possible of this perfume and of this spring.

Gogol' had no difficulty in accomplishing the transposition of these epistolary flights of ecstasy to a literary vehicle, as his Roman story shows.

With the exception of his youthful sketch called "Woman" and his short fragment, *Nights at a Villa*, "Rome" is Gogol''s only prose work with a Western European setting. The hero of this story is a young Italian prince, nameless, who returns to Italy after four years of searching for intellectual refinement in Paris. He falls in love with the dazzling beauty of an elusive young girl, Annunziata, but he never succeeds in approaching her.

Another remarkable feature is that, although it bears the subtitle "fragment," the story is structurally whole and may be considered closer to completion than many of Gogol''s other works. One may recall in this connection the interrupted plot of "Ivan Fedorovič Špon'ka and His Auntie"; the lack of dénouement to Čičikov's adventures in *Dead Souls*; the loaded symbolism of the final mute scene in *The Inspector General*, when the audience learns that only at this point is the real action of the comedy about to begin; the sudden disappearance of the portrait in the homonymous story, with the implication that the contagion of evil (and therefore, the story itself) is without end. There is indeed more in "Rome" than the Romantic's penchant for the "unfinished" work of art, for the fragmented statement, for declaring that the most beautiful songs are those still unsung. There is even more at work than Gogol''s tendency toward flight from reality and the inclination to stop short of the goal, out of a vague fear of consummation. These elements may be present here, as they are almost everywhere with Gogol'. But there may also be seen a balance, a harmony and a symmetry of parts within the very architecture of the story, that would put the stamp of artistic omega on the work.

"Rome" starts out immediately with the beginning of the present action, during carnival time in the city, presumably in late winter. The prince glimpses Annunziata in the throng of pre-Lenten revelers. Then there ensues a swift retreat from this scene of present action to a Vorgeschichte, in which we are given an account of the prince's early education in Rome, of his university studies in Lucca and Paris and finally of his joyous return to Italy and to Rome.[7] And once more the reader is brought back to the time and place of the present action in the story, the moment when the prince first sees Annunziata in the crowd. Again follows an immediate withdrawal from the scene, once more in the form of a brief Vorgeschichte. The reader is here supplied the details of the day's events which have brought the prince to the point of seeing the girl for the first time. Then once more Gogol' presents the scene of the beginning of the present action: the prince's first view of Annunziata is again described. Thus, to this moment in the story no progress in plot has been made beyond the initial point. In a story covering forty-two pages of print Gogol' has taken thirty-two pages to proceed no further than the point at which he began on the first page. "Rome" serves as an example, perhaps by itself extreme, of

---

[7] It is curious that there should be a discrepancy in the facts regarding time in the story. One such instance is provided by the two separate statements about the prince's age: the one that he was twenty-five years old when he went to Lucca to study, and the second that he is still this same age when he returns to Rome. Another *lapsus abaci* may be seen in the two conflicting accounts of his years abroad. A statement at the beginning of the story allots the prince an absence of fifteen years, while a chronological tabulation of the separate portions of his travels yields a sum of only ten years.

Gogol''s general inattention to plot in all his works. The systematic development of story line seems hardly of central concern with the author here, but this focusing off center (and off stage) of the field of incident and adventure is by no means unique in Gogol''s art. In this instance it may be seen as a stark formula, symbolizing his basic approach to reality.

In the last ten pages of "Rome" the action finally begins to develop from the initial point. The prince sees Annunziata again, this time riding in a coach, he loses sight of her in the crowd of carnival revelers and, after an amusing encounter with a group of bantering Roman housewives, he seeks the services of the local factotum Peppe in finding the elusive girl. But ultimately the prince is thwarted even in his fifth and final attempt to find Annunziata. It is ironically significant that the cause of his frustration in his romantic quest is the real heroine of the story, the city of Rome itself.

From the first lines of the story, in the opening description of Annunziata, Gogol' presents not a flesh-and-blood woman, but a painting, a statue, an edifice. Gogol''s involvement in the art world is well known. Some of his stories concern the problems of the artist. All of his works show the effect of this interest: the use of the artist's technique, sudden contrasts of light and shadow, the stress upon form and contour and even the vocabulary of the studio. So in the opening lines of the story the reader encounters a description of Annunziata that is in effect a verbal rendering of a statue. "Try to look at a flash of lightning," the story begins, "when, splitting asunder the coal-black clouds, it shimmers down in a whole flood of brilliance. Such are the eyes of the Albanese girl Annunziata. Everything about her recalls the ancient times when marble came to life and the sculptor's chisel flashed."[8] She has "beauty of lines such as no brush could create." Words like "harmony," "picturesque," "flashing," and "bronze," as well as the various colors of the palette, enter into her portrait. Gogol''s characteristic "Flemish" technique of contrasting light and shadow is everywhere evident: the "thick pitch of her hair" makes a striking frame for the "gleaming snow of her face" and her "sparkling neck" (p. 205). "Everything about her is the peak of perfection, from her shoulders to her classical, 'breathing' leg and to the last toe of her foot. Wherever she goes she creates a painting: when she hurries at eventide to the fountain with a hammered bronze vase on her head" (p. 205), everything around her embraces her in a marvelous harmony.

From this point the description of Annunziata blends almost imperceptibly into a panorama of the Roman landscape, where the same

---

[8] All citations from "Rome" are from N. V. Gogol', op. cit., III, 205-247.

category of descriptive words is used, and the interplay of "sun" and "shadow" serves as a contrasting device. Because of Annunziata "the marvelous lines of the Albanese mountains move more softly off into the distance," "the depth of the Roman sky is bluer," "the Roman pine, that beauty of the southern forests, is traced more precisely and purely against the sky" (pp. 205-206). The vocabulary and tropes used to depict the rustic scene continue to suggest the artist's workshop: "the dark arboreal gallery leading from Albano to Castel San Gondolfo," beneath whose "gloomy vaults the brilliant waistbands and golden flowers" of the peasant girls with their "gleaming white headdress," among whom "sun and shadow run alternately" (p. 206). Then the narrative shifts back to Annunziata. An artist beholding the girl would immediately sense that "she would serve as a marvelous model for Diana, for proud Juno, for the seductive Graces and for all women who have ever been committed to canvas!" (pp. 206-207).

The full significance of this blend and even confusion of woman and art becomes apparent upon the prince's arrival in Italy from France. His first glimpse of Genoa from the steamer sets off a chain of emotions in him that have lain dormant for four years. With his eyes he caresses the plastic beauties of the city as he would a woman: the "undulating lines of the streets" (p. 218), the picturesque bell towers, its domes. In Genoa, Gogol' says, the prince "received the first kiss of Italy" (p. 219). But it is the architecture of Rome that welcomes him home like a beloved. "How many emotions crowd his breast" when he catches sight of the first "marvelously rounded dome" of Rome. Suddenly he is surrounded by the ancient city and is "embraced by that beauty among all the squares, the Piazza del Popolo" (p. 219).

Although Gogol' later asserted that the views of his anonymous prince should not be confused with his own, there is little doubt that there are strong autobiographical elements in the story.[9] Certainly the prince's eager anticipation of the splendors of Paris is reminiscent of Gogol''s own naïve enthusiasm upon leaving the Ukraine for St. Petersburg in 1828. "With impatience," Gogol' writes in his story, "he awaited Paris, he populated it with towers and palaces, he formed his own picture of the city, and with a trembling heart he at last caught sight of the first indications of the capital: the posters, the gigantic letters, the increasing numbers of coaches and buses. Finally the houses of the suburbs flashed by" (p. 210). The prince is dazzled by the "brilliance" of Paris, he gawks at the endless series of "novelties" in this "money-exchange and market-

---

[9] Letter to S. P. Ševyrev, September 1, 1843, ibid., VII, 254.

place of Europe" (pp. 210–211). But all the "glitter" of the capital eventually begins to hurt his eyes, and the "whirling," "bustle," "seething," and constant "motion" of Paris come to weary him. His ears are injured by the dissonance of the streets. In terms of art he sees France as a "brilliant vignette, not a painting by one of the great masters" (p. 216). It is as though "feeling" in him has been sublimated by all the banal tinsel and jarring cacophony of Paris.[10] "Feeling" is reawakened only at his first sight of Italy from the steamer on his return from France. Indeed, Gogol' presents here a significant contrast between the dissonance of Paris and the visual harmony of Italy. "Feeling" and "beauty" are conveyed in terms of architectonics. Gogol' makes clear that for him the Romantic's bridge to the other world of beauty is not music, but the plastic arts.

The exterior architectural design of the story is matched by interior verbal harmony. This inner symmetry results often from series of repetitions, progressions, or summations which, like the fasciae of the architrave, combine to produce harmonious elements that in turn form the unity of the entablature of an architectural column. Thus, in reciting the beauties of Rome, Gogol' uses tight sets of phonic as well as verbal units to create structural balance. The units may consist of simple repetitions of phrase form:

И там, в той церкви, хранится какое-нибудь чудо кисти. И там, на дряхлеющей стене, еще дивит готовый исчезнуть фреск. И там, на вознесенных мраморах и столпах, набранных из древних языческих храмов, блещет неувядаемой кистью плафон. [p. 224]

Or the repetition may vary slightly to conform to grammatical necessity:

Ему нравилось это чудное их слияние в одно. . . . Ему нравилась самая невзрачность улиц. . . . Ему нравились эти беспрерывные внезапности. . . . [p. 222]

and:

Ему лучше нравилась эта скромная тишина улиц, это особенное выражение римского населения, этот призрак восемнадцатого века. . . . [p. 225]

The idea of repetition may be conveyed through the use of negative prefixes:

Тут самая нищета являлась в каком-то светлом виде, беззаботная, незнакомая с терзаньем и слезами, беспечно и живописно протягивавшая руку. . . . [p. 225]

---

[10] See Lucy Vogel, "Gogol's *Rome*," *The Slavic and East European Review*, XI, no. 2 (1967), 145–158.

A sequence of logical progressions may lead symmetrically to summation and conclusion:

Они представляли четыре чудные вида на четыре стороны. С одной . . ., с другой . . ., с третьей . . ., тогда представлялась ему четвертая сторона вида. . . . [p. 226]

and:

Сначала они еще казались зеленоватыми, . . . потом они сквозили уже светлой желтизною, . . . и, наконец, становились пурпурней и пурпурней. . . . [p. 227]

In this inner verbal harmony of the story the architectonic design should, of course, be considered for its audial as well as its visual effect.

The remainder of the story represents a catalogue of the architectural delights of Rome, against which the figure of Annunziata appears frequently in bold relief. It is at times difficult to distinguish the true subject of Gogol''s rapture. The prince's outbursts reveal the dilemma. "Italian women are like buildings," he says at one point. "They are either palaces or shacks, either beautiful or ugly. There is no middle ground with them: there are no simply pretty ones" (p. 234). Later Gogol' comes very close to tipping his hand. Annunziata is "a flash of lightning," he declares, "not a woman. She is a Roman. Such a woman could be born only in Rome" (p. 238). The prince then openly confesses the dehumanized nature of his search. He must see Annunziata again, not to love her, not to kiss her, but only to look at her, to examine her from all perspectives, like a work of art. He has now become through his own words an artist gazing upon a statue, a beautiful caryatid:

> I must see her without fail. I want to see her, not to love her, no—I only want to look at her, to look at all of her, her eyes, her hands, her fingers, her gleaming hair. Not to kiss her—I only want to gaze upon her. And why not? For this is as it should be, it is the natural order of things. She has no right to conceal and remove her beauty. Perfect beauty is given to the world so that everyone may see it, so that everyone may preserve the concept of beauty forever within his heart. If she were simply lovely and not the supreme perfection that she is, she would have the right to belong to one man, and he could carry her off into the wilderness and conceal her from the world. But perfect beauty must be visible to everyone. Does an architect build a magnificent temple in a narrow alley? No, he places it in an open square, so that we may observe it from all sides and marvel at it. [p. 238]

Annunziata is obviously no woman of flesh and blood, subject to the whims of one man, but a work of art, an architectural monument, the patrimony of all ages and of all nations.

Not only as an imaginative artist was Gogol' motivated by architectural forms. In his tract called "Architecture Today," first published in the

Arabesques collection in 1835, he entered directly into an historical commentary on various styles of architecture. Even here esthetic considerations are dominant. In openly declaring his preference for Gothic architecture, Gogol' pays tribute to Sir Walter Scott as the first to "shake the dust off Gothic architecture" and show the world its true merit.[11] Senkovskij objected strenuously to what he saw as Gogol''s tender concern for an essentially non-Russian style of architecture:

> He is extremely fond of Gothic architecture! "Out of kindness, out of compassion," he begs us, "do not destroy it, do not distort it!" This appeal to us Russians not to destroy Gothic architecture, something we have never had, is touching and proves that the author has read with great benefit Victor Hugo's novel. But in general the Middle Ages and Gothic structures are the favorite dolls of our writer's imagination. He would rebuild everything in the Gothic style.[12]

Not content with this sarcastic attempt to debunk Gogol''s understanding of architectural styles, Senkovskij relentlessly pursued his prey, seeing in his predilection for the dome a form of erotic obsession, a species of "mastomania."[13] There is, it is true, something suggestive of breast fixation in Gogol''s rapturous eulogies of the dome in his article on architecture. He considers the "voluptuous" and "airily bulging" dome "the most delightful creation of taste," something that should "embrace" the building and rest upon its mass with "its white, nebulous surface."

> I love the dome, that beautiful, immense, gently bulging dome, which revived the luxurious taste of the Greeks, ... when there was ever visible the dome, bulging out boldly, like the vault of heaven. There is nothing that can impart such voluptuous, such fascinating beauty to a mass of houses as a dome like this .... It should be brighter than the building itself, and preferably it should be completely white. A dazzling whiteness imparts an inexpressible charm and plumpness to the gently bulging form.[14]

Throughout the article caressive reference is made to the dome, "voluptuous," "airy," "gently bulging," and even "lacteal."[15]

The final scene in "Rome" completes and resolves the story's theme and at the same time formulates both the external and internal design of this so-called fragment. Peppe asks the prince how he can serve him in his quest for Annunziata. Instead of giving a reply, the prince turns and looks

---

[11] N. V. Gogol', op. cit., VI, 86.
[12] "*Arabeski*. Raznye sočinenija Gogolja," O. I. Senkovskij, *Sobranie sočinenij* (St. Petersburg, 1858), II, 348. For a modern view of Gogol''s concern with architecture, see Leon Štil'man, "'Vsevidjaščee Oko' u Gogolja," *Vozdušnye Puti*, V (New York, 1969), 279–292.
[13] Ibid.
[14] "Ob arxitekture nynešnego vremeni," N. V. Gogol', op. cit., VI, 79.
[15] Ibid., p. 91.

down from one of the hills at the magnificent city below. He encloses within the embrace of his vision all the harmony of forms found in the city lying at his feet. Images of light and dark are fused to the architectural structure of the passage:

> Before him in a marvelous shining panorama appeared the Eternal City. The bright heap of houses, churches, domes and spires was vividly illumined by the brilliance of the setting sun. In groups and one by one emerged the houses, roofs, statues, airy terraces and galleries. Over there rose a motley mass of delicately topped bell towers and domes with capriciously patterned lanterns. Over there the whole form of a dark palace stood out. Over there was the flat dome of the Pantheon. Over there was the decorated top of the column of Antoninus with its capital and statue of the Apostle Paul. A little to the right rose the tops of the Capitoline buildings with their steeds and statues. A little more to the right, above the gleaming throng of houses and roofs, rose majestically and sternly the Colosseum's dark, enormous mass. There again was the moving throng of walls, terraces and domes, covered by the sun's dazzling brilliance. And above all this sparkling mass appeared in the distance the dark green tops of the stone oaks from the Ludovisi and Medici villas, and standing in the air in a whole flock above them were the dome-shaped tops of the Roman pines, rising upon their thin trunks. And then along the entire length of the painting rose the transparent mountains, light as air, turning azure, embraced by some phosphorescent light. Neither by word nor by brush could one convey the wondrous harmony and blending of all the planes of this painting. The air was so pure and transparent that the slightest outline of the distant buildings was sharply visible, and everything seemed near enough to grasp in one's hand. The last little architectural embellishment, the patterned decoration of the cornice—everything appeared in incomprehensible clarity. At this time resounded a cannon shot and a remote blending cry of the mob—a sign that the riderless steeds had already run past, concluding the day of carnival. The sun was sinking lower toward the earth. Its brilliance upon the whole architectural mass became rosier and hotter. The city kept on becoming darker and more animated. The mountains kept on turning bluer and more phosphorescent. The heavens became ever more solemn and on the point of dying away .... [pp. 246-247]

There can be no doubt that this is a picture of a man in love. The object of his rapture can hardly be questioned. The closing words of this trance scene, and of the story itself, provide the clue to an appreciation of the prince's passion, as well as of Gogol''s: "Lord, what a view! The prince, embraced by it, forgot himself and the beauty of Annunziata and the mysterious destiny of his people and everything else in this world" (p. 247).

THE LUDICROUS MAN-OF-THE-FAMILY
A Recurrent Type in Dostoevskij

BY

OLEG A. MASLENIKOV

DOSTOEVSKIJ is well known for his recurrent character-types[1], such as his criminal Supermen—the Raskol'nikovs, the Stavrogins, the Ivan Karamazovs, the Gazins and Orlovs—men who regard themselves above the human herd and therefore above the laws that govern its morality.

Then there are the Meek and Humiliated sufferers—the Makar Devuškins, the Nellies, the Sonjas—who bear silently the indignities that life has heaped upon them; the masochistic Self-Lacerators—the nameless heroes from the Underground, the Nastas'ja Filippovnas, the Captain Snegirevs—who deliberately seek to fill their bitter cup of insult and suffering to overflowing; the Demonic Women—the Grušenkas, the Liza Xoxlakovas, the Nastas'ja Filippovnas, the Aglajas, the Polinas—who delight in tormenting those who profess to love them; and the Voluntary Buffoons—the Polzunkovs, the Eževikins, the Lebedevs, the Fedor Pavlovič Karamazovs—men who willingly demean themselves in order to entertain others.

Now I should like to focus on yet another category, one which frequently includes that of the Voluntary Buffoons, but goes beyond it. It is a group which for some reason seems to have escaped the attention of Dostoevskij scholars, and which I have called, not quite appropriately, "The Ludicrous Fathers"—the unvenerated, the undignified, the unrespected men-of-the-family.

These types frequently play an important role in the structure of Dostoevskij's narratives, since they provide the comic element to which Dostoevskij resorts in order to relieve the tension and pathos that he constantly builds up in his tales. For all their comic exterior, however, these characters also bear overtones of the tragedy that underlies their all-too-human plight.

Theirs is a large category and numbers among its members most of the fathers one meets in the works of Dostoevskij. Characteristic for them is that few of these fathers command respect even within their own families, and unlike the father characters of Tolstoj and of his predecessors,

---

[1] See Leonid Grossman's splendid study, "Dostoevskij xudožnik," in N. L. Stepanov, ed., *Tvorčestvo Dostoevskogo* (Moscow, 1959), pp. 330–416.

Dostoevskij's appear as ludicrous, undignified creatures—especially to their children.

The clearest case of the Ludicrous Father is seen in *Uncle's Dream* (1859), in the character of Afanasij Matveevič Moskalev, father of the would-be bride Zina and husband of the strong-willed Marija Aleksandrovna. But we can dismiss him rather quickly. He is the stock buffoon in a farce. He is not expected to have any pretensions either to dignity, intellect, or will power. He is completely dominated by his wife, who, recognizing her superiority over her husband, is fond of referring to him as "blockhead" (*bolvan!*). There are no tragic overtones in him—he appears in a purely comic role. Yet it is his ludicrous behavior and inappropriate blurting out of what Marija Aleksandrovna had kept a secret that so embarrass Zina that she explodes and confesses openly her part in the marriage plot involving the old, feeble-minded count. In finding her father's behavior embarrassing, Zina reminds us of many other members of the younger generation in Dostoevskij who react similarly to their fathers' antics.

Anticipating Turgenev's *Fathers and Children* (1862) by some fifteen years, Dostoevskij already in the mid-1840's portrayed the younger generation's rejection of the older, in which it found a source of embarrassment rather than of filial respect. Thus already in Dostoevskij's first independent piece of fiction, *Poor Folk* (1846), we meet the first of his Ludicrous Fathers in Pokrovskij, whom Varvara Dobroselova in the pre-story dealing with her life describes as "soiled, poorly dressed, small, odd, clumsy, in a word, the strangest-looking creature possible" (I, 104).[2]

In the course of Varen'ka's tale we learn that Pokrovskij (like Marmeladov and General Ivolgin after him) has taken to drink, and is frequently subjected to various indignities by his second wife (a *meščanka*, whom he had married apparently beneath his social station). In hopes of currying the favor of his son, whom Pokrovskij adores and admires, he willingly debases himself and plays the buffoon only to find that his behavior arouses in his son a squeamish aversion for his father, and brings him to "hate" the old man's visits. In Pokrovskij we already see various traits that Dostoevskij will eventually exploit in portraying other father-characters.

Thus the comic aspect of the final scene of the Pokrovskij story-within-the-story uncovers the actual pathos underlying the hitherto ludicrous

---

[2] All quotations from Dostoevskij are taken from his 10-volume collection, *Sobranie sočinenij* (Moscow, 1956–1958). Roman figures refer to the volume in question, arabic figures, to the pages.

mien of the old man. Pokrovskij is depicted running after the cart that is taking his son's body to the cemetery and appears doubly ridiculous as his "treasures," his last mementoes of his dead son, his Petin'ka's books, with which he had stuffed his pockets, keep spilling out and falling into the mud. This scene reproduces one of the enduring principles underlying Dostoevskij's esthetics—the ironic use of the comic in order to symbolize the tragic. The ludicrous father, Pokrovskij, one of the "Poor Folk," in essence is meant to be a tragic figure.

Evgraf Larionovič Eževikin (*The Village Stepančikovo*), our next subject, is a horse of a different color. Like Moskalev he also appears as the father of a bride-to-be—of Nastas'ja, the quiet, dignified, but impecunious young woman, who serves as governess in the Rostanev household, and with whom the colonel is in love, with his mother and Foma Fomič opposing the match.

Eževikin is a buffoon, and his antics also prove constantly embarrassing to his daughter, as he forever stresses his poverty and always demeans himself by acting the "voluntary fool" in order to give pleasure to his richer acquaintances.

> Near Baxčeev, Eževikin minced and weaved. As a matter of fact, however, he minced everywhere. He kissed the little hands (*ručki*) of her Excellency, the widow of the General; and of the newly arrived lady visitor; he kept whispering something into the ear of Mlle Perepelicyn; kept looking solicitously after Foma Fomič. [II, 488]

In Eževikin's behavior, we sense something of that of Polzunkov, the prototype of Dostoevskij's "Voluntary Buffoons," who also had the habit of placing himself in an undignified position and deliberately making himself look ridiculous in the eyes of his patrons and benefactors. And yet in Eževikin's behavior there is a discernible note of irony—an underlying protest which escapes the actors in Stepančikovo, but can be felt by the spectators.

Another noteworthy father-character from *Stepančikovo* is Colonel Egor Il'ič Rostanev, who for all his virtues (and physical strength), often, not unlike Myškin, appears as scarcely a dignified figure. The weasel-like Foma Fomič and the domineering mother have the good colonel jumping through hoops at their command. And yet Rostanev, weak-willed though he seems, in sacrificing mere self-esteem preserves what seems to him greater values, and his seeming lack of dignity can scarcely be said to be tragic. In his assertion of his principles he appears as an *heroic*, albeit humorous, figure.

I shall deliberately bypass Foma Fomič Opiskin, the tyrant of *Stepančikovo*, on the justification of lack of space and of the fact that actual physical parenthood was denied him in the novel. I must mention, however, that Foma Fomič, as a substitute father-image, could well qualify as another "Voluntary Buffoon," since he acts the fool and demeans himself in order to get his "betters" to accede to his whims.

One of the most pitiable, unheroic, and pathetic figures in Dostoevskij is the drunkard, Semen Zaxaryč Marmeladov, in *Crime and Punishment*. He inspires neither reverence for himself nor confidence in his own integrity. He has taken to drink in order to escape the horrors of the real world. He has slipped so far down the ladder of self-respect as to allow an outsider to strike his wife, who is in the last stages of tuberculosis. Although he realizes his own degradation and suffers from it, he cannot translate his nobler impulses into action.

"and I lay there—just drunk (*p'janen'kij*)," he admits to Raskol'nikov. And then adds, "But don't think that I didn't suffer." [V, 17]

Marmeladov then openly admits to Raskol'nikov, a stranger, that he has allowed his oldest daughter Sonja to go into the streets—to sell her body to strangers so that she might provide food for his family.

Marmeladov is the object of general ridicule, and his behavior seems only to encourage further insult and derision. Yet he is aware of his own debasement. Thus, when he is heard to say:

"today I dropped in on Sonya—to ask for a little money to help with the hangover (*na poxmel'e*)...."

and admits taking:

"thirty kopecks, which she gave me with her own hands—her last, all that she had," [V, 25]

someone from the side suddenly guffaws, and Marmeladov shamefacedly admits that this ridicule is only just and proper. In fact, it is too mild a punishment.

"I'm not embarrassed by all this head nodding. I do not look upon it with disdain, sir, but with humiliation.... Why should I be pitied? There's nothing to pity me for! I ought to be crucified, not pitied!" [V, 26]

Marmeladov is made to look even more ridiculous when he admits that no sooner will he get home than his consumptive wife, Katerina Ivanovna, in a fit of uncontrolled frenzy, will add to his indignities by starting to pull his hair.

"Why should I worry about my hair. Bother the hair..." [V, 27]

he adds with resignation.

As with Pokrovskij, beneath the ludicrous façade of Marmeladov lies deepest human tragedy, which Dostoevskij brings out by deliberately underscoring the comic element.

In *The Idiot* we meet another ridiculous father. Here it is the ludicrous figure of Ganja's father, of the General Ardalion Aleksandrovič Ivolgin, who reminds one somewhat of Marmeladov. Where Marmeladov, however, is basically honest, Ivolgin appears as an habitual liar, a petty confidence man; thus, he borrows money from Myškin with no thought of repaying the simple-minded prince. As in the cases of Pokrovskij, of Moskalev, of Eževikin and others, his actions repeatedly embarrass members of his family, who despite their poverty cling desperately to their genteel background. Ivolgin is portrayed as a near witless old man—a ludicrous member of the family, one who is allowed to rub elbows with the rest of the world chiefly because his wife lacks Marija Aleksandrovna Moskaleva's means, force, and egoism to have her husband removed for her own peace of mind.

A typical scene of the ludicrousness of the old general is portrayed at his first meeting with Nastas'ja Filippovna, to whom he, a gentleman of the old school, introduces himself.

"Ardalion Aleksandrovič Ivolgin," the general uttered with dignity, bowing and smiling. "An old, unfortunate soldier and father of a family, happy in the hope of including...." But Ivolgin had no chance to finish. Ferdyščenko, one of the boarders, quickly moved a chair up from behind, and the general ... plopped (*slepnulsja*) ... onto the chair. This, however, failed to embarrass him, and with a pleasant smile he slowly and grandly raised her fingers to his lips...." [VI, 124]

Ivolgin, like Marmeladov, can command little respect, especially from among his own immediate family. He, again like Marmeladov, is nevertheless a pathetic rather than a merely comic figure. And Dostoevskij again resorts to depicting the man's ludicrous mien in order to underscore the tragic aspect underlying his portrait.

I shall mention briefly another father in *The Idiot*, this time a secondary character, Lukian Alekseevič Lebedev. Lebedev, like Eževikin, likes to play the buffoon, and like Ivolgin, he deserves and is accorded little honor from the younger members of his family. Even before a total stranger, Myškin, his daughter and nephew openly treat him with a disdain that is scarcely appropriate to a head of the family. The nephew, thus, blurts out to Myškin: "I'll bet he's already trying to swindle you!" (VI, 218). Then as Lebedev shouts "Shut up!" at his daughter Vera, and begins stamping his feet, she—totally unimpressed—only laughs: "I'm not Tanja; you won't scare me!" (VI, 219). The young man further ridicules Lebedev by laughingly telling Myškin that Lebedev, Sr., prays for the soul of the wanton Countess DuBarry. And the older man, surprisingly (and clownlike) admits the allegation.

I shall pass over still another father (this time in *The Possessed*)—Stepan Trofimovič Verxovenskij—with the brief observation that his son, Petr Stepanovič, the evil spirit of the novel, displays a complete disdain for his somewhat ludicrous and naïve, albeit learned, father. Verxovenskij, Sr., is often made to appear as a ridiculous anachronism. Nevertheless, because of a misplaced faith in outworn ideals and principles, he becomes a tragic figure, rather than a mere buffoon.

Finally I come to two symbols of parenthood in the novel *The Brothers Karamazov*: Captain Snegirev and Fedor Pavlovič Karamazov. Nikolaj Il'ič Snegirev, "former captain of Russian infantry—though now put to shame by his vice" (IX, 250), is one of the humiliated little men who are powerless to struggle against fate. He has no alternative other than to submit. In a way he resembles Marmeladov, but unlike the pitiful old drunkard, Snegirev still has pride, a pride which allows him to fling back the money offered him by Mitja Karamazov, who had once mortally insulted him (by publicly pulling him around by his beard). Yet his actions seem to embarrass his children. Like some of his predecessors Snegirev through his behavior often arouses the indignation and reproach of his family. He is torn between pride and a realization of his own shame. He therefore vacillates between outbursts of petty rebellion and mawkish outpourings of self-pity.

As he introduces his family to Aleša Karamazov, he displays a Marmeladovian trait by confessing to a stranger (Aleša) his own worthlessness, as he asks rhetorically: "And while I live, who, except them, will love poor, little worthless me (*menja skvernen'kogo*)" (IX, 252). And as in the case of Ivolgin, and of Marmeladov, and the others, his daughter sounds a familiar note of hurt reproach as she cries out begging him to "Stop playing the fool!" Captain Snegirev with his family of cripples and mental deficients is, like Marmeladov, a pitiful creature, and he deliberately forgoes dignity to appear ridiculous himself.

Finally I come to the figure of Fedor Pavlovič Karamazov, who may be one of the most misunderstood characters in all of Dostoevskij. He is usually regarded as a revolting old lecher, who not only has swindled his own son out of his rightful inheritance, but who will also vie with him for the favors of Grušen'ka. He seems to lack all sense of dignity and commands no respect from anyone. At times, moreover, he displays many of the buffoon-like qualities of his predecessors.

From Karamazov's background we learn, from references that remind us of Marmeladov and of Pokrovskij, that his first wife—once she became convinced that there was no real love between them—took to beating him, but before too long, fortunately for him, she died.

Old Karamazov differs physically from the other fathers in Dostoevskij. There is little that seems pathetic about him. There is something primitive and carnal about Fedor Pavlovič with his enormous Adam's apple, his large, decaying teeth, his nasty little cackle that sounds too suggestive for a man who might demand respect. He therefore is more likely to arouse revulsion rather than compassion or pity in the readers.

Yet in one way Karamazov resembles his predecessors. As mentioned above, he also likes to appear ludicrous to the embarrassment of his children. Even in the sanctity of the monastery cell of Father Zosima, Fedor Pavlovič sets out deliberately to shame his three sons and his neighbor Miusov, who feels constrained to warn him against "playing the clown!" Despite the admonition Karamazov manages to precipitate a scandal, thus trying the patience even of his one remaining filially loyal son, Aleša. Yet his repeated clowning somehow clashes with his profound appreciation of the fullness of life.

Most of the unattractive qualities found in the father images that preceded him find their highest expression in Fedor Pavlovič Karamazov, who thus appears to be a most revolting father figure. And yet....

Russian literature does not give too many portraits of family life. In depicting his fathers, Fedor Dostoevskij seems, nevertheless, deliberately to satirize the traditional image of the venerable head of the family and appears purposely to distort the accepted father image.

From Puškin's elder Grinev and Aksakov's Stepan Mixailovič Bagrov, the grandfather, through Turgenev's Nikolaj Petrovič Kirsanov, and especially down through the various portraits to be found in Tolstoj—the senior Irten'ev, Aleksej Aleksandrovič Karenin, the crusty old Prince Nikolaj Andreevič Bolkonskij, Count Kirill Vladimirovič Bezuxov, Count Il'ja Andreevič Rostov, all these characters as heads of families command respect in their families, ineffectual though some of them (Stiva Oblonskij) may appear.

Contrast them with most Dostoevskian fathers and the picture is startling! It is as though Dostoevskij consciously sets out to caricaturize one of the traditionally most respected segments of society.

Our Western civilization has long recognized as one of its ideological cornerstones the reverence of one's parents. In the old patriarchal order of Russia this meant especially the respect due one's father, and this reverence for the pater familias is conspicuously absent in most of Dostoevskij's portrayals of family life.

That Dostoevskij frequently resorted to parodying the traditions of the aristocratic-manorial social order is now a commonplace.[3] In this light, his irreverential treatment of the customarily venerated heads of the family may well be interpreted as a further indication of his rebellion against the traditions of the gentry culture that ruled his day. Or it may be just a rebellion against the father as symbol of authority (I am deliberately avoiding any reference to an Oedipus complex reflected in Dostoevskij).

There may, however, be yet another aspect to Dostoevskij's Ludicrous Fathers. It may come from Dostoevskij's view of the basic interrelationship between the tragic and the comic. From this point of view could not most of the characters whom we have just observed be therefore essentially tragic? And could not their comic mien belie the tragedy of the disintegration of an old order, which Dostoevskij actually held close and dear? Might not his depiction of the fathers as comic characters therefore be rather an example of Dostoevskij's subtle use of transcendental irony?

And in this light, might not the seemingly merely detestable revolting old lecher and clown Fedor Pavlovič Karamazov, with his almost Dionysian love of life, with all its joys and all its filth be actually a symbol of the disintegrating culture of his day? And as such, especially in view of Dostoevskij's boundless capacity for compassion, may he not be interpreted in reality as one of Dostoevskij's most tragic major figures?

---

[3] Cf. for example, A. S. Dolinin, *Poslednie romany Dostoevskogo* (Moscow, 1963), esp. pp. 133–161.

TWENTIETH-CENTURY AUTHORS AND WORKS

THE DRUM LINES IN MAJAKOVSKIJ'S "150 000 000"

BY

ROMAN JAKOBSON

WHOEVER HAS heard Majakovskij's inspired recital of his epic "150 000 000" will never forget the summit of this performance, the drum motif in the second part of the poem with its train of chiseled exclamatory clauses and with its homogeneous consonantal texture composed predominantly of forty-two sonorants and thirty-eight (thirty-four voiced) labial stops. The entire second part of this work with the twenty-one drum lines was written in Puškino during the summer of 1919. Here they are quoted from the typescript of the entire poem (pp. 18 f.) with numerous handwritten corrections by Majakovskij. I received it from the poet in April, 1920, before going abroad. He wanted me to attempt a Western publication of his poem.

        Мимо
            баров и бань.
        Бей, барабан!
                Барабан, барабань!
        Были рабы!
                Нет раба!
        Баарбей!
                Баарбань!
                      Баарабан!
        Эй, стальногрудые!
                Крепкие, эй!
        Бей, барабан!
                Барабан, бей!
        Или — или.
        Пропал или пан!
        Будем бить!
            Бьем!
                Били!
        В барабан!
                В барабан!
                      В барабан!

As Lili Brik stated in her instructive essay "Majakovskij i čužie stixi," *Znamja*, 1940, No. 3, Vladimir Vladimirovič liked to recite lines which impressed him in other poets. Attracted by Boris Kušner's "Miting dvorcov" ("Rally of the Palaces"), which appeared in Petrograd at the beginning of 1918, he included this "alliterative prose" in the futurist anthology *Ržanoe slovo* which he compiled and published toward the end of the same year. I still remember the passages of Kušner's work which Majakovskij used to quote; these were the beginning and the end of the first section:

« Бил барабан.
Был барабанщиком конный с гранитной глыбы.
Бой копыт Фальконета заставил даже пыль Марсова поля звенеть.
. . . .
— На митинг, на митинг, на митинг . . .
Шли.»

And from the third section:

«Правы ли те, которые правили? Или оравы поведут города?»

Majakovskij's line *Bej, baraban* generates two sets of etymological figures: *Bej—Budem bit'—B'em—Bili*, and *Baraban, baraban'* with a further modification of the same sound pattern—*Baarban'! Baaraban!*—then with a play on homonyms distinguished only by the opposition of /b'/ and /b/: *bili—byli* (cf. *Baraban, baraban'*), finally with a voiceless variation of the /bar/ and /ban/: *Propal ili pan*. Most probably these figures were prompted by Kušner's *Bil—Boj* and *baraban—barabanščikom* as well as by his confrontation *Bil baraban* and *Byl barabanščikom*; also Majakovskij's correspondence of the *b-* and *p-* sequences may be compared with a similar set in the "Miting": *Byl—glyby—boj* and subsequently *kopyt—pyl'—polja*.

Majakovskij's terminal triple prepositional accusative *V baraban! V baraban! V baraban!* is reminiscent of the thrice repeated call in the conclusion of Kušner's first section: —*Na miting, na miting, na miting*. The similar topic of both texts—*deklaracija prav ugnetennoj vešči* ("the declaration of rights of the oppressed object")—finds its expression in the first part of "150 000 000" with its invitations to three kinds of addressees: [115]*Na miting, motocikletki!*—[138-140]*Na miting, parovozy! Parovozy na miting!*—[156-157]*Na miting šli legiony ognja, šagaja fonarnymi stolbami*. Cf. Kušner: *na miting . . . Šli*.

Finally Majakovskij's echo rhyme *ili ili—bili* could have been inspired by Kušner's construction *pravy li—pravili? Ili*.

One of the paronomastic devices in the drum lines of "150 000 000" is not paralleled by Kušner's text, though the latter is rich in diverse paronomasias. The verb *baraban'* is conceived by Majakovskij as a poetic blend of several nouns which emerge in the context: two homonymous roots *bar-* (*bar* "bar" and *barin, bare* "landowner"), *rab, raba* "slave," and *banja* "bathhouse." *Mimo barov i ban'* "while passing by bars and bathhouses"; *Baarbej*, an expressive modification of *bar bej* "beat the landowners"; *Net raba* "There is no slave."

In May, 1919, at a meeting of the Moscow Linguistic Circle, I read my just completed introductory essay to the planned first volume of Xlebnikov's collected works, and this study was published in Prague on the threshold of 1921 under the title "Novejšaja russkaja poèzija: Nabrosok pervyj." Majakovskij took active part in this Moscow meeting and vividly reacted to my paper, in particular to its discussion of his own as well as Aseev's and Xlebnikov's paronomastic devices. A typical fieldwork record enabled me to confront this salient feature of modern poetry with the vital role of paronomasias in folklore: "In the Vereya district an old narrator told us how a vindictive peasant lured a landowner (*barin*) into a bathhouse (*banja*) and there beat him black and blue, as if covering him with drumbeats (*otbarabanil*); and a fellow in the rural audience pointed out with delight: '*Barina da v bane da otbarabanil!* How smart!'" (p. 51).

The series *bar—ban'—baraban'* always appeared to me as Majakovskij's reminiscence from the Vereya folk tale which I had compared in my essay with the play on words in his March ("Naš marš").

MANDEL'ŠTAM'S MONUMENT NOT WROUGHT BY HANDS

BY

KIRIL TARANOVSKY

IN AUGUST, 1836, Aleksandr Puškin, brought to bay by malicious harassment, wrote the lines which entered all schoolbooks:

> Я памятник себе воздвиг нерукотворный,
> К нему не зарастет народная тропа . . .
> Слух обо мне пройдет по всей Руси великой,
> *И назовет меня всяк сущий в ней язык* . . .

A century later, in May, 1935, another persecuted Russian poet, Osip Mandel'štam, wrote the tragic lines that echo those of Puškin:

> Да, я лежу в земле, губами шевеля,
> *Но то, что я скажу, заучит каждый школьник* . . .

The most recent investigator of Puškin's "Monument" writes:[1]

> Едва ли мы погрешим против истины, если предположим, что стихотворение «Я памятник себе воздвиг» мыслилось поэтом как предсмертное, как своего рода прощание с жизнью и творчеством в предчувствии близкой кончины, потому что и самое слово «памятник» вызывало прежде всего представление о надгробии. «Кладбищенская» тема в лирике Пушкина последнего года его жизни была темой навязчивой, постоянно возвращавшейся в его сознание. . . .

The "graveyard theme" is even more directly expressed in Mandel'štam: in his Voronež exile, the poet sees himself as already buried.

> Да, я лежу в земле, губами шевеля,
> Но то, что я скажу, заучит каждый школьник:
> На Красной площади всего круглей земля,
> И скат ее твердеет добровольный,
> На Красной площади земля всего круглей,
> И скат ее нечаянно раздольный,
> Откидываясь вниз до рисовых полей,
> Покуда на земле последний жив невольник.

The image of "moving lips" is Mandel'štam's favorite metaphor for the process of poetic creation. It recurs in the quatrain which directly follows the poem under investigation in the Voronež Notebook:

> Лишив меня морей, разбега и разлета,
> И дав стопе упор насильственной земли,

---

[1] M. P. Alekseev, *Stixotvorenie Puškina "Ja pamjatnik sebe vozdvig . . ."* (Leningrad, 1967), p. 224.

> Чего добились вы? Блестящего расчета:
> Губ шевелящихся отнять вы не могли.

In the "coercive land," in Voronež exile, the poet goes on composing his inspired songs. It will be noted that the image of the sea in this poem is the same Puškinian image of the free element (*svobodnaja stixija*).[2]

The "poetic lips" are an image which Mandel'štam frequently associates with the theme of death. Such a leitmotiv appeared in his poetry as early as November, 1920, in the poem "Ja slovo pozabyl, čto ja xotel skazat'"

> Но я забыл, что я хочу сказать,
> И мысль бесплотная в чертог теней вернется.
>
> Все не о том прозрачная твердит,
> Все ласточка, подружка, Антигона . . .
> *А на губах как черный лед горит*
> *Стигийского воспоминанье звона.*

In the poem "Xolodok ščekočet temja" (1922), this leitmotiv undergoes a modification. Here it clearly expresses the theme of death as the price that the poet has to pay for his poetry:

> Видно даром не проходит
> *Шевеленье этих губ,*
> И вершина колобродит,
> Обреченная на сруб.

This stanza has much in common with the lines from "1 January 1924," which anticipate the mood of the Voronež poems:

> Я знаю, с каждым днем слабеет жизни выдох,
> Еще немного, — оборвут
> Простую песенку о глиняных обидах
> *И губы оловом зальют.*

Almost a decade later, in May, 1933, the poet ends his monologue on the art of poetry, "Ne iskušaj čužyx narečij," with the image of the sponge soaked in vinegar and meant for his lips:

> И в наказанье за гордыню, неисправимый звуколюб,
> *Получишь уксусную губку ты для изменнических губ.*

---

[2] See Puškin's poem "K morju" (1824). Cf. also Mandel'štam's lines written in June 1935:

> На вершок бы мне синего моря, на игольное только ушко,
> Чтобы двойка конвойного времени парусами неслась хорошо.

Thus the autobiographic image of crucifixion, common to a number of twentieth-century Russian poets (Belyj, Blok, Majakovskij, Xlebnikov, Pasternak, *et al.*) finds it way also into the poetry of Mandel'štam.[3]

In the central lines of the poem there appears the image of the Red Square, which is actually a convex surface, its convexity being particularly conspicuous if one looks from the Historical Museum in the direction of the cathedral of Vasilij Blažennyj. The hyperbolic superlative degree *vsego kruglej* clearly indicates that the image is metaphoric; actually, it is but a paraphrase of another stock metaphor, *pup zemli*, the hub of the universe.

In April, 1935, Mandel'štam uses the image of the Red Square in the following poem:

> Наушнички, наушнички мои,
> Попомню я воронежские ночки:
> Недопитого голосá Аи
> И в полночь с Красной площади гудочки . . .
>
> Ну, как метро? Молчи, в себе таи,
> Не спрашивай, как набухают почки . . .
> А вы, часов кремлевские бои —
> Язык пространства, сжатого до точки.

I often had an opportunity to observe that young people who have never seen radio sets with earphones do not understand these lines. Actually, there is nothing obscure in them: at midnight, the poet listens to a news broadcast from Moscow, followed by the Kremlin chimes. Anyone who has heard this broadcast knows that the din of the city, including automobile honks, comes from the Red Square for a few seconds before the clock begins to chime. But the poet also hears other voices, the voices of his past life with its pleasures cut short. While the question which opens the second stanza testifies to the poet's interest in current events, such as the construction of the Moscow Underground, the following sentence, on the contrary, suggests withdrawal from life and turning inward. The swelling buds, a metonymy of spring, appeared in a much earlier poem of Mandel'štam, "Vek" (1923), in which the image is more developed:

> И еще набухнут почки,
> Брызнет зелени побег . . .

I do not think that one should seek any metaphoric meaning in the "swelling buds" of "Naušnički, naušnički moi."

---

[3] Mandel'štam will return to the image of the crucifixion in a Voronež poem dated 1936 or 1937: "Kak svetoteni mučenik Rembrandt," where he speaks of his "burning rib."

The last two lines provide the poem with a pointed conclusion: if the striking of the Kremlin clock is the language of the space condensed to a dot, then the Kremlin itself turns out to be the center of the world. Thus we arrive at the idea of Moscow the Third Rome, the idea which appeared briefly in Mandel'štam's poetry as early as 1916, in the poem "Na rozval'njax, uložennyx solomoj":

> Не три свечи горели, а три встречи —
> Одну из них сам Бог благословил,
> Четвертой не бывать, а Рим далече, —
> И никогда он Рима не любил.[4]

The three meetings of this poem are Rome, Byzantium, and Moscow, that is, the three meetings of mankind and Providence. Our Lord, says Mandel'štam, never liked Rome. Which of the other two meetings did He then bless: Byzantium, the cradle of the true Faith, or Moscow, its heir? It is more likely that Byzantium was the blessed one.

---

[4] In the poem "Na rozval'njax, uložennyx solomoj" Mandel'štam resurrects the Time of Troubles, during which the problem of the Orthodox and the Catholic faith was particularly poignant in Russia. Uglič, mentioned in the second stanza, definitely points at the Time of Troubles, as does the image of the Tsarevich brought to Moscow as a prisoner covered with the "fatal bast mat," his head bare, his hands bound. The historical and philosophical theme of the Third Rome is advanced only in the third (central) stanza, while the other four stanzas develop the "plot" of the poem.

I believe that in the entire poem the narrator speaks in the first person so that the poem is an internal monologue of the Tsarevich, as it were. In the last stanza the Tsarevich speaks of himself in the third person in order to emphasize his royal title: "Careviča vezut, nemeet strašno telo," varying the line from the second stanza: "Po ulicam vezut menja bez šapki."

Mandel'štam's Tsarevich is not a historical personality, but rather a generalized type of those pretenders that appeared during the Time of Troubles (several Dmitrijs, Petr, Ivan, and others). The only Tsarevich that was brought to Moscow as a prisoner under the guard of *strelcy* (in 1614) was Ivan, the son of Marina Mniszek by *Tušinskij Vor*. However, Mandel'štam's Tsarevich is obviously not a three-year-old child, and, moreover, Tsarevich Ivan was hanged, while Mandel'štam's Tsarevich is to be burned (since the straw covering the sledge in the first stanza is apparently the same "yellow straw" that is being set to fire in the last stanza). As is known, the corpse of the first Pretender was exhumed and burned in the winter of 1606. It is possible that from all these historical facts Mandel'štam composed a generalized type of Tsarevich, a victim of inhuman cruelty.

According to the statement of Marina Cvetaeva ("Istorija odnogo posvjaščenija," *Oxford Slavonic Papers*, XI [1964], 134), this poem was written for her in 1916, when she "was giving Moscow as a present to Mandel'štam." Cvetaeva appears to be hinting that the poem reflects somehow their trips together in Moscow. Such a biographical fact can explain the appearance of the poem (the interplay of the names of Marina Cvetaeva and Marina Mniszek may in this case turn out to be more than a coincidence), but most likely has no direct bearing on the poetic message of the poem. It may be noted that Cvetaeva sometimes compared herself to Marina Mniszek: "Takova u nas, Marinok, / Spes', u nas poljaček-to ... " (*Poèma konca*, 1924).

Mandel'štam must have known the legends about the foundation of Constantinople, the miraculous dream of Constantine, and the tracing by the emperor, walking spear in hand, of the boundary of the destined capital: "the growing circumference was observed with astonishment by the assistants, who, at length, ventured to observe that he had already exceeded the most ample measure of a great city. 'I shall still advance,' replied Constantine, 'till HE, the invisible guide who marches before me, thinks proper to stop'."[5] These words are to be compared with the beginning of the poem "Ajja-Sofija" (1912):

> Айя-София — здесь остановиться
> Судил Господь народам и царям!

The church of St. Sophia, too, was founded by Constantine and replaced, after its destruction during the Nika Riot, by a magnificent temple during the reign of Justinian.[6]

However, Byzantium had perished and the Grace of God had passed over to Russia.

To be more explicit in my analysis, I shall examine the metaphors linked with the image of the Red Square. The first epithet characterizing the slope of the Red Square, *dobrovol'nyj*, undoubtedly belongs to the positive semantic field, as do the adjective *kruglyj* and the verb *tverdet'*. The hardening of the Red Square's slope is a metaphor of the growing firmness of the "Third Rome" in its determination to fulfil its historical mission. The second epithet of the slope, *nečajanno razdol'nyj*, describes the unforeseen increase in the scope of this voluntarily assumed mission. In the given context, only the modifier *nečajanno* may have a negative shade of meaning.

The image of rice fields in the penultimate line is a transparent metonymy of China. It will be recalled that in the thirties the semifeudal, semicolonial China was frequently used in the Soviet phraseology as a typical example of the "enslavement of man by man."

The last line, "Pokuda na zemle poslednij živ nevol'nik," clearly foreshadows the end of the poem "Oboronjaet son svoju donskuju son'" (written on February 13, 1937), which is, in its turn, connected with the poem "Naušnički, naušnički moi" by the image of the Kremlin chimes:

> И слушает земля — другие страны — бой
> Из хорового падающий короба:

---

[5] Cf. Edward Gibbon, *The History of the Decline and Fall of the Roman Empire*, II (London, 1929), 157-158.

[6] Cf. Lloyd B. Hoslapple, *Constantine the Great* (New York, 1942), pp. 317-319.

— Рабу не быть рабом, рабе не быть рабой!
И хор поет с часами рука об руку.

The third line, which contains an onomatopoeia of the Kremlin chimes (*bu—by—bom* ‖ *b'e—by—boį*), may be interpreted as "the language of the space condensed to a dot." It should also not be forgotten that in the thirties the midnight striking of the Kremlin chimes was followed by the *Internationale*.

As we see, the main message of Mandel'štam's poem "Da, ja ležu v zemle" is the poet's faith in the historic mission of his country, the faith in the future. This is the testament of the poet, coming from his grave. As for his attitude to his own time, the so-called "period of the personality cult," this attitude was sharply negative, and found a frank expression in both the poetry and the prose of Mandel'štam.[7]

During his lifetime, Mandel'štam could not even dream of having his poem appear in print. Apparently, he addressed it to that "reader in the future generation" of whom he wrote at the very beginning of his literary path (the essay "O sobesednike," 1913). Nor could Puškin think of publishing his "Monument."[8] Nevertheless, both poets were convinced that their poetry would outlive them and reach the generations to come:

Нет, весь я не умру — душа в заветной лире
Мой прах *переживет* и тленья убежит . . .

Да, я лежу в земле, губами шевеля,
Но то, что я скажу, *заучит* каждый школьник . . .

---

[7] Please see note 4, above. There is much in common between the messages of the poems "Na rozval'njax, uložennyx solomoj" and "Da, ja ležu v zemle." Both poems deal with the historical mission of Russia, on the one hand, and the cruelty and the victims of history, on the other. In the first poem, the bound Tsarevich is such a victim; in the second poem, the victim is the poet himself, buried alive.

[8] As is known, the original text of Puškin's poem was published in 1881. Mandel'štam's poem was published for the first time abroad, in *Vozdušnye puti*, II (1961), and, in the Soviet Union, in *Den' poèzii* (1962).

NOTHUNG, THE CASSIA FLOWER, AND A "SPIRIT OF MUSIC" IN THE POETRY OF ALEKSANDR BLOK

BY

ROBERT P. HUGHES

ALEKSANDR BLOK was moved by his father's death in 1909 to begin a long narrative poem entitled *Vozmezdie* ("Retribution"), on which he worked intermittently from 1910 to 1921. It was one of Blok's grandest conceptions, but the *poèma* remained unfinished at his death. The plans and design for the work have links with the poet's ideas about music, both metaphysical (as what he calls the "spirit of music" will be labeled here) and actual. Any attempt to clarify the metaphysical musical aspects of the work must await a discussion of the prose introduction to the work (written only in 1919)—best done, although there is little space here to do so, in conjunction with his contemporary articles and essays. I have chosen first to point out the passages descriptive of actual music and to suggest their symbolic weight.

A most striking reference of a musical nature occurs in the first part of the prologue (1911), which is a modern invocation, the poet's statement of purpose, his definition of his craft and of the function of the poet in the world, and his relation to his fellow human beings. The poet is seen as the most just judge of the world, for he has been endowed with a dispassionate standard for measuring everything he sees. The poet's vision should be firm and clear; the sacred and profane things of the world should pass through the fire of his soul and the coolness of his reason. Then the image of Wagner's Siegfried is introduced, serving as a symbol for the poet:

> Так Зигфрид правит меч над горном:
> То в красный уголь обратит,
> То быстро в воду погрузит —
> И зашипит, и станет черным
> Любимцу вверенный клинок . . .
> Удар — он блещет, Нотунг верный,
> И Миме, карлик лицемерный,
> В смятеньи падает у ног!

In a somewhat different version, this paper was read at the Slavic Section meeting of the Modern Language Association, Denver, Colorado, December 27, 1969.

> Кто меч скует? — Не знавший страха.
> А я беспомощен и слаб . . .
>
> [III, p. 301][1]

The scene of Siegfried's forging of the sword Nothung from the fragments of his father Siegmund's sword, preserved by Brünnhilde and Sieglinde, is, of course, Blok's retelling of act I of Wagner's *Siegfried*. Only Siegfried has the requisite innocence, strength, and fearlessness to reforge the faithful Nothung. The poet, too, according to Blok, should possess those characteristics—even though he himself has little faith in his own strength. Blok's use of this material is highly original, and his knowledge of Wagner—and especially of *Der Ring des Nibelungen*—contributed to the overall conception of the poem. The motifs of "father and son" and the idea of "retribution" are central to both compositions. Siegfried, too, knew no fear at first, and became helpless and weak in a purely human way: because of his love for Brünnhilde. Eventually he must die. He is the archetypal romantic poet—a man who views the world in innocence, but who perishes of too great a knowledge of it.

Siegfried's knowledge comes from his taste of the blood of the dragon Fafner, enabling him to understand the language of the birds, who tell him of Mime's intention to kill him and who direct him to the sleeping Brünnhilde. Blok puts this part of the story to creative use also in the following lines:

> Над всей Европою дракон,
> Разинув пасть, томится жаждой . . .
> Кто нанесет ему удар? . . .
>
> [III, p. 302]

The question ("who will deliver the [fatal] blow" to the dragon[2]—usually read as the threat of the imminent destruction of European culture, to be swallowed up, in Blok's terms, by modern civilization) is not answered, but there is a glimmering of hope. Perhaps music, and its metonym poetry, will sustain mankind in dark moments and will in the

---

[1] All citations from Blok's writings are identified in the text by the volume and page numbers of: Aleksandr Blok, *Sobranie sočinenij v vos'mi tomax* (Moscow-Leningrad, 1960-1963).

[2] In his commentary (III, p. 616) to the prologue, Vladimir Orlov suggests that Blok's image may be an echo of Vladimir Solov'ev's poem *Drakon*, but if this is so, I submit that it is not the only source. Considering the context, it is more likely that Wagner's dragon, the reincarnated Fafner, whom Siegfried slays with the reforged Nothung (*Siegfried*, act II), served as the more immediate prototype. Apropos, perhaps, is George Bernard Shaw's allegoric reading of the impetuous young Siegfried, fearless and unmoral, as the anarchist Bakunin (the composer's friend and companion on the barricades in Dresden in 1848) and Fafner as a stupid, bourgeois money-worshipper (*The Perfect Wagnerite*, *passim*). Blok, too, seems to perceive in Wagner's epic the political and social significance that Shaw details in his study.

end be triumphant; the poet's song will last, even though he has suffered a kind of self-sacrifice:

> Но песня — песнью всё пребудет.
> В толпе всё кто-нибудь поет.³

And, at the end:

> Алмаз горит издалека —
> Дроби, мой гневный ямб, каменья!
>
> [III, pp. 302-303]

It is instructive to see the role of music in the life of the father in the course of the poem. His "sick soul seeks solace" at the keyboard of the "submissive piano," from which he "plucks sounds like flowers" (chap. I, lines 771-780, III, pp. 323-324). "Trash is transformed into beauty" and "hunched shoulders are straightened"; the sounds of Schumann bring rest to the father, "a miser forgotten by men, God, and himself" (chap. III, lines 279-280, 289-299, III, p. 339). And at the playing of the piano, more than music is suggested; again, as so often in Blok, the symbolist, we see that music establishes a connection with another reality:

> И там — за бурей музыкальной —
> Вдруг возникал как и тогда
> Какой-то образ — грустный, дальный,
> Непостижимый никогда . . .
> И крылья белые в лазури,
> И неземная тишина . . .
> Но эта тихая струна
> Тонула в музыкальной буре . . .
>
> [Chap. I, lines 788-795, III, p. 324]

But, I will return to things Wagnerian in Blok's poetry, leaving aside the poet's prose essays and speeches that contain frequent allusions to Wagner's operas and his works of prose, *Opera and Drama* and *Art and*

---

³ These lines are followed by:

> Вот — голову его на блюде
> Царю плясунья подает . . .

Here the sacrificed poet is seen in the guise of John the Baptist. Even though Orlov (loc. cit.) simply glosses this passage with the biblical reference, the origin of the image may again be a musical one: Richard Strauss' *Salome* (1905), his most Wagnerian music-drama. Oscar Wilde's French play also spawned pieces by Glazunov and Florent Schmitt, inter alia. Blok might have seen or heard about any one or all of these; and, in any case, surely must have known Wilde's play. On the other hand, the image of Salome with the head of John the Baptist might have been retained from the time he saw Carlo Dolci's painting in Italy; cf. notebooks of that period and the Italian poem "Xolodnyj veter ot laguny."

Revolution, to which Blok wrote an introduction in 1918 for the Russian translation.

As early as 1898, when the poet was only seventeen, a motif from Wagner's *Tannhaüser* seems to have provided the impetus for a short lyric, "V žarkoj pljaske vakxanalij . . . " (I, p. 373). It is not one of Blok's best efforts, and he did not include it in the basic canon which he later devised. The same is true of another poem, dating from 1900 (although this one was included in his late collection *Za gran'ju prošlyx dnej*). Again on a motif from Wagner—indeed that is the subtitle—the poem entitled *Valkirija* is a fragmentary dramatic paraphrase (it does not follow Wagner's sequence of events) of the first encounter between Siegmund and Sieglinde in the first scene of *Die Walküre*.

Another major incident from the opera's first act, the love duet between Siegmund and Sieglinde and their flight from the hut of Hunding finds reflection in a poem from 1910. In a subsection of *Arfy i skripki* (poems written between 1908–1916) entitled *Čerez dvenadcat' let*, Blok recalls his first love affair, twelve years earlier, with Ksenija Mixajlovna Sadovskaja, (1862–1925, i.e., eighteen years older than the eighteen-year-old Blok), a teacher of voice at the Petersburg conservatory; the infatuation was probably more a crush on an elegant lady from the world of music than a genuine attachment. The poet was at that time in Bad Nauheim, where they had first met—and where, one must imagine, they had attended some Wagner operas. In act I, scene 3 of *Die Walküre*, Siegmund sings a song of spring and love to Sieglinde, his sister and his beloved, with whom he then flees, taking the sword Nothung, which only he, the son of Wotan, has been able to draw from the great ash tree. Siegmund's aria is the famous:

> Winterstürme wichen
> Dem Wonnemond,
> In mildem Lichte
> Leuchtet der Lenz . . .
> . . . .
> Jauchzend grüsst' sich
> Das junge Paar:
> Vereint sind Liebe und Lenz!

Note, then, parts of Blok's lyric:

> Уже померкла ясность взора,
> И скрипка под смычок легла,
> И злая воля дирижера
> По арфам ветер пронесла . . .
>
> Твой очерк страстный, очерк дымный
> Сквозь сумрак ложи плыл ко мне.

И тенор пел на сцене гимны
Безумным скрипкам и весне ...

March, 1910 [III, p. 185]

Thus we have indications—by no means exhaustive—of Blok's knowledge and use of motifs and figures from Wagner's *Ring*. Other operas certainly influenced him. After the experience of hearing *Parsifal* in a concert version (January, 1901), Blok composed the lyric beginning "Ja nikogda ne ponimal / Iskusstva muzyki svjaščennoj...." In one of his finest poems—"Idut časy, i dni, i gody"—written in 1910 (it forms part of the *Strašnyj mir* cycle), he anachronistically employs the image of the dying Tristan, analogue for the love-stricken Blok and for the poet. Here are the final two stanzas:

И перевязан шелком душным
(Чтоб кровь не шла из черных жил),
Я был веселым и послушным,
Обезоруженный — служил.

Но час настал. Припоминая,
Я вспомнил: Нет, я не слуга.
Так падай, перевязь цветная!
Хлынь, кровь, и обагри снега!

[III, pp. 29-30]

Another link between Wagner's *Tristan und Isolde* and Blok's work is to be seen in his poetic drama *Roza i Krest* (1912–1913), first projected as an opera libretto. (It may extend even to the names of the protagonists: Tristan and Bertran; Isolde and Izora, who also happens to share a name with a character in another musically inspired work in Russian literature, Puškin's *Mocart i Sal'eri*—she is the late wife of the poisoner and the source of the poison itself.) Viktor Žirmunskij has suggested that the medieval legend concerning the love of Tristan and Isolde and its modernization in Wagner's musical drama are reflected in Blok's play, and as example he points out a similarity between the "pre-death love ecstasy" of the dying Bertran and the *Liebestod* in Wagner's opera.[4] An even greater similarity, however, may be found between the final scene of Blok's drama and act III, scene I of Wagner's work. It is more likely that Tristan's death, rather than Isolde's, was Blok's model. The three stages

---

[4] *Drama Aleksandra Bloka "Roza i Krest"* (Leningrad, 1964), p. 19. Žirmunskij is exceedingly cautious:

Разумеется, такое художественное влияние эмоциональной темы и музыкально-лирической атмосферы другого, хотя и родственного, искусства не может быть доказано с бесспорной убедительностью, но в свете указанных фактов оно представляется достаточно вероятным.

of Bertran's death and transfiguration (wherein Joy and Sorrow—his physical suffering—do indeed become one) are very like the long dying of Tristan as he awaits the arrival of Isolde. Tristan's death, too, is accomplished in three stages of reminiscence and a final transfiguration in which the joy of understanding becomes one with his suffering.

From his diaries, we know that Blok attended a performance of *Die Meistersinger von Nürnberg* the night before he completed *Roza i Krest*, that he was "swimming in Wagner's musical ocean," and that he "cast into verse the play's final scene to the melodies of Wagner" (VII, p. 208).[5]

The imprint of Wagner, then, was heavy upon Blok; and the power of the music itself was abetted by the poet's philosophical predilections. Again, from the notebooks and diaries, we know that Nietzsche, especially his *Geburt der Tragödie aus dem Geiste der Musik*, exercised a profound influence.[6] Although greatly indebted to Schopenhauer's philosophy, Nietzsche rejected his predecessor's position that tragedy was the product of the serene contemplation of the realm of ideas. (Tragedy was the highest poetical art, but music, in the hierarchy Schopenhauer sought to establish, was the direct expression of the Will—a notion emulated by Andrej Belyj in his *Formy iskusstva*, the essay that prompted the first of Blok's many letters to Belyj, 1903.) In what was to become a tremendously influential reversal of the traditional theory that tragedy in ancient Greece was a harmonious, "classical" art, the result of the Apollonian impulse, Nietzsche assigned the predominant role in its development to the Dionysian impulse, expressed in wild music and the drunken orgy, in which the darker, irrational aspects of men are manifested. The high point of Greek drama was reached in the tragedies of Aeschylus and Sophocles, in which the chorus, the musical factor, represented directly the emotions of the spectators. Nietzsche's conclusion was that tragedy eventually died of the rationalism and skepticism propounded by Socrates and incarnated in the dramas of Euripides, who eliminated the role the chorus had played in the works of his predecessors. Nietzsche does hold that certain other arts are to be

---

[5] R. D. B. Thompson rather too categorically rejects (for the purpose of emphasizing the personal background) Professor Žirmunskij's views (op. cit.), and the parallels with *Die Meistersinger* that he draws seem to me more farfetched than the ones with *Tristan* which are suggested above. The mere fact that Blok had heard *Die Meistersinger* the night before need not mean that it drove from his mind the *Tristan*-like conception (with which the poet had been working for some time) in a single night. Cf. R. D. B. Thompson, "The Non-Literary Sources of *Roza i Krest*," *The Slavonic and East European Review*, XLV, No. 105 (July, 1967), 292–306.

[6] Firm evidence that Blok had thought and worked over Nietzsche's study is provided by his notebooks for December, 1906, into which he copied out extensive passages from the Russian edition (1900) of *The Birth of Tragedy*. Aleksandr Blok, *Zapisnye knižki* (Moscow, 1965), pp. 78–84.

identified with Apollo, but that in tragedy the god of light and vision has only a subordinate role. In music and in lyric poetry, as well as in tragedy, Dionysus' is the dominant spirit.

To the main body of the work, Nietzsche added a preface addressed to Richard Wagner and ten eulogistic chapters glorifying the composer's music-dramas for reestablishing a viable interaction between the Apollonian and Dionysian impulses. In the mind of such a Wagnerian as Blok, the thesis and the figure of its exemplary hero must have taken hold on first reading.

Nietzsche's eventual repudiation of Wagner and his championing of Bizet (announced in *Der Fall Wagner*), glorifying *Carmen* as the greatest opera ever written, was a noteworthy event in the European intellectual world in the 1880's. The building of the Festspielhaus in Bayreuth, considered by the composer's erstwhile friend as a citadel of German imperialism and nationalism, and the composition of *Parsifal*, conceived from a Christian point of view, led Nietzsche to break definitively with Wagner. This final opera of Wagner's was seen as an abjuration of the composer's earlier Greek ideals (so finely manifested, for example, in *Tristan und Isolde*), if considered in the light of the principles through which the Dionysian substance, the all-powerful Will, is expressed in an Apollonian-inspired form.

It is characteristic of Nietzsche's violent temperament that Wagner was to be rejected so completely and to be replaced not, say, with Mozart (whose music surely could just as easily and justly have provided the necessary antidote), but only by Bizet. The choice, however, is indicative of the discerning lover of music in Nietzsche. Bizet in *Carmen* maintains (as does Wagner in his best works, it must be said) that rare equilibrium between the music and the drama that is an indispensable feature of the great operas. The philosopher's choice of epithets in describing the music of *Carmen* is perfectly just and perceptive: "dryness of atmosphere," "*limpidezza* of the air," "African gaiety," "fate hangs over it, its happiness is short, sudden, without reprieve," "southern, tawny, sunburnt sensitiveness," "lascivious melancholy."[7]

Without suggesting that the Russian poet possessed either the musical sensibilities, let alone the metaphysical profundity, of the German philosopher, one may note a curious partial parallel between Nietzsche's change of heart and Blok's similar evolution. If he had chanced to read Nietzsche's rhapsodic remarks about *Carmen* in late 1913 and early 1914, Blok could have welcomed them as wholeheartedly as he must earlier in

---

[7] *The Philosophy of Nietzsche*, ed. Geoffrey Clive (New York, 1965), pp. 259-260.

his life have accepted those about Wagner. Blok never rejected Wagner, indeed continued to honor him as a greater thinker and musician. This Northern poet, however, was already subject to the pull of the South and the Mediterranean; the works written during and after trips to Italy and France are among his finest. And he had reasons of his own for valuing the music of Bizet.

In 1914, Blok composed a cycle of poems with the title *Karmen*, under the impact of meeting and establishing an intimate friendship with the mezzosoprano Ljubov' Aleksandrovna Andreeva-Del'mas (1884– ?),[8] one of the more passionate and enduring in the roster of femmes fatales in his life. She enjoyed especial success for her portrayal of the heroine of Georges Bizet's *Carmen*.[9] Blok first saw her in October, 1913, and was immediately attracted by her red-haired (*ryžaja noč' tvoix kos*, he exclaims[10]), gypsy-like beauty. He finally met her in March, 1914, and their relationship lasted until his death in 1921; during this period he dedicated to her several poems and, for its final publication in his lifetime, *Roza i Krest*, where the dedicatee is designated * * *.[11]

A characteristic poem of the *Karmen* cycle, which is studded with figures, scenes, motifs, and even lines from the opera's libretto, is the one composed on March 26, 1914, where the poet in a crowd of the singer's admirers is inspired to creation; the figures of the infatuated Don José and the poet merge:

---

[8] Now deceased; but I have been unable to discover the date of her death. She was still alive in the spring of 1965, *vide* Lev Šilov, "*Karmen*. Po stranicam blokovskix dnevnikov i pisem" (*Junost'*, no. 10 [October], 1969, pp. 92–99), an account of the author's interviews of Del'mas that includes hitherto unpublished letters and reminiscences of the poet. In a brief note in *Literaturnaja Gazeta*, no. 12 (March 18, 1970), p. 6, V. Enišerlov takes Šilov to task for his naïveté and carelessness and corrects some of his misconceptions.

[9] Although he does not mention Del'mas (nor any other artist) by name, Vjačeslav Karatygin, one of the leading music critics of the day, lavishes praise on the production of *Carmen* in which she starred, at the Theater of Musical Drama in St. Petersburg, during the 1913–1914 season; *vide* "Peterburgskaja opera," *Apollon*, 1–2, 1914 (January–February), pp. 135–138.

[10] Or, in an evocative and vivid stanza (from a poem that echoes the *sorcière infâme* that Don José calls Carmen) descriptive of the voice and appearance of Del'mas:

> Но как ночною тьмой сквозит лазурь,
> Так этот лик сквозит порой ужасным,
> И золото кудрей — червонно-красным,
> И голос — рокотом забытых бурь.

[III, p. 235]

[11] Pavel Gromov, *A. Blok, ego predšestvenniki i sovremenniki* (Moscow-Leningrad, 1966), p. 476.

> Среди поклонников Кармен,
> Спешащих пестрою толпою,
> Ее зовущих за собою,
> Один, как тень у серых стен
> Ночной таверны Лиллас-Пастья,
> Молчит и сумрачно глядит,
> Не ждет, не требует участья,
> Когда же бубен зазвучит
> И глухо зазвенят запястья, —
> Он вспоминает дни весны,
> Он средь бушующих созвучий
> Глядит на стан ее певучий
> И видит творческие сны.
>
> [III, p. 232]

These last lines are an interesting contrast to those of Puškin in *Evgenij Onegin*, chapter I, canto LV (which provides the subtext for Blok):

> Я был рожден для жизни мирной,
> Для деревенской тишины;
> В глуши звучнее голос лирный,
> Живее творческие сны.

The settings are dissimilar: Blok's is urban, in this case outside an opera house, Puškin's is rural. Blok's inspiration came "amidst raging harmonies," Puškin's reflectively in the quiet of the peaceful countryside (on his estates at Mixajlovskoe and Boldino). The juxtaposition is instructive: Blok began his poetic career attuned to the harmonies of nature (at Šaxmatovo, and on the Mendeleev estate at Boblovo, where he produced the most ecstatic and idealistic of the *Stixi o Prekrasnoj Dame*), but he was driven by disillusion to find new, often discordant sounds in the city.

The final poem in the cycle, written March 31, 1914, was designated by Blok as especially important in his notebook under that date. Indeed, it does once again reveal Blok's belief in an ideal existence, in another world of harmony:

> Здесь — страшная печать отверженности женской
> За прелесть дивную — постичь ее нет сил.
> Там — дикий сплав миров, где часть души вселенской
> Рыдает, исходя гармонией светил.

Carmen and Del'mas, her re-creator, are laws unto themselves; and, by analogy, the poet too is a free, creative being. The music of their creations, the opera in performance and the poem in execution, is the most real element of their existence and a means by which they transcend everyday reality.

Сама себе закон — летишь, летишь ты мимо,
К созвездиям иным, не ведая орбит,
И этот мир тебе — лишь красный облак дыма,
Где что-то ждет, поет, тревожит и горит!

И в зареве его — твоя безумна младость . . .
Все — музыка и свет: нет счастья, нет измен . . .
Мелодией одной звучат печаль и радость . . .
Но я люблю тебя: я сам такой, *Кармен*.

[III, p. 239]

It is fascinating to follow the progress of the affair in Blok's diaries and notebooks. His frenzied pursuit of Del'mas takes him about Petersburg in search of her photograph and brings him often to the opera house in hopes of seeing her. In February and March of 1914, he saw *Carmen* several times (once performed by another soprano, when *She* [sic] was in the audience, see the poem beginning "Serdityj vzor bescvetnyx glaz"). It is interesting to note that, in addition, he attended performances of Wagner's *Ring* (to which he had subscription tickets). By a curious coincidence, he finally met Del'mas, the gypsy temptress turned temporary Wagnerian enchantress, on March 28, during the intermission in a performance of *Parsifal*, in which she sang one of the Blumenmädchen.[12]

I have indicated the role of actual music in Blok's life and work. Actual music, principally the operas of Wagner and Bizet's *Carmen*, is to be seen as the outward manifestation of an elemental, metaphysical music which the poet strove always to apprehend.

---

[12] On a less exalted, or delirious, level, Del'mas continued to inspire Blok. Written a few months later, the lyric beginning "Ja pomnju nežnost' vašix pleč— / Oni zastenčivy i čutki" (III, p. 369), inscribed on a photograph that he sent her, is a kind of extension of the *Karmen* cycle. "Ona," from 1916, is also dedicated to her. It is a little known fact that *Solov'inyj sad*, a *poèma* on which Blok was working in this same year, 1914, is also a product of his affair with Del'mas. Šilov, op. cit., pp. 97-99, points to the similarity of images and even lines of verse between *Karmen* and *Solov'inyj sad*, and he reports that the copy of the *poèma*'s separate edition presented to Del'mas by Blok bears the author's inscription, "Toj, čto poet v Solov'inom sadu."

She also helped him with the collecting and editing of the poems of Apollon Grigor'ev and in the writing of the critical article "Sud'ba Apollona Grigor'eva" (1915). Blok presented a copy of his edition of Grigor'ev's poems to her with the following inscription:

От знающего почерк ясный
Руки прилежной и прекрасной,
На память вечную о том
Лишь двум сердцам знакомом мире,
Который вспыхнул за окном
Зимой над Ponte dei Sospiri.

[III, p. 371]

One might look at the foreword to *Vozmezdie* in attempting more carefully to define what the poet meant by "spirit of music." It was written in July, 1919, to accompany the publication of chapter III. Blok notes the musical concerns which preoccupied him during the poem's composition; he wishes to relate "how the poem was born, what were the reasons for its beginnings, whence did its rhythms proceed" (III, p. 295). In 1910, the year Blok outlined the poem and began writing it, the deaths of the actress Kommissarževskaja, the painter Vrubel', and Lev Tolstoj occurred; the same year witnessed the crisis of Symbolism and the rise of the poetic movements inimical to it, Acmeism, Egofuturism, and Futurism. At this time, Blok became convinced of the indivisibility of art, life, and politics. He collates events from various spheres: the murder of Andrej Juščinskij, the Bejlis affair, and the Jewish problem in general; the London railway strike; the Agadir incident in the Mediterranean; wrestling matches featuring a Dutchman whose muscles were "a most perfect musical instrument of rare beauty"; aviation; the assassination of Stolypin. And all those events were viewed by him from a musical point of view:

> Все эти факты, казалось бы столь различные, для меня имеют один Музыкальный смысл. Я привык сопоставлять факты из всех областей жизни, доступных моему зрению в данное время, и уверен, что все они вместе всегда создают единый музыкальный напор.
>
> [III, p. 297]

As the simplest expression of the rhythm of the time, Blok believes the iambus best renders the development of "physical, political and military muscles"; the rhythmical and gradual growth of muscles came to comprise the rhythm of the whole poem, he explains. He concludes the foreword with a note about the leitmotif of retribution which runs through the poem. This, too, is conceived in musical terms:

> ... этот лейтмотив есть *мазурка* ... В первой главе этот танец легко доносится из окна какой-то петербургской квартиры — глухие 70-е годы; во второй главе танец гремит на балу ... в третьей главе мазурка разгулялась: она звенит в снежной вьюге ... В ней явственно слышится уже голос Возмездия.
>
> [III, pp. 299–300]

These "musical" remarks hardly provide a key to the meaning of the poem, but they do indicate the manner in which it was conceived and constructed. The combination of facts from every aspect of life created a "single musical impetus." He was interested in the "musical interrelationships" (far more than the social and political meanings) of events; the most varied phenomena of life are for him the outward reflection of that music.

Blok never finished the poem; his life ended in disillusion and despair—bereft of the ability to apprehend any longer the "spirit of music," he died at forty-one; his death had both physical and spiritual causes.

The "music of the revolution," which he caught fleetingly in his famous *Dvenadcat'*, disappeared almost immediately thereafter. Nothung, the symbol of the poet's mission, was again broken and could not be reforged. Carmen's cassia flower, a symbol of the passionate human element in his life, had faded—and with it "music and light" had disappeared from his world.

SYMPHONIC STRUCTURE IN ANDREJ BELYJ'S "PERVOE SVIDANIE"

BY

SIMON KARLINSKY

A STUDENT of Russian poetry would have to go back to Lomonosov to find another Russian poet whose poetry is comparable to Andrej Belyj's in its scope and variety of erudition, spanning the most diverse fields. Certainly, no other twentieth-century poet has Belyj's grasp of physical and mathematical sciences, of speculative philosophy, of aesthetics, of linguistics, and of musical theory and practice.

Mixail Kuzmin and Boris Pasternak, two poets who originally intended to become composers and who received extensive musical training, would reasonably be expected to write of musical matters with considerable assurance. Yet, neither of them does. Kuzmin can convey his own impressions of musical performances with great charm (e.g., his vivid evocation of a Wagnerian orchestra in the first section of "Forel' razbivaet led"), but he is sparing in the use of concrete musical terminology in his poetry. Boris Pasternak evokes scenes of piano playing in vivid, expressionistic imagery ("Rojal' drožaščij penu s gub obližet" or "Ja klavišej staju kormil s ruki"); yet his one attempt to use technical musical terms, in his translation of Verlaine's "Art poétique," is startlingly inept, considering Pasternak's earlier music studies.[1]

Andrej Belyj, on the other hand, could write of musical theory and practice both in his prose (descriptions of concerts, recitals, and private musical performances in his *Second Symphony*, the chapter on Èmilij Metner in *Načalo veka*, and the numerous passages on music in the rest of the autobiographical trilogy) and in verse (especially in the *poèma* "Pervoe svidanie"[2]) with a consummate understanding of the subject and with fluent use of technical vocabulary. Deržavin and Annenskij have

---

[1] *Zarubežnaja poèzija v russkix perevodax*, E. Vinokurov and L. Ginzburg, eds. (Moscow, 1968), pp. 300–301. In the fourth stanza Pasternak seems to confuse the musical intervals of whole and half tone (*poltona*) with nuances of color (*poluton*). He also does not know the Russian word for bassoon (*fagot*) and uses for it a pointless French borrowing *bason* (from *basson*).

[2] There seems to be no satisfactory way to render the title of Belyj's poetic masterpiece into English. "The First Meeting" and "The First Encounter" have both been tried and both miss the point; "The First Date," although far from ideal, would be somewhat closer to what the Russian conveys, if it did not bring in undesirable Andy Hardy associations. Very reluctantly, one is forced to settle for the pretentious, but reasonably close "The First Rendez-Vous."

written impressively of individual musical instruments, but Belyj is unique in Russian poetry in his detailed and knowledgeable evocations of individual orchestral timbres in "Pervoe svidanie." For all the mystical and symbolic overtones of the scene at the concert, Belyj finds remarkably apt and precise verbal means to convey the tone coloring of a quartet of horns set off antiphonally by bassoons:

> И в строгий разговор валторн
> Фаготы прорицают хором[3]
>
> [429]

or the effect of a trombone crescendo on a single note:

> И стаю звуков гонит он,
> Как зайца гончая собака
> На возникающий тромбон.
>
> [431]

Only a person totally at home with various orchestral timbres could have imagined the nightmarish metaphors and the alliterative howl of *u*'s Belyj uses to convey the auditory chaos of an orchestra tuning up before a performance:

> Возня, переговоры . . . Скрежет:
> И трудный гуд, и нудный зуд —
> Так ноет зуб, так нудит блуд . . .
> Кто это там пилит и режет?
>
> [427]

which is immediately followed by an equally onomatopoetic depiction of a set of kettledrums being tuned up:

> Натянуто пустое дно, —
> Долдонит бебень барабана,
> Как пузо выпуклого жбана:
> И тупо, тупо бьет оно . . .
>
> [428]

Equally apt are Belyj's visualization of an orchestra conductor's typical gestures (429–431) and his felicitous epithet for the chord of the diminished seventh which is about to be resolved: *vozduxoletnyj septakkord*. Belyj's paean to the versatility of the diatonic scale is remarkable for its subtle ambiguity, because the term *zvukorjad* (an old term for "mode") corresponds etymologically to the German *Tonreihe* and is used here in a context that may suggest the dodecaphonic composition systems of

---

[3] "Pervoe svidanie," in Andrej Belyj, *Stixotvorenija i poèmy* (Moscow-Leningrad, 1966). The numbers here and later refer to the page numbers of this edition.

Schönberg and Webern, already evolving, but not yet fully stated or practiced at the time "Pervoe svidanie" was written (1921):[4]

> Интерферируя наш взгляд
> И озонируя дыханье,
> Мне музыкальный звукоряд
> Отображает мирозданье —
> От безобра́зий городских
> До тайн безо́бразий Эреба
> До света образов людских
> Многообразиями неба
>
> [426]

The fivefold paronomastic and prosodic permutation of the stem *obraz* in the above passage suggests a typical procedure of serial musical composition, and is in its way as disconcertingly and inexplicably prophetic as Belyj's famous mention of the atomic bomb in the same *poèma*.

Although familiar with music since infancy, Belyj probably acquired his thorough knowledge of the symphonic form through Èmilij Metner's detailed commentary on Schubert's C-major Symphony during their joint visits to Arthur Nikisch's orchestral rehearsals in 1901.[5]

Four of Belyj's early prose works bear the title "Symphony."[6] The use of the term was not figurative or metaphorical: it was Belyj's intention to apply the principles of musical form to literary, verbal structures. Therefore, while these works can and have been studied by literary scholars,[7] they are unique in world literature in that methods of musical scholarship and analysis are equally applicable to them. For example, the *Second Symphony* (*The Dramatic*) has its themes arranged in the discernible structure of a four-movement classical symphonic cycle, as practiced by Haydn or Beethoven: the first part is a traditional sonata-allegro, the second part a dreamy adagio with religious themes, and also with sonata features. The third and fourth parts can be seen as the scherzo and the

---

[4] Schönberg's first systematic application of the *Tonreihe* dates from his *Five Piano Pieces*, op. 23, and *Serenade*, op. 24 (1923); Webern followed his example one year later in his *Drei Volkstexte*, op. 17.

[5] Andrej Belyj, *Načalo veka* (Moscow–Leningrad, 1933), pp. 78–80.

[6] On all four of Belyj's Symphonies, see Gleb Struve, "Andrej Belyj's Experiments with Novel Technique," *Stil- und Formprobleme in der Literatur. Vorträge des VII Kongresses der Internationalen Vereinigung für moderne Sprachen und Literaturen in Heidelberg* (Heidelberg, 1959), pp. 459–467.

[7] *Third Symphony* was analyzed by Oleg A. Maslenikov, "Andrej Belyj's Third 'Symphony'," *The American Slavic and East European Review*, VII, No. 1 (New York, 1948), 78–92; on *Second Symphony*, see Elena Szilard, "O strukture Vtoroj simfonii A. Belogo," *Studia Slavica Hungarica*, XIII (1967), 311–322.

traditional rondo-finale.[8] The *Third Symphony* (*The Return*), although divided into three parts, is in terms of its musical structure not a symphonic cycle but a vast one-movement sonata-allegro, with the exposition of the themes in the first part, their restatement and development in another tonality (in another universe, in this case) in the second part, and their recapitulation and synthesis in the original key in the last part.[9] These are only brief indications of the kind of musicological analysis that could and should be profitably applied to Belyj's four symphonies in prose.

However, his most thorough and systematic application of the classical symphonic structure was made in a work written in verse and not containing the word "symphony" anywhere in its title. The autobiographical narrative poem "Pervoe svidanie" written in 1921, at the time Belyj was expecting to leave Soviet Russia to join his anthroposophic mentor Rudolf Steiner and the woman he loved (Anna Turgeneva) in Switzerland, is a work permeated with the poet's lyrical joy. The narrative covers the period described by Belyj later in his prose memoir *Načalo veka*: his student days and his realization in May of 1900 that he would become a professional writer. Autobiographical elements that we know from the memoir (Belyj's friendship with the family of Mixail Solov'ev, his infatuation with the wealthy merchant's wife Margarita Morozova, his pilgrimage to the tomb of Vladimir Solov'ev) are interwoven in the poem with themes treated in Belyj's *Second Symphony* (*The Dramatic*)—a mystical encounter at the symphony concert, the ghost of Vladimir Solov'ev hovering over the city of Moscow, the satirical glimpses of Moscow's academic intelligentsia.

Another work of Belyj's connected to "Pervoe svidanie" is his most baffling piece of writing, the long prose poem on language, *Glossolalia. Poèma o zvuke*, written at the time of the October Revolution. Ostensibly a linguistic treatise, the work is in fact a set of inchoate, instinctive, illogical meditations on language, to which, as Belyj himself was the first to admit, scholarly linguistic criticism would not be applicable. The Belyj who wrote "Pervoe svidanie," even more than the author of *Glossolalia*, is no longer the typically Symbolist poet he was when he wrote the Symphonies and his first collection of verse. By 1921 Belyj had read Xlebnikov (including *his* inchoate, instinctive theories of language), Majakovskij, possibly even Boris Pasternak. He was assuredly familiar

---

[8] The authentically musical structure of the *Second Symphony* has been noted by Szilard.

[9] The sonata-allegro structure of the *Third Symphony* was pointed out several years ago in an unpublished paper on this work by my colleague, Professor Erica Brendel.

with the writings of Viktor Šklovskij, Roman Jakobson, and other Russian Formalists. The stylistic and lexical texture of "Pervoe svidanie" show the unmistakable impact of Russian Futurism and Formalism.[10] Combined with this impact is some seepage from *Glossolalia*, which leaves its precipitate in the form of certain verbal devices and of the mystical idea of salvation through language and linguistics, expressed in the Introduction to the poem.

Classical Russian literature provides two additional ingredients: deliberate stylistic reminiscences from Puškin's *Eugene Onegin* in the passages on the Solov'ev family and the Gogolian demon of trivia (*bes pošlosti*) who appears prominently in chapters 3 and 4. All these heterogeneous themes and elements are brilliantly fused by Belyj into a verse texture almost without equal in Russian poetry for its sustained inventiveness and carefully organized into a strict and regular four-movement symphonic cycle consisting of a sonata-allegro (with a separate introduction), an adagio in the form of a three-part Lied, a scherzo with a trio (in which a reprise of the end of the first movement serves as an introduction) and a rondo-finale with a coda.

The brief 32-line Introduction is absolutely astounding in its concentration of numerous levels of meaning. The initial image of the miner-gnome who crushes crunching consonants to form tomes is a clever personification of the mechanical aspects of human language, dead sounds not yet brought to life by spirit and meaning. The gnome is metamorphosed into the "I" of the poem: at first a personified stylistic device then a tired, aging poet, likened to a broken object and to an extinguished bakery oven, baking indifferent verse to order.[11] The tired, extinguished poet starts to pray to God and the poet-oven immediately catches fire. The prayer to God becomes an invocation to language. Images of nature transcending its limitations (an inflated leaf on a dead stick, an ermine in the sky) powerfully convey the idea of spiritual resurrection, central to the entire Introduction. Animals symbolic of the Evangelists—the lion, the ox, and the eagle—which also figure in the Apocalypse, are evoked and the spiritual qualities assigned to them in Christian theology are

---

[10] The author's insistence that "Pervoe svidanie" is a purely symbolist work and his refusal to consider it within the context of the time of its writing weakens Oleg Il'inskij's article on this poem (*Novyj Žurnal*, New York, no. 90, pp. 98–111). Another defect is that Il'inskij repeatedly sees free verbal association in passages that in fact contain profound and multi-leveled meaning.

[11] Il'inskij, p. 103, seems to miss Belyj's witty pun on the word *priem*, which means a stylistic device in line 3 of the Introduction, but refers to the bakers' practice of renting their ovens to customers (*Peku priem: stixi v načinku*) in line 6.

compared to various capabilities of human language. This theological digression culminates in a complex explanation of the Christogram which combines the initial letters of "Jesus Christ" to form the symbol for Life:

«Ха» с «I» в «Же» — «Жизнь»: Христос Иисус —
Знак начертательного смысла

[405]

followed by a paraphrased quotation of an appropriate verse from the Gospel According to St. John and the direct mention of the Evangelists, represented until now by their symbolic animals. In the last four lines of the Introduction, the pedantic gnomes of the inert language matter are left behind, the crunching (*xrust*) of consonants and of dying flames is replaced by crackling sounds of finely-honed sound instrumentation (*instrumentacij grannyj tresk*), and the extinguished oven and the worn-out poet of the beginning are both ablaze with sacred fire. Language is the agent that accomplishes the progression from mineral to fire, from inert matter to vibrant life and is thus assigned divine powers. As in *Glossolalia*, but in a more convincing and successful manner, the Introduction fuses theology and linguistics. Belyj's concentrated poetic art manages to combine into a harmonious whole such seemingly heterogeneous elements as paraphrases from the New Testament and literary terminology of Russian Formalists: *stilističeskij priem* (stylistic device), *jazykovye idiomy* (idioms of language) and *instrumentacija* (sound instrumentation); the latter may refer not only to language phenomena treated in the Introduction but also to the orchestral instrumentation described at length in chapter 3 of the poem.

In Belyj's prose Symphonies distinctive verbal structures were used as equivalents of musical themes (this applies less to his *Third Symphony*, where thematic functions are more likely to be taken by characters or situations). In the sonata-allegro of the first chapter of "Pervoe svidanie," the symphonic structure utilizes complexes of ideas as its basic structural element. The principal theme of this first movement (and in a way, of the entire poem) is the theme of reminiscences of Belyj's experiences in 1900; subsumed within this theme are the ideas of creative imagination and of poetry. The principal theme is stated in the first 22 lines of chapter 1 and is then followed by three related subordinate themes that in turn take up Belyj's activities and interests at that juncture of his life.

Subordinate theme I is his daily and social life as a student at Moscow University. It begins with the lines:

Меня пленяет Гольбер Гент . . .
И я — не гимназист: студент.

[406]

Subordinate theme II has to do with young Belyj's interest in mythology, mysticism, and the history of religions, an interest considered inappropriate and even shocking by his mathematician-father. This theme is brought in with the ironic discussion of Hindu mystics and sacred texts (407) and is soon contrasted with subordinate theme III: the physical sciences that Belyj was then studying:

> Мне Менделеев говорит
> Периодической системой
>
> [407]

The exposition of themes is completed by two humorous restatements of subordinate theme II, which contrast the role of mythology in ancient times and in the modern world.

The development section, beginning with the lines:

> Из зыбей зыблемой лазури,
> Когда отвеяна лазурь,
>
> [409]

combines and varies the principal and the three subordinate themes in various combinations. This section is particularly notable for its inventive use of Xlebnikov-like neologisms:

> Туда серебряные роги,
> Туда, о месяц, протопырь!
> Взирай оттуда, мертвый взорич,
> Взирай, повешенный, и стынь, —
> О, злая, бешеная горечь,
> О, оскорбленная ледынь
>
> [409]

The recapitulation section takes up the subordinate themes II and III (in reverse order):

> И строгой физикой мой ум
> Переполнял: профессор Умов
>
> [410]

(this is the section which contains the celebrated prediction of the atomic bomb), then the principal theme:

> В душе, органом проиграв,
> Дни, как орнамент, полетели,
> Взвиваясь запахами трав,
> Взвиваясь запахом метели.
>
> [411]

and concludes with a developed restatement of subordinate theme I, which this time incorporates some new imagery and syntactic structures that turn out to foreshadow thematic and structural elements of chapter 3 of the poem. The interrupted evocation of the concert hall and of Beethoven at the end of chapter 1 is analogous to the musical effect of an interrupted cadence, the resolution of which has been postponed until chapter 3, where this theme is fully stated and developed. The reversal of thematic sequence in the recapitulation, although not usual in musical practice, is not unprecedented. I. V. Sposobin[12] calls this type of recapitulation *zerkal'naja repriza* ("mirror recapitulation") and cites instances of it in Wagner's overture to "Tannhäuser," Liszt's "Les Préludes," and the first movement of Raxmaninov's Fourth Piano Concerto.

Chapter 2 of "Pervoe svidanie" is, as previously stated, a simple three-part Lied in form. The apartment where Mixail Solov'ev, his wife and their son Sergej opened the new world of poetry and imagination to the young Borja Bugaev, the future Andrej Belyj, is described with wit, humor, and enormous affection. Mixail Solov'ev is assigned as constant background several objects (his "bistre"-colored armchair, his glittering pince-nez, his cigarette) which accompany every mention of his name like refrains. Two principal characters of the poem, Vladimir Solov'ev and Nadežda Zarina (fictitious poetic name for Margarita Morozova), who are later given prominent roles, make their first brief appearances in this first section of chapter 2. The contrasting second section of this chapter, describing Belyj's and Sergej Solov'ev's visit to Vladimir Solov'ev's grave at the cemetery of the Novodevičij Monastery (similar to the analogous episode in the *Second Symphony*), is set off from the rest of the poem by its versification. It is written in couplets of iambic tetrameter, using only masculine rhymes, whereas the rest of the poem freely alternates masculine and feminine rhymes. The final section of the chapter takes the reader back to the Solov'ev apartment, but this time Vladimir Solov'ev is the center of attention. The philosopher and poet, to whom Belyj owed so much of his spiritual development, is, as it were, conjured from his grave, and he appears, not as a ghost (as will be the case later on in chapter 4), but as a memory of Belyj's actual brief encounters with him in his brother's apartment. Fragments of the concert passages from chapter 3 intrude even more insistently than they did at the end of chapter 1 into the portrait of the philosopher, a portrait that is a unique mixture of grotesquerie, satire, and affection. In the last evocation of Vladimir Solov'ev in this chapter, however, grotesquerie and satire disappear for a moment and we are given a tremendously moving brief requiem:

> Он — канул в Вечность: без возврата;
> Прошел в восторг нездешних мест:

---

[12] I. V. Sposobin, *Muzykal'naja forma* (Moscow–Leningrad, 1947), p. 198.

> В монастыре, в волнах заката, —
> Рукопростертый белый крест
> Стоит, как память дорогая;
>
> [424]

which the irrepressible humorist in Belyj cannot resist from topping with a last lapse into the ridiculous a few lines later:

> Так всякий: поживет, и — помер,
> И принят под такой-то номер.
>
> [424]

I have attempted to demonstrate the thoroughness and logic with which Belyj applied the procedures of musical form to the structural organization of his most important narrative poem. The scope of this paper does not allow for detailed examination of the scherzo form in chapter 3, the chapter that is the focal point of the poem, with its final realization of the musical themes presaged in the first two chapters, its dialectical development of the images associated with the Evangelists in the Introduction, and, most important of all, the poet's mystical encounter at the concert (the music serving as a catalyst) with Nadežda Zarina, Belyj's equivalent of Vladimir Solov'ev's Sophia and Blok's *Prekrasnaja Dama*. The trio in the scherzo is realized not only formally, but also symbolically, in the three-fold contrast between the poet, Zarina, and the Gogolian demon of trivia brought into the concert hall by the philistine members of the Moscow society and academic world.

The recurrent rondo theme of chapter 4 is provided by the poet's wanderings through Moscow streets after the concert. Memories of other similar wanderings through snowy streets return throughout the chapter to serve as rondo refrains. The rondo episodes interspersed with these refrains form a retrospective synthesis of the thematic material of the first three chapters. The religious motifs of the Introduction and the theme of Vladimir Solov'ev from chapter 2 dominate the end of the chapter. The final appearance of Vladimir Solov'ev as an invisible ghost in a snowstorm may have been suggested to Belyj by the figure of Christ in Blok's "The Twelve," but this Blokian image is ingeniously fused with the last echo of the concert hall imagery:

> «Ты кто?»
> — «Владимир Соловьев:
> Воспоминанием и светом
> Работаю на месте этом . . .»
>
> И никого: лишь белый гейзер . . .
> Так заливается свирель;

> Так на рояли Гольденвейзер
> Берет уверенную трель.
>
> [441]

The image of the Virgin in the last lines of chapter 4 and the final brief conclusion reaffirm the religious mood of the initial Introduction, not ecstatically and vibrantly as there, however, but on a note of peace and serenity.

"Pervoe svidanie" is an astoundingly successful piece of poetry, rewarding on many levels of perception. It is also a work that could and should be studied from the most diverse angles. Its debt to the Apocalypse and to the Gospel According to St. John; its relationship to *Glossolalia*, to the *Second Symphony* and to Belyj's autobiographical trilogy; its treatment of the person and the writings of Vladimir Solov'ev; its debt to Russian Futurists (especially Xlebnikov) and Formalists—these are some of the problems this complex poem raises. A full-length study of the musical structural devices Belyj used in this poem (which the present paper has only sketched out) could easily result in a book-length treatise.

Such future scholarly attention would be well deserved. Written during a decade when Russian narrative poetry scaled such astounding peaks as Majakovskij's "Pro èto" ("About This"), Marina Cvetaeva's "Krysolov" ("The Pied Piper"), Kuzmin's "Forel' razbivaet led" ("Trout Breaking Through the Ice") and Zabolockij's "Toržestvo zemledelija" ("Triumph of Agriculture"), Belyj's autobiographical verbal symphony can make a valid claim to being one of the two or three most profound, most complex and most verbally dazzling narrative poems in the entire history of the Russian *poèma*.

REMIZOV'S *PRUD*: FROM SYMBOLISM TO NEO-REALISM

BY

ALEX M. SHANE

IN THE PERIOD between the revolutions of 1905 and 1917, Russian literary critics repeatedly spoke of a return to reality, of a new expanded realism that had not only been enriched by impressionistic and symbolic devices, but was characterized by a conception of the artist's function which differed from that of traditional nineteenth-century critical realism. The appellation Neo-Realism, which was encountered with ever-increasing frequency, has been retained today by the literary historian Marc Slonim, who has defined it in terms of the object depicted (provincial life, characters from among the people, national traits, minutiae of everyday existence) as well as certain stylistic features (rhythm, linguistic innovation, the combination of the realistic and the fantastic, stress on irony, grotesque, lyricism, and subjectivity at the expense of a straight narrative).[1]

A considerably more incisive treatment of Neo-Realism can be found in Evgenij Zamjatin's stimulating essay, "Sovremennaja russkaja literatura." Zamjatin, who modestly considered himself a leading proponent of the new direction in Russian prose fiction, viewed Neo-Realism in terms of the Hegelian dialectic as the synthesis of nineteenth-century Realism (thesis) and Symbolism (antithesis).[2] Rejecting the religious and mystical theurgy of the Symbolists who had transcended reality in search of a supreme deity whether positive (Christ) or negative (Lucifer), the Neo-Realists once again focused their attention on everyday reality here on earth, but, unlike the latter-day "Realists" Čexov and Gor'kij, deified neither man nor his potentialities. In this respect, Neo-Realism was in essence anti-religious; hence its predilection for the ironic, for the grotesque, for the exaggerated. Taking their cue from Dostoevskij's assertion that "the real truth is always improbable," the Neo-Realists viewed the world through a cruel, ironic, microscope: where the Realists had seen only smooth skin covered with downy hair, they saw gullies and mounds, thick stems of unknown plants (hair), and huge meteorites (dust particles).

---

[1] Marc Slonim, *Modern Russian Literature; From Chekhov to the Present* (New York, 1953), pp. 228-229.

[2] Originally a lecture delivered at the Lebedjanskij Narodnyj Universitet on September 8, 1918, "Sovremennaja russkaja literatura" was published posthumously in *Grani*, no. 32 (October-December, 1956), pp. 90-101.

By focusing on a few carefully chosen, albeit exaggerated features, the Neo-Realists sought to create a synthetic, symbolic image that would reveal the essence of the depicted object. Many of the other distinguishing characteristics mentioned by Slonim were simply a logical extension of this basic philosophy. The preoccupation with ornamentation, with craftsmanship in the choice and arrangement of words, was a Symbolist legacy to which Remizov added the development of the *skaz* narrative, a unique stylization which reproduced the intonations of colloquial, often dialectal, spoken language in written prose.

In discussing Remizov, the central and most influential figure in the Neo-Realist movement, neither Slonim, Zamjatin, nor Mirskij (who does not use the term Neo-Realism),[3] devoted much space to Remizov's first novel *Prud*. In fact, most of the generalizations made about Remizov's style were based on later works, especially the *povesti* "Krestovye sestry" (1910), "Neuemnyj buben" (1910), and "Pjataja jazva" (1912). *Prud* is unlike them in many respects, and only after extensive revision in 1911 did the novel take on some of the features typical of Neo-Realist prose. A comparison of the two editions will graphically illustrate Remizov's transition from Symbolism to Neo-Realism.

Prud was written in 1902–1903 while Remizov was still living in exile in Southern Russia. Shortly after his return to Petersburg in February of 1905, the novel was serialized in *Voprosy Žizni* (nos. 4–11). Two years later, in November, 1907, *Prud* appeared in book form (hereafter referred to as the first edition) with a few alterations, most of which consisted in dividing some of the longer chapters of the serialized version into separate chapters.[4] Neither style nor content was modified significantly. *Prud* did not inspire general critical acclaim. Perhaps it had been overshadowed to some extent by the simultaneous serialization of Sologub's *Melkij bes* in the same journal, but ultimately the reason for its poor reception was the very nature of the work itself: it lacked any semblance of plot development typical of major fiction, its extremely fragmented structure made it difficult for the reader to follow, and the frequency of base, ugly, and depraved actions created a pall of gloomy horror which repulsed all but the most intrepid of philosophers. Aleksandr Blok, for example, upon completing the first installment wrote Remizov that fear had gripped him

---

[3] D. S. Mirsky, *Contemporary Russian Literature*, 1881–1925 (New York, 1926), pp. 281–291.

[4] Aleksej Remizov, *Prud. Roman* (SPB: Izdanie Sirius, 1908), 284 pp. Although the title page bore the date 1908, it was registered in the Dec. 1, 1907, issue of *Knižnaja Letopis'* (which listed books received during the last week of November), and the first reviews appeared in December.

when he read the novel and later admitted that after *Prud* he had been unable to read Remizov for a good two years.[5] In his summary review of Russian literature for 1907, Blok described *Prud* as something "ponderous, asphyxiating, and tortuous."[6] In contrast to Blok's genuine terror, Andrej Belyj viewed the novel in a considerably lighter vein and rather waggishly declared in a devastating review: "I must say something about *Prud*. Oh, how I don't want to! It would be better not to talk about *Prud*! I don't like *Prud*. Remizov didn't know how to compose *Prud*. Say what you will, but Remizov's *Prud* fell short." He then went on to criticize the novel's abstruseness and fragmentary character, finding only one redeeming feature: "it was a talented writer's first major work!"[7] Translating these strictures into a traditional dichotomy of criticism, Blok found the content to be insufferably distasteful, while Belyj felt that the form left much to be desired. But let us consider the novel itself.

The first edition of *Prud* was divided into two parts equal in length: the first—an episodic account of the four Finogenov brothers' life from childhood until, after graduating from secondary school, they were turned out into the street to shift for themselves; the second—an extended description of Nikolaj's (the youngest Finogenov) imprisonment, exile, return, and subsequent crime. There is very little action; when events take place, they are haphazard, without preparation and without apparent motivation. The general tone of part I is that of unbearable gloom, beginning with the description of the Ogorelyšev (maternal) grandfather who delights in raping orphan girls who ask for alms at his door; continuing with the children's cruel and blasphemous diversions (scalding of rats, maiming of frogs, crushing of plump white worms, religious processions with a hen's head instead of a cross); and including their mother's suicide as well as that of Sergej Molčanov, the leader of a revolutionary group to which the oldest Finogenov brother belonged.

The events of part II serve only to intensify the gloom: an extended description of Nikolaj's despair and nightmares while in prison, his rape of Aleksandr's betrothed, his visit to an insane asylum, and Arsenij's murder. The lack of plot development, of an ordered actional sequence, as well as the general disregard of motivation of characters indicate that Remizov had not intended *Prud* to be a narrative in the nineteenth-century realistic tradition. Rather, it was a thoroughly modernist work combining extreme impressionism with a symbolist orientation.

---

[5] A. Blok, *Sobranie sočinenij*, VIII (Moscow-Leningrad, 1963), 126, 257.
[6] A. Blok, "Literaturnye itogi 1907 goda," *Sobranie sočinenij*, V (Moscow-Leningrad, 1962), 226.
[7] A. Belyj, "Aleksej Remizov. *Prud*," *Vesy*, no. 12 (December, 1907), pp. 54–56.

As Čiževskij has pointed out in his discussion of Čexov's role in the development of Russian literature, the content of impressionistic literary works is characterized, on the one hand, by the renunciation of thought formulations (particularly in the form of aphorisms or maxims) that are intended to communicate the purpose of the work, and, on the other hand, by the creation of a general mood through which the effects of the artistic presentation are suggested to the reader's feelings.[8] And in terms of form, Remizov not only adheres to impressionistic canons by combining vagueness of the total picture with the prominence of detail and trivia, but goes considerably further, undoubtedly under the stimulus of the Polish modernist Stanisław Przybyszewski, with whose works he was familiar, and creates a fragmented lyric "where the sense is not in the whole, but in each page, and the sense of each page is in separate phrases, and the sense of phrases is in special words." [9]

In *Prud* Remizov, like the Symbolist poets, exhibits a complete lack of humor. But more important, the characters and their actions, in addition to being a description of a segment of Russian "reality," were intended as expressions of the author's own spiritual state much as were Baudelaire's morbid images of Parisian life. In this respect, *Prud* with its mood of pain, of despair, of frustrated hopes, and of violence, represents an intimate, lyric revelation of Remizov's feeling for the suffering and misfortunes of others, which comprises the fountainhead of all his art as the following self-characterization well illustrates:

> Bitterness struck me and pain sank into my heart. I observed the world, and pain did not leave me. I had not heard about this from my brothers; I did not know whether deprivation had touched them. But within me I heard: "How is it possible not to notice, and in noticing, not to feel? You must either sink in misfortune yourself or change the course of life. How is it possible to see everything and remain with hands folded?" I entered life being neither indifferent, nor peaceable. My soul would not accept the misfortune of others![10]

This aspect of the novel takes on even greater significance because *Prud* is essentially an autobiographical novel, certainly to a much greater degree than any other piece of Remizov's prose fiction. One has only to read Natal'ja Kodrjanskaja's brief fifteen-page biography of Remizov[11] in order to realize how closely the life of Varen'ka (suicide excepted)

---

[8] Dmitri Chizhevsky, "Chekhov in the Development of Russian Literature," *Chekhov: A Collection of Critical Essays*, ed. Robert L. Jackson (Englewood Cliffs, N.J., 1967), p. 54.
[9] A. Belyj, p. 56.
[10] Natal'ja Kodrjanskaja, *Aleksej Remizov* (Paris, 1959), p. 73.
[11] Ibid., pp. 65–80.

parallels that of Mar'ja Aleksandrovna Najdenova, Remizov's mother; or that Nikolaj Finogenov is patterned after the author himself and, presumably, experiences the same insults and joys, thinks similar thoughts, and poses the same questions; or that the huge white house with red outbuilding, the factory and pond, as well as the St. Andronicus Monastery in the background were actually an accurate description of the house and cotton mill of Remizov's maternal grandfather in Moscow on the Jauza River.

The philosophic nucleus of the novel rests on typically Dostoevskian antipodes: rebellion, a blasphemous indignation and unrestrained protest against the amoral structure and needless pain of the world, as opposed to humility, the desire to rise above life through self-effacing meekness.[12] Nikolaj, and to a lesser extent his oldest brother Aleksandr, are the chief rebels. The misery of others, the arbitrary violation of earth's humble creatures whether animal or human cause Nikolaj to repeatedly ask the question: "Why?" His brother Aleksandr, an alter-ego in the sense that he embarks on alternatives open to Nikolaj, first chooses humility through prayer, rejects it in favor of bloody rebellion, and finally follows in the footsteps of their uncle Arsenij, a typical Dostoevskian strong-willed, demonic personality who desires to take, to grasp anything that cannot be rightfully taken. The embodiment of humility and the bearer of the message that one must unselfishly give of oneself completely to others is Father Gleb, the monastery *starec* who was undoubtedly inspired by Dostoevskij's Father Zosima. However, the conflict between rebellion and humility remains unresolved, for in Remizov's world Christ passively watches from the heavens while the Devil with his demons rules the earth. It is significant that most of the tragic events of part I (Varen'ka's suicide, Rozik's hurt paw, Aleksandr's rebellion against God, and his arrest) all occur at Easter time, the sole joy in the Finogenov brothers' life. And in part II, the focus on Nikolaj both in prison and in exile, occurs at Christmas (synonymous with the birth of new hope), while Arsenij's murder and Nikolaj's arrest take place with the onset of Spring. Is not the Devil mocking the Master?

In preparing the second edition of *Prud* for inclusion in his eight-volume *Sočinenija*,[13] Remizov made extensive changes which entailed recasting

---

[12] For a more extensive discussion of this point see A. Dolinin, "Obrečennyj," *Reč'*, no. 163 (June 17, 1912), p. 2. The Dostoevskian legacy of pain, as acknowledged by Remizov himself, was stressed by Gleb Struve in his *Russkaja literatura v izgnanii* (New York, 1956), pp. 259, 261-262.

[13] Aleksej Remizov, *Sočinenija* (SPB: Izd. Šipovnik, n.d.), 8 vols. The second edition of *Prud*, which comprised volume 4, was written early in 1911 and appeared by October of that year. *Knižnaja Letopis'*, no. 43 (Oct. 29, 1911), item 25679.

every page. It was surprising that of all the reviewers only one, the poet Mixail Kuzmin, noticed the difference, commenting that "one could almost speak of a new work."[14] Despite massive alteration in form and some rather noticeable changes in substance (Nikolaj, for example, is killed rather than imprisoned after Arsenij's murder), the philosophical essence of the work remained unchanged but was brought into sharper focus. Frequently the lyrically implicit becomes explicit epic statement. Consider, for example, Remizov's treatment of the Devil. In part I of the first edition the Devil crops up six times: Arsenij's workers speak of him as Anti-Christ (p. 11); a laughing petty demon suddenly appears in the snow (p. 37); the Devil crawls into the bathhouse and, giggling voluptuously, licks his warm, open wounds (p. 42); the Devil lazily stretches out in the quiet sky (p. 55); a green devil with laughing, sparkling eyes rocks on a swing (p. 79); and, finally, part I ends with a hungry demon sitting on a fence, gnawing a hoof (p. 142). Each appearance, with the exception of the green devil who actually is a poster painted by the Finogenov brothers, is accompanied by neither motivation nor explanation; nonetheless, it is presented as a real, visual phenomenon from which the reader must deduce the existence of a Devil, an evil force or destiny that rules the world depicted by Remizov. In the second edition, an "explanatory" paragraph, fifteen lines long, is appended to the appearance of the petty demon:

> Он-то знал, . . . [there follows an enumeration of specific names and actions—A.S.] . . . почему так складывается, одним одна жизнь, а другим другая, одним легкая и удачная, другим трудная и несчастная. Да знал ли он? И кто он — демон, один ли из бесов или просто бесенок? И демон, и бес, и бесенок, он знал и горько и криво смеялся с сжатыми губами. [pp. 64-65]

And the description of the demon's appearance at the end of part I (p. 232) is identical to that of this first appearance and again is followed by an explanatory paragraph beginning with "On-to znal" and ending with the refrain "Da znal li on? etc. . . . " The refrain recalls the first appearance, the reader perceives it as a repetition of a known fact, and through this subjective technique becomes convinced not only of the demon's existence, but of the predetermination of man's fate. This theme of predetermination was enhanced by the insertion of a God's fool, Sema the oven-maker. (Perhaps "Devil's fool" would be more appropriate in Remizov's case.)

In the first edition, an unnamed beggar-fool (*niščij-jurodivyj*) spits in Nikolaj's face just prior to his murder of Arsenij (p. 263). The relation of

---

[14] M. Kuzmin, "Zametki o russkoj belletristike," *Apollon*, no. 9 (1911), p. 74.

this action to Arsenij's murder is tenuous. In the second edition, however, the beggar becomes Sema (p. 345) and is introduced in part I (pp. 83–84) prior to Varen'ka's suicide: he interprets the appearance of a thief as the delivery of a death sentence (*mertvaja gramota*), an interpretation reinforced by the addition of a final paragraph to the chapter (p. 87) suggesting that the unidentified knocking at the window may be that of a petty demon with a death sentence. In addition, Sema brings a calf to the Finogenov home (p. 155) on the eve of Varen'ka's suicide; the symbolism of the sacrificial calf, when coupled with the death sentence prognosis, clearly endows Sema with the prophetic vision of God's fools traditional in Russian literature and lends considerably greater significance to his spitting in Nikolaj's face (p. 345), an action that presages not so much Arsenij's murder as it does Nikolaj's own death. This expansion and closer interrelation of characters' roles and incidents is typical of the second edition. The vast majority of changes, however, are stylistic ones.

Most stylistic changes were motivated by Remizov's desire to achieve some degree of clarity and continuity in narrative, thereby mitigating the excessive lyric impressionism of the first edition. The most obvious alteration was the addition of chapter headings which served as directional guides for the reader's attention and frequently were accompanied by an expansion and rearrangement of the material within the chapter. In the chapter entitled "Rozik," the Finogenov's companion-overseer, dubbed Prometej by his wards, awakes from a drunken stupor and for no apparent reasons grabs a log and strikes the dog Rozik, breaking its leg. In the first edition (pp. 123–124), the incident was simply one of many narrated in the chapter. In the second edition the incident is moved to the chapter's end (pp. 206–207), the image of Rozik silently crying is repeated a second time as the final paragraph in order to embed it firmly in the reader's mind, and the motif of innocents' suffering is explicitly introduced (*nu v čem že on-to byl vinoven?*). Nikolaj recalls this incident while imprisoned, relating it to the suffering of other innocent creatures and to his own guilt feelings (pp. 256–257, 305). The Rozik theme is also tied to Aleksandr's rebellion against God, the description of which is considerably expanded to include a rejection of Christ (no doubt inspired by Ivan Karamazov's) on the grounds that his coming to earth entailed the death of so many innocent children (pp. 215–216).

The description of the monks at the St. Andronicus Monastery (including the Vorgeschichte of Father Gleb's life) and the Finogenovs' first visit to Father Gleb provide another excellent example of chapter headings' elucidative effect on textual rearrangement. In the first edition, the description of the various monks and the Finogenovs' visit to Father Gleb, included together in chapter IX, were followed by the Vorgeschichte of Father Gleb's life (chapter X). In the second edition, a considerably expanded description of all the monks with the exception of Father Gleb was set off as a separate chapter ironically titled "Earthly Angels—Heavenly People" (all of the greedy, drunken, and debauched monks had been dubbed by the Finogenovs with denigrating nicknames such as Louse, Nipple, Snot, Hen's Neck, and others) and was followed by Father Gleb's life history, appropriately and contrastively titled "The Guardian of God's Truth." Some changes in Father Gleb's past enhanced his role as the sole positive figure in the novel and his message of humility was spelled out in italics: "One must accept all of fate—all kinds of misfortune, and accept it freely and humbly, and bless all of it to the last degree" (p. 115).

The polarization of Father Gleb and the rest of the monks was heightened in the following chapter, which juxtaposed the Finogenovs' perverse pleasures with the monk Jaška-Elephant to their visit with Father Gleb, in whose presence for the first time in their life they trustingly unburdened themselves from the bottom of their hearts. And the chapter heading "Cherubims' Incense," the senseless phrase muttered by Father Gavriil upon awakening (p. 121), also symbolizes the spiritual relief experienced by the Finogenovs in Father Gleb's presence.

A second major stylistic change consisted in shifting emphasis from phrases and single sentences to whole paragraphs. Frequently this was accomplished by combining separate sentence-paragraphs into larger paragraphs with the aid of connective phrases, as graphically illustrated by the example below:

Ушел кононарх.
Садилось солнце.
Вдруг спохватились.
И страсть не хотелось идти, да неловко.
И вот вошли они в башенку после вечерни.
Гомон на угомон шел. На лестнице уж поджидала ночь.
Вошли они, скорчившись, дикими, голоса потеряли.
Молча подошли под благословение.
Старец благословил. Благословил и засуетился, будто оробел не меньше.
                                                    [1st ed., p. 62]

Compare the above with the results of the 1911 revision:

Так весь день и провозились с кононархом. И ушел кононарх от о. Гавриила, стало солнце садиться, вдруг спохватились: пора уж было итти к старцу знакомиться. А страсть не хотелось итти после веселого кононарха.

И вот вошли они в белую башенку. Гомон на угомон шел. На узенькой темной лестнице, казалось, уж поджидала ночь, чтобы выйти на волю.

Вошли Финогеновы в келью, скорчившись, дикими, голоса потеряли. Молча подошли они под благословение. Молча благословил их старец, благословил и засуетился, будто и оробел не меньше. [2nd ed., p. 118]

The fragmentary, impressionistic strokes of the first edition have been replaced by an expanded, flowing prose that has taken on the peculiarly Remizovian rhythm of a *skaz* narrative. The use of conjunctions in the initial position, of particles associated with the spoken language, the recurrent inversion of subject and verb, the repetition of key words, the musicality of alliteration and assonance—all these devices and more were consistently utilized in rewriting *Prud*.

Another significant characteristic of the second edition was Remizov's increased concern for the revelation of his personages' motivation. Sometimes this was accomplished on a stylistic level by the insertion of brief phrases:

— Мамаша-то ваша, здорова?
— Ничего, — не сразу ответил Саша, ответил затихшим голосом, — иногда... ничего... хворает.
Уткнулись в стаканы [1st ed., p. 63]

Note the explicit motivation inserted in the revision:

Старец спросил Сашу о Вареньке.
— Ничего, — ответил Саша, ответил не сразу затихшим голосом, — иногда... — он хотел сказать: пьет..., но спохватился, — ничего... хворает.
Финогеновы уткнулись в стаканы, им было неловко, что старец знает о матери. [2nd ed., p. 120]

In other instances, entire paragraphs describing a character's innermost thoughts and feelings were inserted in order to make him stand out in greater relief and in order to provide better internal motivation for future actions. This was true of Varen'ka (compare the detailed treatment of her marriage, the thoughts of suicide, and flight from her husband in the second edition, pp. 17–26, with the considerably scantier, external description in the first edition, pp. 12–14) and especially of Nikolaj, who emerged as the protagonist much more clearly in the second edition than in the first. This was accomplished not only through expanded analyses of his first childhood memory (p. 53), his first love (pp. 91–92), his interest in literature (p. 131), and a summation of his loves (p. 240), but also by attributing solely to him actions that had previously been attributed to all four Finogenov brothers: consider, for example, the dream of a better future (pp. 141, 179) or the burial of the cat Naumka (p. 145).

Continuity between chapters was provided by the inclusion or expansion of existing descriptive passages that usually indicated the passage of time or seasonal changes. The most striking example of this device was the inclusion of an entire chapter at the beginning of part II, which in the first edition had abruptly begun with Nikolaj being ushered into a prison cell without a word as to why he had been arrested. The inserted chapter bridged the year and a half hiatus between the novel's two parts by summarizing major events (Arsenij's ever-increasing activity, Nikolaj's employment at the Suxoplatov's and his love for Tanja, Maška's death, Aleksandr's release from prison and his interest in Tanja) and ended by stressing the theme of fate determining the course of human events. In addition, by focusing on Arsenij's reputed ties with the Devil (emphasized by the chapter heading: "Demons Serve Him") and by serving as a Vorgeschichte to all that follows, the inserted chapter achieved a structural symmetry with the first chapter of part I.

One of Remizov's most successful and innovational devices was the studied use of refrains, sometimes entire recurrent paragraphs. Although this device had occasionally been utilized in the first edition, it was systematically extended in the second, in part to counteract the fragmented quality of the original version. At its briefest, the refrain took the form of an epithet, such as the unusual *dikij* in "the *desolate* Finogenov house," inserted and repeated four times on consecutive pages (pp. 20–23), and thrice accompanied by some form of *čužoj* (alien). Varen'ka's constant use of *prokljatye* (accursed) as a form of address to her children and in reference to her own life does much to enhance the general atmosphere of doom. More frequently, the refrain took the form of a phrase or sentence, sometimes several lines in length. The device was particularly effective in hallucinatory scenes such as Varen'ka's suicide, where refrain and repetition (added only in the second edition) act as an incantation in evoking a feeling of delirium in the reader. Before the reader was admitted to Varen'ka's bedroom a triple repetition in the space of two dozen lines lulled his senses: "u Varen'ki bylo tixo, i tol'ko nagorevšij fitil' lampadki pered kiotom potreskival"; and then he was suddenly confronted with the apparition facing Varen'ka:

> Монах с красивым лицом и рассеченной бровью, из которой тихо, капля за каплей, сочилась густая темная кровь, монах в ярко-зеленой шуршащей, шелковой рясе, держал перед ней деревянный темный крест, обшитый неровной зазубренной жестью. [p. 159]

Within the space of three pages, the refrain was repeated once in its entirety, and four times in truncated form as the monk pursued Varen'ka about the room, driving the sharp end of the cross into her brain. And her final vain attempts to escape were accompanied by the thrice-repeated refrain: "No už pozdno, net ej zaščity."

The interconnection of symbols not explicitly related to one another in the first edition was occasionally effected through the use of refrains or recurrent imagery. Pljamka is an excellent case to point; a name on a doorcard, Pljamka impinges on Nikolaj's memory and is senselessly repeated during his cruel treatment of Maška in the tavern (pp. 133–136). Toward the very end of the novel a man in a thick cloth coat appears (p. 260), steadies Nikolaj (p. 269), reveals that he is Pljamka (p. 275), and the ring of the phone prior to Nikolaj's arrest sounds like "Pljamka" (p. 280). Pljamka's introduction in the second edition is essentially the same, but the meaningless repetition in the tavern scene (pp. 220–224) is more artistically sustained as is the expanded refrain of a man "v drapovom pal'to, nasmešlivo ulybajas' tonkimi ptič'imi gubami" (pp. 342, 351, 357). However, the initial appearance of the man in the cloth coat is followed by the refrain: "Kto on—demon, odin-li iz besov ili prosto besenok, samo Gore-Zloščastie ili Pljamka? I demon, i bes, i besenok, Pljamka, on xodil po dorožke, slovno podžidal kogo-to na svidanie" (p. 342), which recalls the twice-repeated refrain accompanying the appearance of the demon in part I, and which has already been quoted above in the discussion of Remizov's conception of the world. The identification of Pljamka with the demon opens new perspectives: the senseless importunate repetition of the name represents the senseless, importunate repetition of pain and violation in man's life, while the demon-Pljamka in a thick cloth coat symbolizes man's ultimate and inexorable fate, death, which reveals his life to be no more significant than the teeming of muck worms in impenetrable darkness (pp. 358–359).

All of the stylistic devices above represent additions to the text; however, the deletion of material found in the first edition was also significant. Chapters IX and X of part II, which contained inserted tales of fellow prisoners as well as a description of the prisoners' transfer from jail to the railroad station, were deleted in entirety as extraneous material. Whole sentences were dropped throughout part II, especially in the passages dealing with Nikolaj's imprisonment, as were verbose and abstruse passages, ranging in length from a modest paragraph to a whole page (pp. 154–155, 170–171, 212, 230, 234, 242–243, 259). Some were considerably condensed (pp. 240–241). Authorial lyric invocations, whether to God (pp. 216, 283), the Virgin (pp. 67–68), or on the necessity of love (p. 111) were consistently omitted in order to mute the personal, lyric quality of the novel. And in divesting *Prud* of its amorphous vagueness, Remizov consciously deleted typically decadent devices such as the use of pronouns without antecedents ("Ona, nevidimaja i gorjačaja ...," presumably a reference to Spring, p. 251), the appearance of legendary beings ("A bednaja Sneguročka plakala, taja ...," p. 259), excessive anthropomorphism ("Da! pomniš', pomniš'!—kričalo serdce ...," p.167; "Krivila tišina svoi suxie, zelenye guby," p. 171), and the use of neuter indefinite pronouns (compare "I čto-to, budto grjaznoe, seroe telo, čut' prikrytoe loxmot'jami, rasplastannoe na krovati, polezlo v glaza," 1st ed., p. 145, with "Smjatyj tjufjak i poduška s uzkoj krovati polezli v glaza, i kazalos' emu, ševelilos' èto seroe mesivo, trjaslis' loxmot'ja, kak studen' po kusočkam raspolzalis' ..., 2nd ed., p. 245).[15]

The numerous changes brought out in the comparison of the first and second editions of *Prud* point to a significant evolution in Remizov's art. The first edition, both in conception and execution, was clearly a product of the Symbolist era. The second edition, although not markedly different in conception, was quite dissimilar in execution. The concern with motivation, the development and use of chapter headings, of refrains, of *skaz* narrative, of musicality and rhythm, the reduction of verbosity, of lyric digressions, and of some typically Symbolist devices, eloquently testify to a general movement from the abstract to the concrete, from vagueness to clarity, from lyric fragmentation to epic continuity in narrative, from extreme impressionism to an impressionistic realism, in short—a transition from Symbolism to Neo-Realism.

---

[15] This tendency from the abstract to the concrete was also reflected in the replacement of common nouns by proper nouns in the second edition: Varen'ka for mother or she, Finogenovy for *deti*, Mixail Ivanovič for *stariček-prikazčik*, Vas'ka Kon'kov for *palač*, Jaškov for *časovoj*, and so forth. In passing, it should be noted that many of the names were changed in the second edition. Although the change from St. Andronicus to Bogoljubov monastery could be interpreted as an attempt to avoid using the actual name of the prototype, there was no apparent reason for changing Voroninskij sad to Kolobovskij, or grandfather Pavel and grandmother Serafima to Nikolaj and Evfrosin'ja, or two of Nikolaj's three uncles from Aleksej and Nikolaj to Arsenij and Nikita.

MIXAIL ZOŠČENKO AND THE PROBLEM OF *SKAZ*

BY

I. R. TITUNIK

THE MOST CURIOUS thing about the problem of *skaz* is how infrequently it is recognized as a problem.[1] Handbooks, encyclopedias, histories, monographic studies, reviews, etc., devoted to Russian literature use the term freely, but either without any specification of its meaning (assuming its familiarity to the readers) or with ad hoc thumbnail definitions (for the benefit of the "uninitiated"). Boiled down to their common denominators, the various implicit and explicit acceptances of the term skaz may be said to refer to a technique or mode of narration, in prose fiction primarily, in which the author is replaced by a fictional narrator who tells the story in his, the narrator's, own words.

With respect to the telling of the story, skaz is conceived to be specifically oral in its stylistic organization, that is, designed to produce the illusion of spontaneous, "living" speech. With respect to the teller of the story, it is conceived to be individualized in its stylistic organization, that is, it reproduces or imitates speech supposedly characteristic of a particular human being, the given narrator. Hugh McLean, in his article, "On the Style of a Leskovian *Skaz*," identifies skaz with "the 'story within a story' of venerable epic traditions" (though "of new stylistic dimensions") and adds that "the technique itself is familiar enough in English literature from the *Canterbury Tales* onwards,"[2] thereby, all other things aside, informing the reader that the technique in question is neither a recent development nor the exclusive property of Russian literature, the Russians being only at the enviable advantage of having a term for it.

---

[1] This does not mean, of course, that skaz has never been treated as a problem. Boris Èjxenbaum may, apparently, be credited with having initiated the serious study of skaz in his two early articles, "Illjuzija skaza" and "Kak sdelana 'Šinel'' Gogolja" (both 1918). Among scholars who have devoted attention to the problem of skaz, V. V. Vinogradov has made by far the most sizable and most important contribution. A list of Academician Vinogradov's works bearing on the problem, as well as of similar literature by other scholars, is given in the bibliography to my doctoral dissertation, "The Problem of *Skaz* in Russian Literature" (Department of Slavic Languages and Literatures, University of California, Berkeley, 1963), pp. 160–161. My dissertation was an attempt to devise a theory of narration and to derive from it a theory of skaz, relying largely on investigations into the problem of reported speech. I take this opportunity to express my special gratitude to Gleb Petrovitch Struve for his graciousness in having served as the chairman of my dissertation committee.

[2] *Harvard Slavic Studies*, II (Cambridge, 1954), 299–300.

In the history of Russian literature, though it can be claimed that the technique has existed from at least the mid-seventeenth century (Avvakum) and continues to the present day (Solženicyn, Sinjavskij-Terc, and others), skaz has come to be associated most commonly with Gogol' and the so-called "Natural School" (1830's and '40's), with Leskov in the last third of the nineteenth century and with the "ornamental" prose fiction of the early decades of the present century when, especially in the twenties, there was hardly a prose writer who did not write "using skaz or a manner close to skaz in one form or another."[3] Aleksej Remizov, Evgenij Zamjatin, Isaak Babel', Vsevolod Ivanov, Leonid Leonov were a few among the more prominent writers in whose verbal art at that time skaz was a factor of major importance.

However, the name most likely to occur to mind at mention of the term skaz is Mixail Zoščenko (1895-1958). If there is one Russian writer to be singled out as the *auctoritas et exemplum* of skaz technique, one Russian literary master whose credentials are based predominantly, if not, in fact, exclusively, on expertise in skaz, it is Zoščenko. Yet, any critical attention, even slightly above the superficial, to the stories of Mixail Zoščenko must acknowledge an odd paradox: the almost total inadequacy of the usual, popularly held conception of skaz outlined above. Of course, interpretation of the terms "narrator," "oral speech," and "individualized speech" immediately comes into question. Conceivably, it is simply a matter of adjusting and refining those terms. But such a procedure inevitably encounters insuperable difficulties and generates insoluble confusions. The fact is that "narrator," "oral," and "individualized speech" lead off in the wrong direction—into the realm of problems associated with the speech and functions of characters in a work of fiction ("narrator" not being an exception in this regard because, by and large, "narrator" is understood to mean a "personality," a "point of view," a "special source of information"). Meanwhile, the right direction is into the realm of problems associated with "author" speech and function in a work of fiction. The words "right" and "wrong" are being used here for mildly provocative purposes. Actually it is not an either/or matter; both realms do apply, but they are not complementary and coequal. The essential point about skaz is that it carries out author function and relates directly to author speech. Therein lies its principal difference from character speech, and, therefore, all such features as personality, point of view, oral or individualized speech, etc., applied to skaz, must be viewed

---

[3] B. M. Èjxenbaum, "Leskov i sovremennaja proza," *Literatura: Teorija. Kritika. Polemika.* (Leningrad, 1926), p. 222.

from a different angle. The study of skaz can proceed only when the context of study itself is properly constituted.

This essay pursues very limited and modest aims: merely to demonstrate that skaz may be something somewhat different from, and more complex than, what it is usually assumed to be. Works by Mixail Zoščenko, an acknowledged master of the technique, will be used to prove the point.[4] In other words, the direct aim of this essay is to put the problem of skaz in relief as a problem for literary analysis. No attempt will be made to construct a "theory of skaz," though, needless to say, something like such a theory will inevitably and necessarily be implied.[5]

I

Mixail Zoščenko never pretended to be a literary theorist or even a theorist of his own literary art, but in one of his few outright instances of "autoanalysis" he had extremely interesting things to say:

Я только хочу сделать одно признание. Может быть оно покажется странным и неожиданным. Дело в том, что я — пролетарский писатель. Вернее я пародирую своими вещами того воображаемого, но подлинного пролетарского писателя, который существовал бы в теперешних условиях жизни и в теперешней среде. Конечно, такого писателя не может существовать, по крайней мере, сейчас. А когда будет существовать, то его общественность, его среда значительно повысятся во всех отношениях.

Я только пародирую. Я временно замещаю пролетарского писателя. Оттого темы моих рассказов проникнуты наивной философией, которая как раз по плечу моим читателям.

В больших вещах я опять таки пародирую. Я пародирую и неуклюжий, громоздкий (Карамзиновский) стиль современного красного Льва Толстого или Рабиндранат Тагора, и сантиментальную тему, которая сейчас характерна. Я пародирую теперешнего интеллигентского писателя, которого, может быть, и нет сейчас, но который должен бы существовать, если б он точно выполнял социальный заказ не издательства, а той среды и той общественности, которая сейчас выдвинута на первый план....[6]

---

[4] The edition of Zoščenko's works used here is *Sobranie sočinenij* [= SS] (Leningrad: Priboj, 1930); since the third volume of that edition was not available to me, I have added: M. Zoščenko, *Povesti i rasskazy* [= PiR], Izdatel'stvo imeni Čexova (New York, 1952). Citations of sources will appear following quotations.

[5] Here I can only refer the reader, with some latter-day misgiving, to my above-mentioned dissertation, in particular to chapter 2, entitled "Narrative structure and theory of *skaz*."

[6] "O sebe, o kritikax i o svoej rabote," *Mixail Zoščenko. Stat'i i materialy* (Mastera sovremennoj literatury, I) (Leningrad, 1928), pp. 10–11. "Karamzinian" is, of course, a blatant misnomer, but as Zoščenko is fond of remarking in his stories, *ne v ètom delo*.

Parody of "that which might be but is not" is extraordinary kind of parody indeed. But it provides the key to what precisely Zoščenko was up to—not creation of special characters or even narrators (understanding "narrator" in the usual sense) but creation of a special "image of author," that is, that component of a work of fiction which governs the structure as a whole, which commands and implements the language of narration, subjecting to its control and manipulation all instances of character (reported) speech, and which serves as the basis of authority in the work. Characters and narrators can command only their own speech and only their own points of view. What Zoščenko created was not character or narrator but author—an author of a special kind, precisely a parodic author who assumes the powers and functions of authorial norms and operates with them in some way (comic, ironic, grotesque, etc.) contrary to expectations. Indeed, not only is a parodic author created, a parodic reader is created as well. V. V. Vinogradov, referring specifically to Zoščenko's story "Strašnaja noč'," but with applicability to Zoščenko's skaz technique in general, remarks: "the author, having donned an anonymous verbal mask, ascribes to the reader, as the accepted norm, forms of speech from which the latter must recoil in dismay."[7] No character, no narrator has any such privilege vis-à-vis the reader.

Zoščenko distinguishes between the parodic author of his short pieces —"the proletarian writer"—and parodic author of his longer works —the "modern-day red Lev Tolstoj, . . . the intellectual writer"—but no sharp dividing line, as Zoščenko himself insists, can be drawn between them. The direction of shift, to parody, is the same in both cases, and only the forms of the stories—the very short story or feuilleton, on the one hand, and the long story or novelette (*povest'*), on the other—are dictated by the particular parodic focus.[8]

When we examine Zoščenko's works, it becomes abundantly apparent that "narrator," in the usual sense of the word, is indeed very little used. Of course, there is Nazar Il'ič, gospodin Sinebrjuxov. Evenija Žurbina, in her perceptive introduction to Zoščenko's collected works, properly points out the "experimental" nature of *Rasskazy Nazara Il'iča, gospodina Sinebrjuxova*; it is the work in which "Zoščenko's skaz jelled and took

---

[7] "Problema skaza v stilistike," *Poètika*, I (Leningrad, 1926), 35. The point is elaborated in his "Jazyk Zoščenki," *Mixail Zoščenko, Stat'i i materialy*, op. cit., pp. 75-77.

[8] What Zoščenko says on this point (op. cit., p. 9) is also extremely interesting —in part, that his longer works are more tied in with the traditions of "big" literature. Indeed, in the *povesti* Zoščenko's parodic author most fully displays literary professional pretensions.

true shape."⁹ The Sinebrjuxov cycle represents a distinctive shift of structural center of gravity as against the Čexov-style comic anecdote, skit, or "document," with almost its entire weight in reported speech (dialogue or "letter to the editor" and the like), that characterizes much of Zoščenko's work belonging to the same early period of his career (e.g., "Geroj," "Molitva," "Niščij," "Pis'ma v redakciju," and others). Sinebrjuxov is no narrator in the ordinary sense of the word; he does have "personality" and a "point of view," but they are wholly subsumed in lingo. Sinebrjuxov is first and foremost a style of narration which fills out the entire image of author in the cycle and constitutes its exclusive linguistic system, not only serving as author speech but also "renarrating" into its own stylistics all instances of character speech. I. V. Kolenkorov, the "author" of *Sentimental'nye povesti*, is already a step onto a different level; the narrator concept no longer applies to him even to the degree it might in Sinebrjuxov's case. I. V. Kolenkorov is just such another "literary man" as Ivan Belkin or Rudyj Pan'ko,¹⁰ the possessor of literary professional pretensions. I. V. Kolenkorov is, of course, the name of the "verbal mask" that the writer Mixail Zoščenko dons in *Sentimental'nye povesti* (a fact, incidentally, which Zoščenko found himself obliged to make explicit in the third preface to the cycle). The next step was to operate without any assumed name or, rather, to assume the already established image of author associated with the name Mixail Zoščenko (*Vozvraščennaja molodost'*, *Golubaja kniga*).¹¹

In Zoščenko's shorter pieces we do find a number of examples of motivated narrators—the glazier Ivan Fomič Testov in "Sčastie; Vasja, the amateur actor, in "Akter"; Efim Grigor'evič, the "victim" in "Žertva revoljucii"—and a number of cases of unmotivated but self-identified narrators (in "Ruka bližnego," "Aristokratka," "Slučaj" and a host of others where the narrator tells a story about himself). The majority of the stories have addressers who are neither motivated nor identified. Finally, the addressers of a number of stories are in some way identified as "author" (e.g., "Vor," "Userdie ne po razumu," "Puškin," and others). The point about all these motivated and unmotivated, identified and unidentified narrators and authors is, of course, that they are not discretely different

---

⁹ *Sobranie sočinenij*, op. cit., p. 7.
¹⁰ His forebears in Russian literature go even further back—to "Nižajšij i učtivyj sluga obščestva i čitatelja Rossijanin," the "author" of Mixail Čulkov's *Peresmešnik* (1766); the "Preduvedomlenie" by the Rossijanin and Ivan Kolenkorov's "Ot avtora" share a remarkable resemblance.
¹¹ *Pered vosxodom solnca* is still another step in the same series but now in a different direction—into autobiography.

personalities or points of view or even different styles; they together constitute a collective verbal mask or, perhaps better, a collective "mouthpiece" through which Zoščenko parodies his "proletarian writer." It is highly significant that in most cases where a motivated narrator is used the author's context doing the motivating is just as "skaz-ified" as the narrator's narrative. So, for instance, in the author's introduction to "Drova," which motivates the "inner narrative" as a conversation over a bottle of beer, we read the following remarks addressed to the reader by the author:

> Читатель — существо недоверчивое. Подумает: до чего складно врет человек.
> А я не вру, читатель. Я и сейчас могу, читатель, посмотреть в ясные твои очи и сказать: «не вру». И вообще я никогда не вру и писать стараюсь без выдумки. Фантазией я не отличаюсь. И не люблю поэтому растрачивать драгоценные свои жизненные соки на какую-то несуществующую думку. Я знаю, дорогой читатель, что жизнь много важнее литературы.
> [SS, II, p. 34]

In "Akter" we find another highly significant feature: here the author briefly introduces the inner narrative as a story told to him by the hero-narrator: "Rasskaz ètot—istinnoe proisšestvie. Slučilos' v Astraxani. Rasskazal mne ob ètom akter-ljubitel'. Vot čego on rasskazal." But the skaz inner narrative itself, despite its supposedly being told to the author, begins with exactly the same sort of address to an "audience at large" as do a great many Zoščenko stories without motivated narrators:

> Вот вы меня, граждане, спрашиваете, был ли я актером? (Compare "Vory": «Что-то, граждане, воров нынче много развелось» [SS, II, p. 50]; "Muž": «Да что ж это, граждане, происходит на семейном фронте?» [SS, II, p. 53]; and many others.)

Moreover, this opening generates exactly the same sort of proem on the topic of the story (in "Akter"—the art of acting) as do stories addressed by unmotivated narrators or the author, in the latter case often including the author's remarks about his attitude, as author, toward the topic of his story, for example:

> Только теперича вполне чувствуешь и понимаешь, насколько мы за десять лет шагнули вперед! *Etc.* ["Šapka," PiR, p. 222]

> Театр я не хаю. Но кино все-таки лучше. *Etc.* ["Kino-drama," SS, II, p. 98]

> Очень даже удивительно, как это некоторым людям жить не нравится. *Etc.* ["Ne vse poterjano," PiR, p. 233]

Пущай читатель за свои деньги чувствует — я печатаю этот рассказ прямо с опасностью для здоровья.
Это есть истинное происшествие. Все, так сказать, взято из источника жизни. И я побаиваюсь, как бы главное действующее лицо не набило бы мне морду за разглашение подобных фактов. *Etc.*
["Xorošij znakomyj," PiR, p. 237

II

The question of individualized speech has a number of aspects that require special attention. The assumption is made that the skaz narrator's speech is speech characteristic of him as a certain particular kind of person with a certain particular point of view or even "mentality." As has already been indicated, the addressers of Zoščenko's stories do not command a speech distinctly and individually their own. But even taking their speech as the collective speech of a collective narrator, can notions of personality, point of view, mentality, etc., be directly applied? They have, of course, and one speaks of Zoščenko's narrator as the special type of "new Soviet man," "Soviet vulgarian," or, from a different position, "typical Soviet man of the NEP period," and so on. The legitimacy of making such conclusions is not now being called into question, but these characterological or typological considerations do overlook or overshadow the central literary fact that the speech of a skaz addresser relates directly to author speech, and perceptibility of skaz, as such, may depend precisely on some mixing or interplay of features associated with the standard literary language (the norms of author speech) and features divergent from it. If the essence of Zoščenko's skaz is parody, then the postulation of some special type of "man" as narrator simply misses the point. Zoščenko's humor, that aspect of his art most commented on and enthused over, consists in just such a mixing or interplay of stylistic features which results not in personality but verbal mask.

In his shorter pieces the sources for "standard" language are, of course, the language of sloganeering, of political manifestos, poster language, newspaper rhetoric, officialese, etc.—all those elements that make up the new code of literary expression which Zoščenko's parodic proletarian writer presumably takes seriously. In the longer works, with their shift to overt literary professional pretensions, the standard language is the more traditional language of literature in its canonized compositional forms. This can be seen in the following illustrations taken from a single work, "Strašnaja noč'" (the series below could be extended and analogous series cited from practically all of Zoščenko's *povesti*):

Description of nature:

Природа была не ахти какая замечательная, однако — небольшие сады у каждого дома, трава, и канавы, и деревянные скамейки, усыпанные шелухой подсолнухов, — все это делало вид привлекательным и приятным.
[SS, IV, p. 138]

Biographical dossier:

Вот, бывают такие люди, о которых можно в десять минут рассказать всю ихнюю жизнь, всю обстановку жизни, от первого бессмысленного крика до последних дней.

Автор попробует это сделать. Автор попробует очень коротко, в десять минут, но все-таки со всеми подробностями, рассказать о всей жизни Бориса Ивановича Котофеева.

А впрочем, и рассказывать нечего. [SS, IV, p. 140]

Description of a character's appearance:

Это был седоватый, сухонький старичок в длинном худом сюртуке, без жилета. Грязная рубашка без воротника выпирала на груди комком. И медная, желтая, ужасно яркая запонка выдавалась как-то далеко вперед своей пупочкой. [SS, IV, p. 147]

Philosophical and/or psychological analysis:

Так вот и все в нашей жизни, даже в нашей худой — до слез скучной — жизни и то все случайно, нетвердо и непостоянно.

Об этом Борис Иванович Котофеев вряд ли, конечно, думал. Был он хотя и неглупый человек, со средним образованием, но не настолько уж развит, чтобы обобщать с научной точки зрения.

И все-таки, в каком-то мелком плане, в повседневном своем существовании он и то заметил какой-то хитрый подвох в жизни. И даже стал с некоторых пор побаиваться за твердость своей судьбы. [SS, IV, p. 145]

Another aspect of individualized speech, curiously enough often passed over in discussions of skaz, is the individualized reported speech of characters. Every skaz addresser, whether identified as the author or not, carries out the author's function of reporting the speech of the characters in his narrative (their uttered statements or sub-vocal thoughts). In Zoščenko's short stories reported speech is given almost exlusively in the form of renarrated direct discourse, that is, character speech, though presented in a formally autonomous way (direct discourse), is marked by exactly the same features as is the lingo of narration. The result is that individuality of character speech—one of the hallmarks of, at least, modern fiction—is done away with. The most egregious instances of this are to be found in *Rasskazy Nazara Il'iča, gospodina Sinebrjuxova* with its mixed population of aristocrats and peasants, Russians and Poles all delivering themselves in Sinebrjuxov's lingo. But even in the short stories that make up the bulk of Zoščenko's literary output, where the population is somewhat more homogeneous, the same principles are operative, as can be seen, for instance, by the repetition in reported speech of certain "tag" words or expressions of the narrative, for example.

Narrative:

На кондукторшину сумку, скажем, засмотрелся — и баста — стырили уж. Ёлки-палки . . . ["Vor," SS, I, p. 175]

Reported speech:

»Эх, ёлки-палки! — подумал Васька, — Не туда, честное слово, залез. Не иначе как в детскую комнату я залез. Ёлки-палки.« [Ibid., p. 178]

(Compare "Černaja magija" [SS, V, pp. 213–230] where the skaz addresser and all the autonomous addressers in his narrative "share" an inordinate fondness for such expressions as: *imejte v vidu, zamet'te, predstav'te sebe* and the like; many other examples could be cited.) These stories, moreover, do not lack instances of the more egregious kind where the reported speech is bizarrely out of keeping with what is expected from a given character. The professional utterances of doctors provide a set of very striking examples:

Доктор говорит:
— Ожирение — главная причина вашей неподвижной жизни. Или наоборот. Побольше, — говорит, — ходите взад и вперёд, может быть, от этого факта похудеете. ["Ljubitel'," SS, II, p. 156]

— Органы, — говорит, — у вас довольно в аккуратном виде. И пузырь, говорит, вполне порядочный и не протекает. Что касается сердца, очень еще отличное, даже, говорит, шире, чем надо. Но, говорит, пить вы перестаньте, иначе очень просто смерть может приключиться. ["Limonad," PiR, p. 207]

In the longer works we find a somewhat different situation. Directly reported character speech there may be regarded more or less the characters' own words, individuality of speech being maintained at least by the fact that the characters do not deliver themselves in the author's lingo. But direct discourse is not the principal mode of reported speech in these stories; instead, we find the predominance of indirect discourse or, more often than not, of quasi-indirect discourse, bearing distinct evidence of interference in reported speech by the author (analogous to renarrated direct discourse). The following illustration from *O čem pel solovej* should make apparent what is involved here:

Былинкин принялся стыдить мамашу, говоря, что он, побывавший на всех фронтах и дважды обстрелянный тяжёлой артиллерией, может же, наконец, рассчитывать на покойную жизнь.

— Стыдно, мамаша! — сказал Былинкин. — Жалко вам комода. А в гроб вы его не возьмете. Знайте это.

— Не дам комода! — визгливо сказала старуха. — Помру, тогда и берите хоть всю мебель.

— Да, помрете! — сказал Быликин с негодованием. — Жди!..

Видя, что дело принимает серьезный оборот, старуха принялась плакать и причитать, говоря, что в таком случае пущай невинный ребенок, Мишка Рундуков, своими устами скажет последнее слово, тем более, что он единственный мужской представитель в ихнем Рундуковском роду, и комод, по праву, принадлежит ему, а не Лизочке. [SS, IV, p. 182]

Compare in the author's narrative (as regards Bylinkin):

И он, Былинкин, дважды побывавший на всех фронтах и обстрелянный тяжелой артиллерией, как бы впервые слушал эти дребезжащие звуки беккеровского рояля. [SS, IV, p. 172]

И Былинкин, этот слегка циник и прожженный жизнью человек, оглушенный снарядами и видевший не раз лицом к лицу смерть, этот жуткий Былинкин слегка ударился даже в поэзию,.. [SS, IV, pp. 174–175]

И тогда Василий Былинкин, потрясенный необычайностью существования на земле и удивительными ее законами, падал от избытка чувств на колени перед барышней и целовал землю вокруг ее ног. [SS, IV, p. 176]

Individualization of speech in connection with skaz thus becomes extremely problematical: for just as the supposedly individualized speech of the skaz narrator is qualitatively different from, and more complex than, any instance of individualized character speech, precisely because skaz carries out author function and relates directly to author speech, so the individualized speech of characters under the control and manipulation of a skaz addresser is always in jeopardy of losing its individuality through some form of interference or renarration. When the skaz addresser is an author with literary professional pretensions, as in Zoščenko's *povesti*, techniques that depend on discrimination between author and character speech, such as certain forms of "interior monologue," may result in total ambiguity.

Still another, and perhaps the most common, association of individualized speech is with "cast of mind." It should be readily apparent from arguments already presented that skaz, in this respect, involves something else again than a given narrator's peculiar mentality or set of values—what V. Erlich would like to identify as "the worm's eye view of reality."[12] The skaz addresser, as author mask or surrogate, bears the author's authority for the message as a whole. The discrepancy between "true"

---

[12] "Notes on the Use of Monologue in Artistic Prose," *International Journal for Slavic Linguistics and Poetics*, I/II (1959), 226.

authority and the pseudo- or quasi-authority of the skaz addresser may be made explicit, as often is the case with Leskov's skaz, for instance. But, again, this is by no means the case with Zoščenko. Zoščenko's skaz addresser is not a point of view but *the* authority. It is not a special mentality that Zoščenko parodies but the norms implicit in a work of fiction, the parody resulting from attribution to those norms of a content that is improper or contrary to expectations. The proems in the short stories, especially those concerned with the author's attitude toward his topic of discourse, all have precisely this function. But it is, of course, in the longer works that play on authorial authority achieves consummate expression, reaching at times the very limits of comic absurdity (à la Gogol'), as, for instance, in *O čem pel solovej* where we read:

> Конечно, автор не взялся бы писать художественные повести, если бы были у него только такие скудные и ничтожные сведения о героях. Сведений у автора хватает. Например, автору очень живо рисуется ихняя жизнь. Ихний небольшой Рундуковский домишко. Этакий темненький, в один этаж. На фасаде — номер 22. Повыше на досочке багор нарисован. На предмет пожара. Кому что тащить. А только есть ли у них багор? Ох, небось, нету . . . Ну да не дело художественной литературы разбираться и обращать на это внимание уездной администрации. [SS, IV, p. 163]

Vozvraščennaja molodost' has a proem seventeen chapters long (!) in which the author "scientifically" expatiates on his topic and discusses his qualifications as an "authority."

III

Of all the features associated with skaz, however skaz be defined, oral speech would seem to be the indispensable one. Yet, no aspect of skaz is so muddled as the question of its "orality." Since we are dealing here with a literary technical term, etymological and genetic arguments cannot help much. There is no dispute that the term itself denotes orality and suggests, as Boris Èjxenbaum declares, "extemporaneous oral recitation," "free improvisation," etc.[13] But it must be remembered that we are talking about skaz in literary works of art presented through the medium of printed words, where "oral speech act" and "written speech act" are equally potential as illusions which a writer may or may not exploit. Èjxenbaum's proposal to apply *Ohrenphilologie* to the study of narrative style, skaz narration in particular, was clearly a mistake.[14] As for the

---

[13] "Illjuzija skaza," *Skvoz' literaturu* (Voprosy poètiki, IV) (Leningrad, 1924), p. 152.

[14] "In B. M. Èjxenbaum's work [i.e., "Kak sdelana 'Šinel'' Gogolja"] resides the indisputable value of an acute description of the pantomimic-declamatory aspect of

supposed origin of skaz in oral (=folk) literature, the connection must be recognized as of the most tenuous kind. We are concerned with skaz as a property of "sophisticated" literature, and no folk literature origin, even if one can definitely be established, historically speaking, can possibly explain its nature and functions in that literature. Indeed, in the sphere of sophisticated literature the imitation of oral folk skaz with its reciter (*skazitel'*) is only one in a wide range of possible forms for concrete implementation of skaz technique. The fact that the most prominent form for such implementation in the early stages of modern Russian literature (eighteenth century) was the canonical literary genre of the verse fable (the *pritči* of the Sumarokov school[15]) speaks for itself.

Part of the difficulty here stems from a failure to recognize clearly that at least two different things are meant by "oral speech": (1) speech represented as uttered aloud, signalized through the use of various devices in the written code (e.g., phonetic spelling, intonational punctuation, phoneticized non-verbal sounds and gestures, and the like) and often framed compositionally in an oral speech situation (usually, a "conversation"), and (2) speech "oral" in a metonymic sense, that is, composed of features associated with conversation, everyday, colloquial speech or speech outside the codification of the standard language— dialect. Clearly the latter, oral speech in the metonymic sense, plays the crucial role in skaz. Thus, the "illusion" of oral speech in skaz is illusion by association and need not be interpreted as speech uttered aloud, orally delivered. A frame motivating an oral speech situation has no determinative value in itself; a narrative motivated as orally delivered may not result in perceptibility of skaz at all, as many stories by Turgenev amply demonstrate. On the other hand, narratives motivated as written (letters, memoirs, diaries, etc., which serve as the form of a story, or story forms as such—"this story, this novel, I, the author, am writing") may be rife

---

one of the forms of comic *skaz*. But the concept of *skaz* itself in its full dimensions is not elucidated thereby. The more so because there is room for notes of scepticism; for the perception of *skaz*, fixed as it is in written form, is the primary and overall factor indeed that of articulatory reproduction and acoustical interpretation? *Skaz*, after all, is embedded in the verbal-semantic design of a work of art which is intended not only for dramatic presentation or declamatory stage performance but also has its own objective nature for any reader ... This objective nature of prose fiction in its phenomenological essence is the same for everybody. But when realized by expressors of a motor-acoustical type of inner speech on the plane of 'aural philology,' the factor of utterance, of the, so to speak, artistic-vocal performance, deforms the objective nature of a literary work in its own peculiar and individual way." V. V. Vinogradov, "Problema skaza v stilistike," op. cit., p. 26.

[15] See G. A. Gukovskij's article on Rževskij in his *Russkaja poèzija XVIII veka* (Voprosy poètiki, X) (Leningrad, 1927), esp. pp. 155–160.

with "oral" features.[16] All of Zoščenko's *povesti* and a good number of his short pieces are motivated as written, that is, as addressed by author to reader.

However, this is not the main point. The main point is, rather, that oral speech is not the conditioning but a conditioned feature of skaz technique. Skaz relates directly to author speech and carries out author function; at the same time, it is a play on authorial norms. The user of skaz technique never merely displays oral speech as an object, as would be the case in a "normal" narrative where oral utterances of characters are reported, but manipulates it, makes it serve a different purpose than any instance of character speech. The essential point is, then, that skaz cannot be viewed apart from authorial norms. Skaz is, as M. M. Baxtin has convincingly argued, an instance of "bi-vocality" (*dvugolosost'*, *dvugolosoe slovo*); it carries, as it were, two voices at once.[17] Therefore, oral speech cannot be in and of itself the *differentia specifica* of skaz but must be regarded as a means (perhaps, indeed, the chief means, certainly the most common means) of generating bi-vocality of narration itself, that is, of generating skaz.

If we follow Baxtin a bit further and claim that parodic skaz in general, and Zoščenko's skaz in particular, consists in a conflict between the two intersecting voices,[18] we can, among other things, come to a conclusion that must seem paradoxical and highly controversial: for all its supposed and much-acclaimed "orality," Zoščenko's skaz cannot be rendered orally, is unperformable, unrecitable. This conclusion flies in the face of the immense popularity (at least at one time) of Zoščenko's skaz works among Russian professional reciters (*čtecy*) and the fact that Zoščenko himself gave public readings of his own stories (though it would be interesting to know exactly how he read them).[19] It would be prodigiously silly to argue that the *čtecy* and Zoščenko himself have "done wrong"; all that is entirely beside the theoretical point. In theory, the conflicting bi-vocality, what Baxtin calls *raznonapravlennoe dvugolosoe slovo*, of parodic skaz is realizable only to the "mental" ears of an attentive silent reader.[20]

---

[16] For example, Vinogradov quotes N. N. Straxov's reaction to Dostoevskij's *Bednye ljudi*: "The letters are written in a language possible only in conversation." *Èvoljucija russkogo naturalizma* (Leningrad, 1929), p. 268 n.

[17] *Problemy tvorčestva Dostoevskogo* (Leningrad: Priboj, 1929), pp. 113–117.

[18] Ibid., pp. 118–119.

[19] An intriguing clue, indicating indeed, *difficulties*, is given in *Pered vosxodom solnca*; see, in the edition of the Meždunarodnoe Literaturnoe Sodružestvo (1967), pp. 113–114.

[20] In his analysis of Dostoevskij's "Skvernyj anekdot," V. N. Vološinov comes to

To prove the case on the material of Zoščenko's stories, with their already firmly established reputation in the reciter's repertoire, would be an extremely difficult and, for a non-Russian, hazardous, maybe even impossible task. But I would, instead, like to point out an analogous example in American literature. The American writer Damon Runyon, like Zoščenko, has been acclaimed for the oral speech, the special slangy lingo, of his narration. Indeed, Runyon stories are also often recited and, what is more, made into plays and even musical comedies. Yet, for all of Runyon's so-called "Broadway-ese," his style of narration blatantly depends on mixture with standard written, even, in part, specifically "business-letter," English. The total absence of elision (e.g., always "cannot," never "can't," always "let us," never "let's," etc.), fixation on the *praesens historicum*, the use in great abundance of "furthermore," "as follows," "undoubtedly," "indeed," "under such circumstances," etc., are features of written language styles in English that Runyon's author-narrator uses and plays on—indeed, exaggerates—as such because he is writing stories. To utter this mixture aloud, as if it were a special kind of oral speech, is to produce an effect wholly unjustified by the text. Again like Zoščenko (in his short pieces), Runyon, too, consistently uses re-narrated direct discourse in rendering character speech. The characters in Runyon stories speak the way they do not because that is how they are supposed to sound but because that is the way the author-narrator writes. Surely something approaching ridiculous nonsense is produced by having a performer, playing the role of the gangster Gentleman George, from the story "Cemetery Bait," say or sing (!) such lines as:

"They are vexed with me ... because one night I take Lou Adolia's automobile out on the salt meadows near Secaucus, N.J., and burn it to a crisp, and it seems that I forget to remove Lou Adolia first from same."[21]

The conclusion of this essay can only refer back to the point from which it started. There are no safe assumptions about the term skaz. The technique in question must be regarded as a problem on the agenda of modern literary scholarship still under fundamental investigation.

---

similar conclusions regarding its bi-vocality; see the chapter, "K istorii form vyskazyvanija v konstrukcijax jazyka" (from his book, *Marksizm i filosofija jazyka* [Leningrad, 1930]), reprinted in *Readings in Russian Poetics*, Michigan Slavic Materials, no. 2 (Ann Arbor, 1962), esp. pp. 89–91.

[21] *A Treasury of Damon Runyon*, The Modern Library (New York, 1958), p. 324.

THE ROLE OF NATURE IN
THE QUIET DON

BY

HERMAN ERMOLAEV

THERE ARE about two hundred and fifty descriptions of nature in *The Quiet Don*, not counting those less than two lines in length. Over two hundred species of the animal and vegetable worlds appear in the novel, some of them (willows, poplars) as often as fifty times. Such abundance is eloquent testimony to the author's love of nature, particularly that of his native Don region. This affection is expressed in the strongest terms at the end of a lengthy lyrical digression on the "beloved" steppe: "Low I bow and as a son kiss your fresh earth, O you, Don Steppe, soaked with unrusting Cossack blood!"[1] The patriotic theme of the Cossack land is forcefully sounded in the metaphorical portrayal of the "mounds rising in wise silence, guarding the buried Cossack glory" (IV, 64), or in the old Cossack song about the heroic past of these free people (V, 279). The Cossacks' devotion to their country is conveyed through the popular symbol of the dear and bitter wormwood, which in foreign lands has a different odor (III, 113; V, 356, 478).

Šoloxov's attachment to the Don region and its people was so strong that at times he looked at historical events through the eyes of the White Cossacks. At the beginning of the third book in the earliest editions of *The Quiet Don* he wrote that the Cossacks drove the Reds out of the Don territory "liberating through battle every inch of their native land," and a few lines later he asserted that by the end of April two-thirds of the Don region "was cleared of the Bolsheviks."[2] These phrases quoted above were purged from the 1945 edition and from subsequent ones.

A sort of "Cossackization" of nature is evident in the fact that natural scenes are frequently imbued with imagery associated with the Cossack way of life and folklore. One sees "the proud starry ways trodden by neither hoof nor foot," and "the moon—the Cossacks' little sun." The

---

[1] Mixail Šoloxov, *Sobranie sočinenij v vos'mi tomax* (Moscow: Gos. Izdat. Xud. Lit., 1956–1960), IV, 64. Cited hereafter in the text and notes by volume number and page. (Volumes II through V of this edition correspond respectively to books I through IV of *The Quiet Don*.) Translation of this and subsequent passages is based on Mixail Šoloxov, *And Quiet Flows the Don*, tr. Stephen Garry [H. C. Stevens], rev. and completed by Robert Daglish (Moscow: Progress Publishers, 1967). Passages from this translation are quoted with my occasional corrections.

[2] *Oktjabr'*, no. 1 (1929), p. 63; Mixail Šoloxov, *Tixij Don*, book III (Moscow: Gos. Izdat. Xud. Lit., 1933), p. 7.

Milky Way girdles the sky "like a silver-studded Cossack belt," clouds and waves "move in herds," fog and floes "rear," lightning "does trick riding," and the new moon and the easterly wind go "Cossacking." And faithful to folk poetry, Šoloxov uses *mesjac* for the moon, hardly ever *luna*.

For what is regarded as a socio-historical or epic novel, the part played by nature in *The Quiet Don* is exceptionally great. In its narrow function, nature is introduced to lend to descriptions an air of reality or to provide a parallel or a contrast to separate occurrences, human actions, conditions, and emotions. In its broader function, nature takes strategic places in the novel's structure, or accompanies the development of an event or relationship, or serves to express the author's philosophy of life.

The first indication of the structural importance of nature is given by the suggestive and symbolic title of the novel. The two epigraphs, which precede the first and second halves of the novel, consist of old Cossack songs about Father Don. In these songs natural processes occurring in the river are allegorically related to the Cossack past and to the momentous events of the novel: World War I, the Revolution, the Cossack uprising of 1919, and the disappearance of the Cossacks as a distinct social integer that had formed during centuries of unique environment. Four of the novel's eight parts and over one-fourth of its chapters either begin or end with sketches of nature. The landscape at the end of the second book carries Šoloxov's philosophical message, and the sun, in the novel's last sentence, sheds light on the fate of its protagonist. The depiction of nature in the opening lines of a chapter often foreshadows its subject matter and tone, whereas nature appearing at the close of a chapter reveals the author's attitude toward its content.

The role of natural descriptions that accompany the unfolding of human relationships or various events can be best examined by following the love story of Grigorij and Aksin'ja, Grigorij's relationship with Natal'ja, and the progress of the Cossack uprising. In such cases one may speak of the participation of nature in the plot, which, as the Soviet scholar Anatolij Britikov justly observes, is the most distinguishing trait in Šoloxov's treatment of nature.[3]

Natural imagery attends the love story of Grigorij and Aksin'ja from its very inception to the tragic end. It is a story of passion and unfulfilled hopes. Its leitmotif is floral blooming, the symbol of love in folk poetry.

---

[3] See A. F. Britikov, "Pejzaž u Šoloxova," *Voprosy sovetskoj literatury*, ed. P. S. Vyxodcev and V. A. Kovalev (Moscow–Leningrad: Akademija Nauk SSSR, 1959), VIII, 312.

The first natural image to allude to the main feature of the budding relationship is the henbane. "Your hair," Grigorij says to Aksin'ja, "smells like henbane. You know, that white flower" (II, 35). The point is that Grigorij calls henbane by a vernacular name, *durnop'jan*, that suggests intoxication. And the motif of love-intoxication permeates the next—and crucial—statement on the style of Aksin'ja's love: "Not like a red flower of the tulip, but like that loco weed, the roadside henbane, blooms a woman's belated love" (II, 53). This sentence opens the chapter portraying the changes in Aksin'ja brought on by her passion. In addition to *durnop'jan*, the henbane is called here by the local term of *sobač'ja besila* that implies madness. When Grigorij decides to break up his affair with Aksin'ja, her crushed love is symbolized by the chewed-up petals of the bindweed flower which he spits out, and by a smoky shadow which falls on her head and on the pink cup of the bindweed flower (II, 81).

Grigorij rudely pushes Aksin'ja away, and the devastating result of his action is highlighted through parallelism. A field of flowering corn, its ears powdered with golden dust, is flattened by a herd of cattle in the same way that Grigorij "had trampled [Aksin'ja's] feelings that had ripened to golden flower with his heavy, raw-hide sandals. He had sullied them, burned them to ash—and that was all" (II, 98).

Grigorij's parents marry him off to the unloved Natal'ja. But he soon leaves his wife for Aksin'ja, dreaming of a happy life in the Kuban region with her: "And beyond the rolling hills, beyond the grey road lay, as if in a fairy tale, a welcoming land of blue skies, with Aksin'ja's passionate, late-flowering love, to boot" (II, 171). A motif of hopeful dreaming has been added here to the dominant theme of blossoming.

Toward the end of the first book, Grigorij returns from the front on leave and learns that Aksin'ja has been unfaithful to him. Without saying a word to her about it, he goes to sleep. She spends all night standing on the porch, listening with a heavy heart to the "funeral dirge of the northern wind" that symbolizes the futility of her hopes for a reconciliation with Grigorij (II, 400).

Though deceived by Aksin'ja, Grigorij continues to love her and thinks of her at the front. Here the motif of henbane is revived in the episode in which he mistakes the scent of fallen leaves for the "fine intoxicating aroma" of her hair (III, 47).

Three years have passed, but "the feeling blossomed and fermented" in Grigorij, "he loved Aksin'ja with old, exhausting love" (IV, 165).

Finally, after more than four years of separation, a reunion takes place on the shores of the Don, against a lyrical natural background in which "the poplars stood with their pale grey trunks in the water, rocking their naked boughs, and the willows, fluffy with blossoms—girls' earrings, luxuriantly rose over the water like thin wondrous green clouds" (IV, 326). This subtle watercolor drawing harmonizes with the tender sadness of both characters and simultaneously represents a variation of the love and blooming theme which is developed further in Aksin'ja's observation that "a tree only blossoms once a year" and in Grigorij's question: "And you think ours has already blossomed?" (IV, 326).

Two pages later we learn that it has not. Aksin'ja's long-suppressed feelings burst out in streams of happy tears. The accumulation of feelings and their release are likened to the formation and downfall of an enormous crag of snow which hangs over a cliff until it is dislodged by a gust of wind, and then plunges downward crushing every bush in its way and "dragging in its wake a foaming, skyward-leaping, silvery train of powdered snow" (IV, 329). In the case of Aksin'ja, the "gust of wind" happened to be Grigorij's tender greeting, and the avalanche of her reciprocal feelings turned out to be as destructive as the plunging crag of snow. It was the night rendezvous with Grigorij, which Aksin'ja had arranged after their meeting, that induced Natal'ja to have an abortion, resulting in her death.

In the opening chapter of the fourth book Aksin'ja, on her way to Grigorij, is shown taking a rest surrounded by luxuriant late spring vegetation. The languorous aroma of a lily of the valley—"already touched by mortal decay"—attracts her attention. Looking at the flower and inhaling its "mournful scent," Aksin'ja is unwittingly moved to tears and recalls all her long and difficult life (V, 16). Then she falls asleep under a bush of eglantine and is gradually covered by its withering petals, broken away by the wind.

Both the dying lily and the fading bush of eglantine not only symbolize the approach of old age for Aksin'ja but also introduce the motif of her impending death, which is enhanced by the presence of a cuckoo that "faintly and mournfully counted out someone's unspent years" (V, 15).

During the retreat of the defeated White Army in the Kuban region, Grigorij had to leave Aksin'ja behind because she caught typhus. Upon her recovery, at the beginning of the eighth part, the early-spring nature appears to her as marvelously fresh and enchanting. "All seemed incredibly beautiful to her, all was blossoming with heavy yet delicate tints, as though haloed in sunlight" (V, 297). This is more than a heightened physical perception of a person who has just recuperated from a serious illness. This also reflects Aksin'ja's emotional condition, the revival of her bright hopes for a speedy reunion with Grigorij.

Though not immediately, Grigorij does return to her. Expectations of happiness rise in her again, but a strong feeling of anxiety replaces them. She peers through the window, and "the darkness only faintly lit by the snow" (V, 366) suggests the frailty of her hopes. It turns out that Grigorij is forced to leave her again, fleeing from persecution by the Reds.

Several months later Grigorij returns, and now they escape to the Kuban region. The early motif of seeking happiness in this land of plenty is reiterated. The entire world seems to Aksin'ja exultant and bright. Her long-cherished hope of life with Grigorij seems to be coming true. During a halt Grigorij lies down for a sleep amid thick grass and flowers, listening to the sounds of birds, animals, and insects. Aksin'ja weaves a wreath of gay sweet-smelling flowers and lays it at Grigorij's head (V, 486). This wreath has a double meaning. As a wedding accessory it symbolizes a joyous union of the two characters; on the other hand, as a funeral accessory it indicates their imminent death. It is possible that the latter aspect is stressed by Aksin'ja's thrusting a few flowers of the prickly eglantine into the wreath, which can be taken as an allusion to the crown of thorns.

The death motif receives an added emphasis as soon as the fugitives resume their journey. As in folklore, nature foretells disaster. A bittern booms hollowly in the distance, the orchards look black and unfriendly in the mist, and the stillness of night imbues Grigorij with anxiety and fear. A few lines later a Red soldier's bullet kills Aksin'ja. Grigorij buries her, "firmly believing that they will not be parted for long" (V, 490). Then, at the end of the chapter, he raises his head and sees "above him the black sky and the blindingly glittering black disk of the sun" (V, 490). This black sun symbolizes more than the depth of Grigorij's grief. With Aksin'ja's death, he loses his will to live. Thus the sun—the generator of life in Šoloxov's view—has burned out for him.

The motif of blackness is immediately developed in the next and last chapter that starts with a poignant comparison of the black barren steppe, scorched with fire, with the black life of Grigorij whom death has deprived of everything dear to his heart (V, 491).

In a few months Grigorij returns to surrender himself to the Soviet authorities. The cold sun in the concluding line of the novel emphasizes his alienation from the living world. The only thread tying him to it is his son, whose appearance in the final scene of the novel asserts the perpetuation of life. But Grigorij is already dead spiritually and resigned to his physical destruction.

The descriptions of Grigorij's relationship with Natal'ja are not marked by recurrent images of flowers and blossoms or by richness and poetry of natural scenery, except for purposes of contrast. All the beauty of nature belongs to Aksin'ja, for in Šoloxov's own words, he likes her better than any of his other female characters.[4] Natural imagery associated with Natal'ja serves to underline the plight of a devoted but unloved wife whose desperate actions run contrary to the basic laws of nature. Right after her wedding the coming rain may be taken as a sign of good luck, but the flickering lightning seems to presage eventual destruction (II, 105).

Soon after the wedding, in the steppe at night, Natal'ja learns from Grigorij that he does not love her. At that point the inaccessible stars, the ghostlike cloud, the fresh snow, and a sad dead smell of withered grass are all combined to underline the vanity of her hopes and the coldness in her marital life (II, 146).

Abandoned by her husband and humiliated by her fellow villagers, Natal'ja attempts to take her own life. The news and description of the suicide attempt are preceded by the portrayal of the Don liberating itself from winter ice. The roar of the bumping floes merges with the ringing of the Easter bells (II, 196). This scene is intended not only to create an appropriate atmosphere for the arrival of the news that Natal'ja is near death, but also to suggest the incompatibility of her action with Christian faith and—more importantly—with nature's coming to life in spring. This can be substantiated by the fact that the scene of Natal'ja cutting her throat is immediately followed by the repeated reference to the drifting floes and tolling church bells. The chapter ends with the observation that "the joyous, full-flowing, liberated Don was carrying its icy fetters away down to the Sea of Azov" (II, 212). Here the indifference of the joyous nature to Natal'ja underscores the unnatural character of her act.

Five years later the continuing coldness between Natal'ja and Grigorij is set off against a vigorous spring landscape, full of life-giving strength and fruitfulness, eagerly awaiting the rain announced by distant thunderclaps (IV, 300). The fecundity of nature in this instance foreshadows, by means of contrast, the motif of Natal'ja's self-imposed infertility embodied in her forthcoming abortion, whereas the mention of faint thunderclaps is a prelude to the violent thunderstorm in the fourth book.

During the thunderstorm Natal'ja curses the unfaithful Grigorij, imploring God to punish him with death. Black thunder clouds, majestic and wild; burning white flashes of lightning; murmuring grass and bitter dust—all are in tune with the mood, posture, and action of the outraged

---

[4] Since Šoloxov said this at the end of 1958, he had in mind all his female characters, including those in the second book of *Virgin Soil Upturned*. See Vasilij Il'in, *Naši dobrye sovetčiki. Literaturnye portrety* (Moscow: Moskovskij Rabočij, 1966), p. 58.

woman (V, 158). The subsequent rain reactivates the life-generating forces of nature. The steppe turns wonderfully green. At the same time Natal'ja makes the decision to kill the life within herself (V, 160).

The last appearance of nature in connection with Grigorij and Natal'ja is one of the subtlest in *The Quiet Don*. Grigorij, working in the field, suddenly experiences an urge to see his orphaned children. Natal'ja's last wish that he should take good care of them rings in his ears. On his way home he passes the stubble field full of rooks, with the old birds feeding the young ones (V, 178). Here, for the first time in the story of Grigorij and Natal'ja, nature appears in constructive harmony with the characters' action. Until now natural vitality contrasted with Natal'ja's rejection of life, a tragic behavior for a woman who physically was "like a young apple-tree in blossom—beautiful, healthy, strong" (V, 166). This single "blossom" image was bestowed upon Natal'ja when she was in her deathbed.

The juxtaposition of natural phenomena with the central event of the novel—the 1919 uprising of the Upper Don Cossacks against the Bolsheviks —begins with an almost two-page portrayal of nature that, in the style of folk poetry, conveys the Cossacks' anxiety before the arrival of the Red Army and predicts war and destruction for them. A typical excerpt from it reads: "In the evening the red-hot shield of the moon arose from behind the spears of the naked forest. It glowed mistily with the bloody light of war and fire over the silent villages. And under its merciless, unfading light an inarticulate alarm was born in the hearts of men. The animals fidgeted anxiously; the horses and bullocks wandered restlessly about the yards until dawn"[5] (IV, 113-114).

The Red fighting troops have passed through the Upper Don region, and the Cossacks are fearfully expecting the arrival of the Bolshevik authorities. The condition of the Cossacks is compared to that of the "ancient" and "dear" steppe (again Šoloxov's attachment to his native land) which is covered with snow and seems dead. But under the icy cover the winter rye clings tenaciously to life, and "it will rise in its time! The quails will struggle in it, the April skylark will sing above it. The sun will shine on it and the wind will send it swaying, *until the master comes and looses the rattling (čekakajuščie) blades of the mowing machine to cut*

---

[5] As soon as Šoloxov approached the subject of the Cossack uprising, the serialization of the novel in the literary monthly *Oktjabr'* was interrupted for nearly three years so that the quoted passage (chapter XIII, book III) was published in *Oktjabr'*, no. 1, only in 1932. The main reason for the interruption was the objective portrayal of the Bolsheviks' brutal treatment of the Cossacks which caused the uprising.

and kill the wilted, moribund stem."⁶ It may be that the rising of the winter rye alludes to the Cossack uprising which was to erupt in the spring. It is more likely, however, that the winter rye is symbolic of the perpetual self-renewal of life. Therefore the life of the Cossacks will continue in spite of the bloody repression by the Bolsheviks, that is, the master with the rattling (*čeka*kajuščie) blades. The italicized letters of this onomatopoetic word do undoubtedly stand for CHEKA—the Extraordinary Commission for Combating Counterrevolution, Sabotage, and Speculation. This can be borne out by several facts. First, the immediately following paragraph contains a direct reference to the "Extraordinary Commissions and tribunals" that "were holding brief and unjust trials of the Cossacks who had served with the Whites .... An accusation, a couple of questions, sentencing—and then machine-gun death" (IV, 148). Second, in all of Šoloxov's writings the term *čekakajuščie*, in combination with "blades," occurs only once, in the passage in question. On two other occasions where Šoloxov speaks of the rattling blades of a mowing machine he uses the verb *čečekat'*.⁷ The same verb or its derivatives, are used several times in *The Quiet Don* and once in *The Tales of the Don* to reproduce the sounds of birds, people, hoofs, and a machine gun. Third, the rattling (*čekakajuščie*) blades of the mowing machine are to be found only in the earliest printed text of the passage in question, that is, within the excerpt from *The Quiet Don* published in the magazine *Krasnaja Niva*, no. 16, June 10, 1930.

In all editions of the novel, including the text printed in *Oktjabr'*, the word *čekakajuščie* is no longer there, and the sentence in which it appeared is recast. In *Oktjabr'* it reads: "Until ripe full ears, rumpled by downpours and ferocious winds, guiltily bow their moustached heads and fall down under the scythe of the master, humbly dropping their grain on the threshing floor."⁸ In this version, however, the word "guiltily" still contained a hint of the punishment of the Cossacks for their opposition to the Bolsheviks. It was removed from all subsequent editions of the novel, as were the italicized words in the sentence that immediately followed: "The entire right bank of the Don, *like the steppe in winter*, lived a secret, suppressed life." The deleted words, which appear only in *Krasnaja Niva*, drew an obvious, and uncomfortable, parallel between the subterranean life of nature and the anxious stillness of the Cossack villages expecting the arrival of the Bolshevik punitive organs. The

---

⁶ *Krasnaja Niva*, no. 16 (June 10, 1930), p. 12. Italics mine.
⁷ "Batraki," I, 266; *Tixij Don*, II, 84.
⁸ *Oktjabr'*, no. 1 (1932), p. 20.

allegorical portrayal of the winter steppe and rye must have been of particular importance to Šoloxov, since he decided to include it in a short excerpt that he was able to publish at the time when the serialization of the novel in *Oktjabr'* was banned.

The main reason for the Cossack uprising is reflected in the behavior of the Don. Where its bed is wide and shallow the river flows quietly and peacefully. But where "the banks are narrow the imprisoned Don gnaws a deep channel for itself and drives on its foam-clad waves with a muffled roar. Whirlpools form in the deep water around headlands. The water races there in such an enchanting frightening circle that one can hardly take his eyes away" (IV, 177). The same is true of the Cossacks: "From the calm shallows of peaceful days life had flowed into a narrow channel. The Upper Don district started to seethe.... The young Cossacks and the poorer ones still lay low and hesitated, still hoped for peace from the Soviet regime, but the old men were on the offensive and were already saying openly that the Reds intended to destroy the Cossacks to the last man" (IV, 177). The entire chapter goes on to describe the mounting unrest caused by arbitrary executions, though Šoloxov did not dare to disclose their true dimensions.[9]

The beginning of the uprising is symbolically likened to the Don freeing itself from its icy fetters: "Get up! The Don has broken its ice!" Grigorij learns from the Cossack who had hidden him from the Reds (IV, 195). The rapidly growing scope of the Cossack action allows Šoloxov to speak of "the wide flood of the uprising" (IV, 208). "Like flood water the uprising swelled and spread, inundating" the Upper Don district that produced 25,000 horsemen and 10,000 foot soldiers (IV, 238). The ravaging effects of the insurrection and the annihilation of the Cossacks and their own atrocities are neatly summarized in a brief simile: "Like an all-devouring steppe fire the uprising raged" (IV, 277). This and all but one of the preceding references to nature in connection with the uprising appear at the very beginning of chapters and have a direct bearing on their content.

---

[9] "I have intentionally omitted such facts—which constituted the immediate cause of the uprising—as the senseless shooting of sixty-two old Cossacks in Migulinskaja village, or the shootings in Kazanskaja and Šumilinskaja villages where the number of the Cossacks who were shot (former elected village elders, holders of the Cross of St. George, sergeants major, honorary village judges, curators of schools, and other bourgeois and counterrevolutionaries on the village scale) has reached within six days the impressive figure of more than 400 men." See Šoloxov's letter to Maksim Gor'kij of June 6, 1931, in *Literaturnoe Nasledstvo*, vol. 70 (Moscow: Akademija Nauk SSSR, 1963), 696. To my knowledge, this is the only place where Šoloxov's letter was published without omission of the chilling statistics. This was done at the peak of de-Stalinization.

The hopeless situation of the defeated Cossacks is mirrored in the weather during their retreat in the Kuban region: a "pitch-dark night," a "black steppe," clouds, wind, rain, cold. The retreat into darkness assumes the proportions of an historical landmark. It indicates the disappearance of the old Cossack way of life. At this point Šoloxov reveals his duality. A nostalgic Cossack admirer, he makes the Cossacks sing an old epic song that is "wide like the Don in flood"—a song about the glorious past of their free ancestors. A stern Communist, he passes a political judgment: "And now the descendants of these free Cossacks, shamefully retreating after being defeated in an inglorious war against the people of Russia, listened to the mighty song in gloomy silence" (V, 279). It is wrong to identify the Cossacks' resistance to the Bolshevik terror with a war against the Russian people, and it is unjust to brand their retreat shameful in view of the vast numerical and material superiority of their enemy. Šoloxov had been less ideologically orthodox in the first three books of *The Quiet Don*, written when he belonged neither to the Communist party nor to the Komsomol.

A clue to Šoloxov's philosophy of life is given in the closing paragraphs of the second book which describe the grave of Valet, a Red soldier killed by the Cossacks. The killers buried Valet in Christian fashion, with his head to the west. In two weeks the small mound was overgrown with fresh, gay, and fragrant grasses. An old man set up at the head of the grave a little shrine with an affixed image of the Virgin and an inscription in Old Church Slavonic: "In the years of strife and trouble, / Brothers, judge not the brother" (III, 397). Šoloxov goes on:

> The old man rode away and the little shrine remained in the steppe to sadden the eyes of passing travellers with its eternally mournful aspect, and to stir in their hearts a strange and sad longing.
>
> Later on, in May, bustards fought around the shrine. They beat out a little bare patch in the blue wormwood, crushing the green flush of ripening quitch grass, fighting for the hen, for the right to life, for love and fertility. And again after a little while, under a mound, right by the shrine, in the shaggy shelter of the old wormwood a hen bustard laid nine speckled, smoky-blue eggs and sat on them, warming them with her body, and shielding them with her glossy wings. [III, 397]

Here Šoloxov expounds a sort of a pantheistic outlook on the eternity of life. Man is a part of nature even if he is dead. To paraphrase Puškin, young life plays at the entrance to man's grave. Christian teaching is congenial neither to the spirit of man nor to the laws of nature. It imbues man with dejection and is incompatible with the natural principle of fighting for the right to live, love, and procreate. The grasses on Valet's grave are not the flowers on Bazarov's grave which speak of an "eternal reconciliation."

A question arises: Does Šoloxov apply the laws of struggle in nature to human society? To a certain extent he does. The fight of the bustards has something in common with the human fight in which Valet perished. At the same time one feels that the natural struggle is presented as something more justified, spontaneous, and constructive than the human struggle. It is the struggle for the perpetuation of life. The biological aspect of this struggle is more acceptable and attractive than are the political and ideological motivations of human wars. In this respect Valet's grave acquires a particular significance, since the preceding chapter deals with a mass execution of the Red Cossacks.

In a number of the important natural descriptions associated with war, the emphasis is laid not on the struggle in nature but on its beauty and the abundance of vital forces. Nature is contrasted with man's actions and placed above him in a way reminiscent of Tolstoj's condemnation of war in "Sebastopol in May" through the juxtaposition of putrid corpses and flowery vale. The cruel extermination of people during the Upper Don uprising takes place against the background of the spring which "in that year was brilliant with unusual beauty.... The steppe, green-tinted and drenched with the ancient scent of the thawing black earth and the eternally youthful odor of the new grass, was filled with inexpressible charm" (IV, 277–278). Detailed depictions of ugly, mutilated, and decomposing bodies of the Cossacks killed in action give way to either a "quiet, gracious" autumn landscape dominated by "the stern, silent beauty of the forest" (V, 233) or to a page-long portrayal of the steppe in April when "made fecund by the spring, an invisible, almighty, and palpitant life was unfolding in the steppe," when "the grass was growing luxuriantly," and when "hidden from the rapacious human eye, conjugal couples of birds and beasts, big and small, were mating in their secret steppe lairs, and the ploughed lands wore a fine brush of innumerable young shoots" (IV, 339).

As if the contrast between human self-destruction and the life-creating forces of nature were not sufficiently sharp, the author brings in "the rapacious human eye," implying that indeed it is not birds and animals that are rapacious but man. This is not the only case of man's humiliation when compared to animals. Of a character who observes the lives of horses Šoloxov says that "he gained a profound respect for their intelligence and their non-human nobility" (IV, 65). The mating of horses, "this primeval act, accomplished in primitive conditions, was so naturally wise and simple that it involuntarily aroused in Koševoj's mind a comparison with human beings that was not in the latter's favor" (IV, 65). The deepest, even sarcastic, degradation of man before nature is made in the passage describing the vigorous life in the steppe right after the burial of the old man Saška, who was senselessly murdered by the Reds:

> on the earth which had just taken the merry ostler and drunkard Saška to itself, life was still seething as furiously as ever. From the steppe that crept in a flood of green to the very edge of the orchard, and in the tangle of wild flax around the borders of the old threshing-floor, one could hear the incessant pulsating call of the quail; gophers were whistling, bumble-bees were humming, the grass rustled under the wind's caresses, the skylarks sang in the spirtling air of the hot day, and, to confirm the grandeur of man's place in nature, from somewhere a long way off down the valley came the persistent angry mutter of a machine gun. [V, 51]

The machine gun is anonymous. It does not matter whether it belongs to the Whites or Reds. It is a symbol of human malice, arrogance, and destructiveness.

Typical of Šoloxov, the sentence with the machine gun closes the chapter, and equally typically, the vigorous natural life unfolds itself next to a human grave. The life goes on regardless of whether the Reds kill the Whites or vice versa. The same indestructible life dominates the natural imagery in the scene of the atrocious murder of the Red commander Lixačev (IV, 207) and in the description of the grave of the executed Petr Melexov, a White Cossack officer (V, 207). There is no exaggeration in saying that if one wants to know Šoloxov's view of life, one should go to his graves. It is there that he transcends his ideological limitations and raises his art to the level of universality, treating the eternal subject of life and death with a purely human touch. This is also true of descriptions of graves and nature in his latest and most orthodox work, the second book of *Virgin Soil Upturned* (1960), in the final scene in particular.

For the atheistic Šoloxov, the sun is the source of life. He speaks of "life which repeats itself under the solar cycle" just before the Cossacks go to cut down Lixačev with their sabers (IV, 207). At another point a lengthy portrayal of a spring landscape brimful with life is capped with a respectful reference to "a proud and lofty sun" (IV, 301). Elsewhere landscapes appear as "haloed in sunlight" (IV, 339; V, 51, 297).

Natural life under the sun goes on parallel to human life. In this lies the unity of man and nature. Because of a firm belief in this unity, *The Quiet Don* is permeated with analogies relating actions and inner experiences of man to the world of nature. One encounters among them numerous personifications of nature, especially when it is called upon to highlight wounds and grief caused by human wars. Distinguishing traits, behavior, and exterior of the characters are constantly likened to those of animals and plants. Thus the merchant Moxov's mind is "tenacious as bind-weed" (II, 119). Bunčuk, a Bolshevik, resembles "the corkelm, the tree of a stern, iron hardness that grows on the grey, loose soil of the inhospitable Don-side earth" (II, 350). Valet's face looks like that of a porcupine (III, 333), whereas the commander of a Cossack squadron, "a hook-nosed fierce looking man with a bristly ginger beard covering his face to the eyes, had a striking resemblance to a wild boar" (IV, 394). The Cossack officer Medvedev combines in himself a bear and a wolf. He is a sullen man, "of wolf-like appearance and wolfish habits, "with tiny ... bear-like eyes" (IV, 247, 276). Comparing human actions and exterior to those of a wolf is a favorite device of Šoloxov. It is used at least thirty times in *The Quiet Don*.

Man, of course, has his own peculiarities not inherent in the world of nature. He can surpass nature in cruelty and destructiveness. On the other hand, the complexity of his spiritual and emotional life is unknown to nature. After sabering four Red sailors in combat, Grigorij writhes in a fit of remorse on the rich black earth, imploring his subordinates to kill him. This eruption of feelings is contrasted with the insensitivity of the grass that "grows on the earth, indifferently accepting the sun and the rain, feeding on its life-giving juices, humbly bowing under the destructive breath of the storm. And then, scattering its seeds to the wind, it dies as indifferently, with the rustle of its withering stalks welcoming the death-radiating autumn sun" (IV, 283). Placed at the end of the chapter, this observation plays the role of a philosophical résumé.

Nature also shows no compassion when a Cossack and a goose—both mortally wounded—and the grief-stricken Natal'ja (twice) press themselves to "the unaffectionate earth" (II, 375; IV, 284; V, 36, 156). Equally unconcerned is the Don at the close of the chapter, where after a detailed description of the "bitter-sweet life" of a Cossack village with all its love, hate, and politics, the author sums it up: "And over the village slipped the days, passing into the nights; the weeks flowed by, the months crept on, the wind howled over the hill, warning of bad weather to come, and, glazed with the clear greenish-blue of autumn, the Don flowed on indifferently to the sea" (II, 135).

The bond between man and nature is, however, more significant for Šoloxov than the difference between them, and this bond is not merely biological. For Šoloxov (as for Maksim Gor'kij) nature is the field of man's work. This is why Grigorij longs for ploughing the land instead of trampling the grain in the maneuvers of war (IV, 95). As for Pasternak, life for Šoloxov is a miracle, though not in the Christian sense. He simply marvels at natural life as such. Therefore he does not hesitate to characterize nature with such clichés as marvelous, enchanted, wonderful, magic, fantastic. These epithets are applied not so much in their esthetic or everyday connotations but more in their original meaning, and the use of them drastically increases in the second half of the novel. Here are some examples: "in the sunlight the hoar-frost gave off iridescent, fantastically rich combinations of colors" (II, 223); "the withering autumn forest, feathered brightly as in a fairy tale" (III, 131); "the magically silent forest" (III, 328); "filled with a marvelous and multivoiced sonority, the forest lived its mighty, primordial life" (V, 16); "the most wonderful entwining of flowers and herbs" (V, 16); "the flood water stood motionless as though charmed, reflecting the twilight of the starry heaven" (V, 306); "the steppe lay in a dead silence as though enchanted" (V, 357).

Since every form of life is a miracle, man cannot force his artificial laws upon it. Jurij Živago ridicules attempts to reshape life like a lump of raw material, in accordance with political blue prints: "But life is never a material, a substance. Life, if you want to know, is the principle of uninterrupted self-renewal, it is eternally remolding, remaking, and transforming itself, and it is far beyond your or my dull-witted theories about it."[10]

Šoloxov entertains a similar view when, at the beginning of a chapter, he asserts the impossibility of predicting the course of human life or of guiding it: "When swept out of its normal channel, life scatters into many branches. It is difficult to foresee which direction it will take in its treacherous and winding course. Where today it trickles, like a rivulet over sandbanks, so shallow that its ugly shoals are visible, tomorrow it will flow rich and full" (II, 362). Elsewhere Šoloxov says, "Life dictates its own unwritten laws to man" (II, 387), and numerous examples in the novel illustrate this point, including the confessions of the characters themselves. Bitterly, Grigorij laughs about "his queerly twisted life" (II, 397), and Anna Pogudko spends a long time "thinking about her strange and drastically changed life" (III, 298).

Šoloxov is devoid of the officially optimistic view of life. The fates of his principal characters are tragic. Grigorij does in life not what he wants but what he is forced to do, and he perishes. He is also involuntarily involved in the tragic deaths of Natal'ja and Aksin'ja. Grigorij's life is described as "rich in sorrow and poor in joy" (IV, 283) and that of Aksin'ja as "long and poor in joy" (V, 16). Direct references to bitter, difficult, and joyless lives are made with regard to such different characters as Bunčuk (III, 385), Grigorij's mother (V, 325, 328), and an Austrian

---

[10] Boris Pasternak, *Doktor Živago* (Ann Arbor: The University of Michigan Press, 1959), p. 348.

soldier (II, 275). To explain the hard lives of Šoloxov's characters exclusively in terms of social and economic conditions would be nearsighted. He treats life in its complexity and his conception of its driving force—love—is tragic. "The two sad friends and companions of almost every true love," he asserts in the second book of *Virgin Soil Upturned*, "are separation and loss" (VII, 335). This view is borne out in both of his novels.

Tragedy may be a purely human phenomenon, but human life in the broad sense, as an ingredient of natural life, is governed by love, procreation, and self-renewal. These forces constitute the core of life—its inherent truth. Šoloxov's closeness to nature in *The Quiet Don* played an important part in permitting him to portray life as it is and to tone down his ideological bias. Truth of life and originality of craftsmanship combine in *The Quiet Don* to produce an outstanding literary work.

SOLŽENICYN AND THE LEGACY OF TOLSTOJ

BY

KATHRYN B. FEUER

THE RECENT, almost simultaneous, appearance of Aleksandr Solženicyn's two long novels, *In the First Circle* and *The Cancer Ward*,[1] the news of the forthcoming *Arkhipelag Gulag*[2], the publication of various stories and sketches—this sudden emergence of a voluminous mass of new fiction, by a writer of extraordinary ability, creates an unusual situation for literary criticism, which is accustomed to great works more deliberately spaced. Views proposed now must inevitably be subject to later revision, while the novels are so masterly that judicious silence is difficult. In a new situation one looks for familiar guideposts; in the terra incognita of the Solženicyn novel the traces of Tolstoj create constantly recurring moments of recognition. One approach to Solženicyn then is to survey his "Tolstoyanism" with the secondary aim of defining an influence but primarily to point up by this narrow light some features of his own literary landscape.

I

In several ways Tolstoj seems to have provided models for Solženicyn's fiction. Since a writer's first published work is usually significant of his elective affinities, it is worth noting that the account of a day in the life of Ivan Denisovič recalls "The Woodfelling" in its chief organizing devices: men of various class and attitude, caught in a common situation of stress which belongs to and is yet outside the ordinary life of their society, joined together by membership in a group within the larger whole, conducted through a day which begins before dawn and ends in moonlight, with the position and heat of the sun used to define forward movement and also to demarcate shifts in mood or focus.

In Solženicyn's novels some Tolstoyan structural features are also apparent. Both use extremely large casts of characters whose coming

---

[1] Aleksandr Solženicyn, *V kruge pervom* (New York: Harper & Row, 1968). A. Solženicyn, *Rakovyj korpus* (Paris: YMCA Press, 1968). All references in this study are to these editions, abbreviated as VKP and RK respectively. I have consulted and sometimes followed *The First Circle*, translated by Thomas P. Whitney (New York: Harper & Row, 1968), *The Cancer Ward*, translated by Rebecca Frank (New York: Dial Press, 1968) and *Cancer Ward*, translated by Nicholas Bethell and David Burg (New York: Bantam Books, 1969). All references to Tolstoj are to volume and page of *L. N. Tolstoj, Sobranie sočinenij v dvadcati tomax* (Moscow, 1960-1965).
[2] *Time Magazine* (March 21, 1969), p. 40.

together, however unlikely, is made to seem natural and believable—in Tolstoj by an intricate system of family relationships, in Solženicyn by the common extraordinary situation of sharashka and cancer ward. Like Tolstoj, Solženicyn involves the reader in the destinies of both primary and secondary protagonists among these characters, although in this respect Solženicyn is more "egalitarian" than Tolstoj, who tends to reserve important spiritual development for his major heroes and heroines. Moreover both writers incline toward the expansive roman-fleuve, in which external action has only a minor role. Both the minimalization of plot events and their open-endedness are particularly notable in Solženicyn because they are unusual features in novels whose time structures are so rigorously controlled—four days for *In the First Circle*, about six weeks for *The Cancer Ward*.³ In this respect Solženicyn may seem to resemble his other great predecessor, Dostoevskij, but there is this important difference. When finishing, for example, *The Brothers Karamazov*, the careful student who adds up how much time has passed is astonished at the result of his calculations. Time sequence in Dostoevskij is usually correct, but the illusion of temporal realism is sacrificed to dramatic unity. Both Solženicyn and Tolstoj, on the other hand, manifest strong concern for the sequential treatment of depicted time. They like to provide the reader with internal temporal references, and they find it hard to elide, to break out of continuous time—indeed the depiction of the four "days" of *First Circle* continues through the three intervening nights. Occasionally minor timetable errors even occur in their novels, but never to the reader who does not track them down. Rather, the reader's impression is that time has been carefully accounted for and that the duration of hours or days or weeks has been experientially sustained.

As to narrative structure, the similarities between the two authors are perhaps outweighed by the differences. Solženicyn's use of the first person in "The Right Hand"⁴ a story which seems in all other respects a rejected

---

³ *First Circle* begins at 4:05 P.M., December 24, 1949, and ends in the early afternoon (after lunch) of December 27. Midnight of the 24 probably comes around the division between chaps. 15 and 16; midnight of the 25 probably comes in chaps. 65 and 66; midnight of the 26 in chap. 83 or 84. Part I of *Cancer Ward* goes from Thursday, February 3, 1955, to Thursday, February 10. Part II can be dated exactly from Thursday, March 3, to Friday, March 11 (chaps. 22-26). Thereafter dating is not entirely clear. The novel ends (chaps. 35-36) on a Saturday which seems to be March 26, but could be the 19. The latter is more likely since Kostoglotov arrived at the hospital on January 23 and is said (several times) to have been there eight weeks and Rusanov, who arrived on February 3, is said to have stayed six weeks.

⁴ Alexander Solzhenitsyn, "The Right Hand," *The Atlantic Monthly* (April, 1969), pp. 45-49.

fragment of *Cancer Ward*, suggests that he may have worked his way from *Ich* to *Er* by the same kind of meticulous experimentation as the young Tolstoj. Neither writer explicitly abjures omniscience yet both prefer to narrate within the specified points of view of their characters, shifting easily from one to another but adhering faithfully, while with a particular character, to his experience, attitudes, and limitations. Perhaps because their heroes are so recognizably "autobiographical" both Tolstoj and Solženicyn tend to mark clearly their own authorial appearances as un-characterized narrators or commentators. Solženicyn, of course, does not reason with the reader about causes or meanings, but both writers make themselves felt as constantly hovering presences of critical intelligence, and both make frequent injections of biting social irony, more massive in Tolstoj, more mordant in Solženicyn—the irony of the observer, perhaps, versus that of the participant. And it can be noted also that both authors' voices are primarily those of moralists, with the great difference that Solženicyn's modesty and compassion never acquire the insistently didactic Tolstoyan accent.

Whatever the tone, both Solženicyn and Tolstoj know well the effectiveness of flat interjections in their own voice. When Solženicyn begins a chapter with the statement: "Strange are the relationships between a man and a woman: they cannot be predicted, they possess no direction, they have no laws" (VKP, 361) he is surely recalling the opening of *Anna Karenina* (and note the typically Tolstoyan concreteness in generalizations: "*a* man and *a* woman"). But far more often, as in his notable chapter endings, or in the passage near the end of *First Circle* when he suddenly addresses the reader as "you," Solženicyn achieves an immediacy and force which is strikingly his own—for reference in the latter case to "Sevastopol in December" would probably be more pedantic than true:

> And so . . . the zek puts his hands behind his back, and . . . surrounded by dogs and convoy guards, he goes to the railroad car.
> You have all seen him at that moment in our railroad stations—but you have hastened to look down at the ground like a coward, to turn away like a loyal subject, so that the convoy lieutenant will not suspect you of something and arrest you.
> The zek goes into the car. . . . [VKP, 491–492]

Potapov's highly stylized narration of "Buddha's Smile" is a sustained mock epic brilliantly evocative of both "Graf Nulin" and "Istorija sela Gorjuxina" (after all Potapov is the camp Puškinist) and the tale's most effective point comes at its only interruption:

> "But the next thing—not one of you could guess! They brought in potatoes—not frozen, not rotten, not black—simply, what one might call ordinary potatoes."

"That's impossible!" the listeners protested. "Now that's not true to life!" "But that's just what happened!" [VKP, 295]

Such moments in Solženicyn owe nothing to Tolstoj. They are, however, reminiscent of Tolstoj's power to manipulate his own realistic surface with a twist of narrational change-of-pace.

Solženicyn has adapted and put his own stamp on many other traits of the Tolstoyan novel. Both portray real historical men of power and introduce current public events, with a similar awareness of the havoc they can bring to individuals and a similar refusal to accept them as determinative of men's ultimate moral choices. There is a like desensationalization of inherently dramatic situations and at the same time the ability to renew the commonplace, to make the petty concerns and familiar sentiments of ordinary people vital, fresh, and extraordinary. Tolstoj's and Solženicyn's protagonists are genuinely comparable: unheroic heroes, whose adventures are in the realms of conscience and thought; wonderfully individualized heroines who nevertheless exist most powerfully in the novels as objects of temptation or tenderness or saving love for the men. This kinship is all the more striking when one considers that two important aspects of Solženicyn's feminine portrayals derive from conditions inconceivable to Tolstoj: the theme, developed with sensitivity and compassion, of an entire generation of women "widowed" by the war and the terror; and the custodial role (nurses, doctors, MGB officers) of almost all the loved women.

Finally, Tolstoj was a significant exemplar for Solženicyn in a number of important secondary characterizations. A detailed comparison could be made, for example, of Solženicyn's security officers and those of *Resurrection*. Kondrašev-Ivanov in *First Circle* recalls Mixajlov in *Anna Karenina*, by the function and the very construction of their scenes. The two authors' diffident, even humble, yet mystically idealized conceptions of art are expressed by an interplay of three elements: what the visitors see, what the paintings show, what the artists think. Most interesting, however, are the characterizations in which Solženicyn not only uses but deliberately recalls a Tolstoyan model. Three notable examples are Rusanov and Ivan Il'ič, the Makarygin family and the Rostovs, Stalin and Nicholas I.

Solženicyn has emphasized the Tolstoyan source of these characterizations by supplementing their numerous parallel passages and motifs with a detail taken from another, related Tolstoj character. Thus Rusanov, the Soviet true believer, follows each step trod by Ivan Il'ič, yet in his encounter with the unknown he also recalls Tolstoj's other great bureaucrat, Karenin:

Aleksej Aleksandrovič was confronted with life ... and this seemed meaningless and incomprehensible to him, because it was life itself. All his life he had lived and worked in official spheres, which deal only with reflections of life. [VIII, 170]

And Rusanov, caught unaware by this stealthy approach of death, not only could not fight it but he could not in general think or decide about it or pronounce on it in any way.

It came illegally, and there were no rules, no instructions to defend Pavel Nikolaevič. [RK, 223]

Thus the Makarygin family dinner party is so reminiscent of the Rostov nameday party that the prosecutor takes his male guests to his study to see his "tobacco-altar" (VKP, 318) as the count takes the men to his study to see his "choice collection of Turkish pipes" (IV, 80), and Nataša's cry, "Mama! what will there be for dessert?" (IV, 89) is echoed by Klara's, "Mama! Can't our table have an intermission till tea?" (VKP, 314). In addition to such Rostov details, however, there is Klara's sister Dotty whose English nickname recalls Tolstoj's other daughters of the nobility —Kitty, Dolly, and Missy. And Stalin, seen on (Western) Christmas day, while Nicholas I was seen on New Year's day, is like Nicholas in his senility, gloom, intellectual pretensions, capriciousness, sensuality, malice, and above all in his egomania:

"Yes, what would Russia be without me," he said to himself, sensing again the approach of a feeling of discontent. "Yes not Russia alone, but what would Europe be without me. . . . "

Returning . . . he saw the carriage of Elena Pavlovna ... [who] was to him the personification of those futile people who discussed not only science and poetry but also the governance of men, imagining that they could rule themselves better than he, Nicholas ruled them. He knew that however much he crushed these people they would again come to the surface, they would keep crawling out. . . . And a vexed and gloomy feeling gripped him. [XIV, 94]

Vexation which nothing could overcome burned inside him. Like a legendary bogatyr Stalin had all his life been chopping and cutting off the sprouting heads of the hydra . . . [but still they] kept proposing some kind of new, better socialism.

Better socialism! *Different* from Stalin's! Snot! Who could build socialism *without Stalin?*

The collected works of Lenin had already been revised three times, and those of the Founding Fathers twice. They had all been asleep for a long time now, those who had disagreed, who had been cited in old footnotes, all who had thought of building socialism *in some other way*. And now when even in the rustling of the taiga there were no critics, no doubts to be heard—Josef Tito crawls out ... and says that things should be done *differently*. [VKP, 84–85]

Solženicyn's Tolstoyan emphasis is double in Stalin's portrait. "Even to his intimates, he must appear as he would to history" (VKP, 86) is a clear recollection of the Napoleon of *War and Peace*, while "He must be a mountain eagle always, always" (VKP, 91) is an echo of Nicholas I's alter-ego in tyranny, Šamil'.[5]

With these underlined prototypes Solženicyn is not so much labeling a literary influence as he is creatively reshaping a literary material. Rusanov emerges as a Soviet Ivan Il'ič whose life is indeed "most simple, most ordinary and therefore most terrible." The Makarygins are not only a Soviet family of privilege; they enjoy their prerogatives less gracefully and more hypocritically than their predecessors. And although it is not "easy to be the Greatest of All the Great," Stalin, when measured against a favorite Soviet image of evil despotism, overtakes and surpasses.

II

In language and style Solženicyn is a descendant of Tolstoj, but a living creative descendant whose voice is distinctively his own. The extraordinary pathos which Solženicyn achieves in Spiridon does derive something from the Tolstoyan method (in his novels) of portraying peasants as they look and sound to educated men, without entering into their consciousness, without reporting their admirable or petty ambitions, their touching or unworthy fears. The language of Ivan Denisovič and of Spiridon, however, is more subtle than that of Tolstoj's peasants, whose speech seems always stylized to externalize their simple virtues, while in Solženicyn's usage of peasant speech it is the complexity of the inarticulate which is revealed.

Solženicyn's short sentences contrast with Tolstoj's complex ones as sharply as his use of conversation contrasts with Tolstoj's avoidance of it. Indeed, Solženicyn's colloquial mastery is remarkable. As he moves from one to another character's consciousness, the language becomes unmistakably Neržin's or Rubin's or Kostoglotov's or Rusanov's. Tolstoj only occasionally achieved this; in his novels the content of a character's thought and speech is adapted to his consciousness with such massive and precise detail that each is definitively individualized, but Nikolaj and Pierre think their different thoughts in a common vocabulary, Dolly and Anna conceive their different worlds in the same sentence structures. Solženicyn has learned from Tolstoj, but he has also incorporated into his style the delicacy of Čexov's language of nuance and the achievements

---

[5] Compare from *War and Peace*: "With the characteristically Italian ability to change the expression of his face at will . . . [Napoleon] assumed a look of reflective tenderness. He felt that what he said and did now would be history" (VI, 245). And from *Hadji Murad*, the description of Šamil' as "a mountain-man. And in those mountains eagles live" (XIV, 77).

of the great practitioners of *skaz*. Vinogradov's notable study of Tolstoj's language was based on his works of the fifties and sixties; the Solženicyn oeuvre is already sufficient to make a similar study rewarding.

The two features of Solženicyn's style which seem specifically Tolstoyan are his powerful physical language and, stemming from this, his ability to present external objects and settings in such a manner that without losing their existential integrity they irradiate the novel with meaning. Solženicyn is not a Tolstoyan poet of the healthy body, and indeed only a few of his characters have sharp corporeal immediacy: red-haired Neržin's wrinkled face; the almost translucent two triangles of Vega; Šikin with his globular head and tiny feet in boys' shoes; shaggy Rubin in his underwear. Yet from the Tolstoj who created Vronskij's toothache, Serpuxovskoj's "putrescent worm-infested body in its new uniform and polished boots" (XII, 44) and Ivan Il'ič's gnawing pain, Solženicyn is a remarkable inheritor. Both use healthy flesh to convey the horror of diseased flesh: as the doctors prepared to amputate Anatole Kuragin's shattered leg, his *other* "large, white plump leg kept rapidly, constantly twitching with febrile tremors" (VI, 290). "And Federau ... with his still smooth, white but already condemned neck lay curled up on his side ... " (RK, 122–123). But Solženicyn eschews Tolstoj's relentless visual detail (such as Nikolaj Levin's emaciated hand and arm "like a huge rake ... attached to a long, thin, untapering spindle" [IX, 70]) for images which are just as stark, even more concentrated, but dynamic rather than descriptive: through five weeks of his life Rusanov had been "pulled along by his tumor like a hooked fish" (RK, 316); Vadim's "leg was caught in a trap—and his whole life with it" (RK, 320); Innokentij, reading on the warrant for arrest his own name, "was pierced throughout the whole length of his body as if by a single, huge needle" (VKP, 460).

It was not necessary for one translator of *Cancer Ward* to "Tolstoyanize" Solženicyn's language by having Šulubin call his cancer "it,"[6] in echo of chapter VI of "The Death of Ivan Il'ič." Although this tale provided a major theme for the novel, Solženicyn found his own methods for conveying what Tolstoj achieved with his pronoun—the personalized malice and mindlessly impersonal menace of cancer:

[Kostoglotov] immediately felt how that toad inside him, his life's companion, burrowed itself deep within him and pressed down. [RK, 54]

[Perhaps even as a child Vadim] was already striving to outdistance the future tumor, but he was racing into darkness, not seeing where his enemy was—while it

---

[6] Rebecca Frank, p. 359.

saw everything and at the most ardent moment of his life it struck and bit! Not a sickness—a snake! And its snakish name—melanoblastoma! [RK, 216]

the striped panther of death which had settled down in the same bed beside him. . . . [RK, 217]

Death had already made her nest in him—and he would not believe it! [VKP, 106]

It should be noted that Solženicyn's animal imagery (which is only one of many varieties of his physical language) is by no means confined to disease. Indeed in this realm he is as vivid as Leskov and as versatile as Tolstoj (although far less knowledgeable—one is not sure that he has ever really watched a panther). Tolstoj's constant observation of real animals in human settings imbues his fiction with the sense of man's moral strivings as part of the world of nature, while Solženicyn's animals, metaphoric in hospital and prison, remind us that the spiritual aspirations and sufferings which are his prime concern are borne not by moral abstractions but by men of flesh and blood.

The use of a recurrent and unifying symbol in *Anna Karenina* was exceptional for Tolstoj, and similarly, the bird symbolism of *First Circle* seems unusual for Solženicyn.[7] When they do employ it however, both writers use sustained symbolism in the same way. In *Anna Karenina* the railroad has a primary meaning, the destruction of natural good by man's devisement, and the symbolization does not transform the railroad image or expand the meaning, but rather introduces the meaning into various contexts, through different manifestations of the image: an important locale for Anna's and Vronskij's fatal passion; an intrusive children's game in the "upset" Oblonskij and Karenin households; the focus of Levin's study of the land and peasant; the profession of a man named Malthus. The birds of *First Circle* have a primary meaning of human freedom, physical freedom from captivity and spiritual freedom within captivity. Like Tolstoj's railroad, Solženicyn's birds are not transmuted or distorted as images, but are rather presented in many guises, introducing the idea of freedom into different situations: the bird plumage robe of the Hungarian partisan girl, caged in a Moscow dormitory; Sologdin's "bird-words," bearers of alien concepts; "the great beating wings" of true intellect and the "winged language of allusion" which can speak freely even in prison; courageous Gerasimovič, "puny as a sparrow, . . . the sparrow in the proverb, whose heart was as brave as a cat's" (VKP, 416); Ščevronok, who will be arrested because of Rubin's eagerness for "scientific" success

---

[7] At the end of *First Circle* the departing zeks are compared to Christ at Gethsemane, and Neržin's birthday is December 25. Nevertheless, the novel does not seem to me to contain *sustained* Christian symbolism.

and whose name makes Rubin think of a skylark (žavoronok [VKP, 174]); Innokentij's green enamel Lubjanka mug on which a cat (in reading glasses) menaces a bird; Simočka, shy as a quail, whose heart liberates her mind from MGB indoctrination; Innokentij, who has learned to distinguish between good and evil, going to his interrogation "with his head thrust back, as a bird drinks water" (VKP, 488).

Far more than he used single, unifying symbols, Tolstoj developed the device of endowing individual scenes or particular physical objects with human meanings which infuse the entire novel, and through them giving simple, concrete expression to complex and ambiguous emotions or reflections: Dolly's visit to Anna, Katjuša at the railroad station, Karenin's ears, Pierre's bare feet, Liza Bolkonskaja's tombstone, etc. Solženicyn has made these techniques his own and such scenes as the mock trial of Prince Igor, the visit of Gleb and Nadja, the blood transfusion, Kostoglotov's letter to the Kadmins and his "day" in Tashkent should soon be competing with Frou Frou's last ride as subjects for "intrinsic and extrinsic analysis." And for Solženicyn's readers a whole host of material objects will never again be merely themselves: Zoja's *moulinet* (recalling Dolly's and Kitty's embroidery); Kostoglotov's army belt; the oxygen bag; the clothes of casual lovers strewn around a bedroom; a skewer of smoking shashlik; the blossoming apricot tree (which Vega seeks and Kostoglotov finds, and which unites them as their common dream united Anna and Vronskij); the blinded rhesus monkey; a black imitation-caracul coat; fluffy pink bath towels and a cake of "Lilac Fairy" soap; a parquet floor; a book of poetry with oak leaves on the cover; a neatly labeled "Meat" truck, and many more.

Solženicyn has even invented his own special categories of meaningful objects. First, those which are empty or absent or simply not there: the rhesus monkey is not in its cage and is never seen; there is a sliver of moon but no bird in the cage which Ivan the glassblower spins (for the New Year's tree which is barely glimpsed by the departing zeks as it is being delivered); the spot on the stairs over which Klara cannot walk is invisible; the music which Agnija strives to make Jakonov hear comes after the church bell has ceased to ring, while the bell to whose tolling Neržin listens is "mute." And Solženicyn has a special sensitivity for the pathos and meaning which can be transmitted to objects by the human bodies which have touched them: the cancer ward's "tarnished door handles, rubbed by the hands of the sick" (RK, 14) and its veranda "polished by thousands of feet" (RK, 92); the little table behind which generations of prisoners have sat, its surface warped and marked "with strange wavy or angular figures, unconsciously drawn, which in some mysterious way preserved the secret twistings of the soul, ... the little table which had seen many tears" (VKP, 199, 202); the stairs in Lubjanka which Innokentij notices: "From the edge to the middle they were worn down in oval hollows to half their depth. He shuddered: in thirty years how many feet! how many times! must have shuffled across here, to so wear down the stone!" (VKP, 482). In Solženicyn's novels these worn objects embody the accumulated suffering of those who have touched them while the absent objects signify the non-material reality of such moral entities as freedom, guilt, injustice, truth.

Even in the realm of the physical language of bodies and objects Solženicyn's accomplishments cannot, of course, always be related to Tolstoj's. Pondering his recovery from cancer, which threatens him with impotence, Kostoglotov reflects: "The honey in the barrel was equally mixed with grease, and now it was no good, either to eat or to oil a wheel" (RK, 382). Both the coarseness of the imagery and the second explanatory clause are reminiscent of Tolstoj, but such is not always the case. For example, Čalyj's explanation of why bigamy is convenient for traveling men: "in every city there's a room with a chicken leg" (RK, 270). Or the portrayal of the marriage of Innokentij's Bolshevik father to his gentle mother who lived in a world of symbolist poetry and idealistic ethics, "that world into which his father, in a black raincoat, his belt hung with grenades, entered with a search warrant" (VKP, 306). For such expressions as these no useful specific comparison to Tolstoj can be drawn. What can be concluded is that in ways sometimes similar, sometimes different, Tolstoj and Solženicyn are probably the two greatest practitioners of that variety of Russian realism which uses the concrete, physical, everyday entities of the external world to represent the intangible, spiritual, personal yet universal phenomena of the inner world. A realism in which the puddle not only reflects but *is* the cloud:

> The strange, palely-sunshiny spot on the ceiling suddenly rippled, sparkled in brightly silver dots, and then disappeared. And with this running rippling, with these tiny wavelets, Oleg finally understood that the mysterious, lofty cloud on the ceiling was simply the reflection of a puddle which had not dried up, near the fence outside the window. A transformation of a simple puddle. [RK, 286]

III

School children write compositions: On the Unhappy, Tragic ... Life of Anna Karenina. But was Anna really unhappy? She chose passion—and paid for passion, that's happiness! She was free and proud! But what if, in peacetime, men in caps and overcoats come into the house where you were born, where you've lived all your life, and order the whole family to leave the house and the city in twenty-four hours, taking only what your weak hands can carry? ... And nosy speculators ... shamelessly offer you a hundredth of its value for your mother's piano,—and your little daughter in a hair-ribbon sits down to play Mozart for the last time, but bursts out crying and runs away,—why should I re-read *Anna Karenina?* Where can I read about *us, about us?* [RK 401–402]

The closest kinship between Tolstoj and Solženicyn is philosophic, and when significant differences appear they seem to stem from two sources, one temperamental and one biographical. Where instinctive pride made Tolstoj an answerer, intrinsic modesty casts Solženicyn as a questioner, but the terms of his queries are Tolstoyan. The questions which preoccupy Solženicyn have arisen from realities which he has experienced and Tolstoj never dreamed of: prison camp, cancer, lives cruelly disrupted, helpless people unjustly tormented—not by war or by "society" but "just simply so".

First one may note how many favorite Tolstoyan attitudes, even quirks of thought, Solženicyn assumes or assigns to his characters. Sologdin reminds us of Tolstoj of the diaries when he punishes himself with "faultmarks" for transgressions of his private intellectual or sexual rules. And there is still another bond between the two, for although Tolstoj frequently used not only the language but even the syntax of "Apparent Clarity" he sounds very much like Sologdin when he argues in *What Is Art?* that *krasota* should not be used for words or sounds or deeds because its old Russian meaning was purely visual (XV, 56–57). With regard to doctors and medicine the realities of his own experience have led Solženicyn to a reasoned and reasonable acceptance: gratitude for the relief of pain and sympathetic indignation at the persecution to which dedicated, overworked physicians are subject in the Soviet Union. But his instinctive attitude is very much like Tolstoj's, as in the description of Klara's illness, which recalls both Nataša's and Kitty's, or in Kostoglotov's plea that his recovery be left to "the defensive forces of the organism" (RK, 56). Another shared attitude is their uncompromising insistence that whatever the circumstances love cannot survive the violation of a woman's faithfulness and purity. Thus Kostoglotov cannot return to the girl he had loved. Thus Prince Andrej's bitter paradox—"I said that a fallen woman ought to be forgiven, but I didn't say that I could forgive her. I can't."
—is echoed by Rubin and Neržin: "Theoretically Glebka is right," Rubin comments on Neržin's former belief that if a husband can be forgiven for unfaithfulness, so can a wife. "But to make love to your wife after someone else has made love to her? Brrr! Biologically, I can't!" (VKP, 286–287)

Other, perhaps more fundamental views are also shared by Solženicyn and Tolstoj. Kostoglotov's idyll of the Kadmins' simple life in Uš-Terek produced his most Tolstoyan animal, the dog Žuk, and even recalls Tolstoj's tender description of another exiled, elderly husband and wife as "Baucis and Philemon".[8] The woodchopping scenes of *First Circle*, with their expression of the elementary pleasure of physical labor, recall Levin mowing with his peasants, despite Solženicyn's remark in another context that war correspondents are as different from front line soldiers "as a count who plows the soil is different from a real *mužik*" (VKP, 334). When Kostoglotov advises Demka that "education doesn't make you smart. . . . Trust your own eyes, not what you hear [from others]" (RK, 30) he is warning him of the morally stultifying effect of received doctrine, a basic Tolstoyan tenet. The same point is made through Vadim, who partly from reverence for his father and partly from his scientific ambition (as selfless yet egoistic as Andrey's quest for glory) has refused the wisdom of his own insight into Stalin. (It is striking how Solženicyn the writer shows through—recognition of Stalin's turgid literary style is a revelatory experience for several of his characters, and distaste for poor quality paper and ink is one of the rare complaints about material hardships repeated in the novels.)

Nothing is more basic to Tolstoj's thought and art than the conviction that only one's own experience can be trusted and that the inner voice of conscience must be trusted. But no single character in Tolstoj exemplifies this principle as perfectly as Lev Rubin of *First Circle*. Generous, kind, honorable, selfless, Rubin is a figure of tragic stature, blinded by political dedication. Rising above his personal suffering "for the good of the cause," he betrays the humanity he has sacrificed all to serve, and it is a measure of Solženicyn's artistry that Rubin is never more appealing than when entrapping Innokentij for his decent impulse, scorning food and sleep in his enthusiastic pursuit of "the fountainhead of science." Although Rubin's first reaction on hearing Innokentij's tape was to like the "simple fellow" who tried to warn the philanthropic doctor, he then suppressed his own inner voice: "But *objectively*—objectively that fellow, wanting to do good, had in fact acted against the progressive forces of history" (VKP, 173).

The terms of Rubin's fatal self-delusion are pure Leninism: *objectively* humanity is the working class, the working class is the party, the party is its vanguard, the vanguard is Stalin; objectively sadism and injustice are progressive if they serve Stalin's will, decency and honor must be crushed if they impede it. Solženicyn's fundamental counter-premise—trust your

---

[8] L. N. Tolstoj, *Polnoe sobranie sočinenij*, LX, 113. The reference is to the exiled Decembrist, M. I. Puščin, and his wife, whom Tolstoj visited in Switzerland in the spring of 1857.

own eyes, your own experience, your own inner feelings—has led him to other beliefs to which Tolstoj also proceeded from the same starting point. First is ultimate reliance on the private, individual conscience, not because it is perfect but because it is the least faulty of men's governors. From this follows the ardent, personal quest for truth through sincerity. To Elizaveta Anatol'evna's question as to how to bring up her son: "to hide the truth or to reconcile him with life?" Kostoglotov's reply is staunch: "Burden him with the truth!" (RK, 400). And it is notable that except in his portrayal of Stalin, Solženicyn's sarcasm is most devastating in his treatment of writers who have betrayed this great Russian literary tradition. As Alla Rusanova triumphantly proclaims:

[Writers adjust smoothly to a change in the official literary line]—it's one of those sharp reversals life is so full of. ... If there were disharmony, if some said the old things and some the new, then you would notice that something has changed. But as it is, right away, everyone starts saying the new thing together. ... Sincerity cannot possibly be the chief criterion in literature. When there are untrue ideas or alien tendencies it only strengthens the harmful effect of a work; sincerity is *harmful*! Subjective sincerity can detract from the truthfulness of the portrayal of life—that's dialectics. [RK, 245-246]

Subjective sincerity in the quest for truth, reliance on one's own experience and conscience, are doctrines which exalt the individual but circumscribe the self. Both Tolstoj and Solženicyn value the healing humility which comes from the acceptance of compassion to oneself, and Solženicyn's attempts to "rehabilitate" pity provide several of his most moving passages. And both stress the presumptuous egoism of judging for others: "A circle of wrongs! A circle of wrongs! ... Where should one begin to set the world right? With others? Or with oneself?" (VKP, 377). Between trust in oneself and humility toward oneself the link is a conception of man as not merely a physical organism but as the possessor of a soul. Kostoglotov repeatedly protests the idea that life is man's highest value, "at any price," and in this Solženicyn joins himself to Tolstoj in opposition to Russian literature's chorus of life-worshipping yea-sayers. Indeed Solženicyn's first mention of the soul comes with a characteristically ironic reference to Tolstoj: "It is well known that when a French soldier would not permit Pierre to cross the road, Pierre roared out laughing: 'The soldier did not let me across. Who—me? It's my immortal soul he did not let across!'" (VKP, 152). As Solženicyn moves forward in *First Circle*, and then in *Cancer Ward*, this affirmation loses its touch of self-consciousness and becomes strong and explicit.

Tolstoj told Gork'ij:

about the soul I know one thing: the soul desires nearness to God. And what is God? That of which my soul is a particle.

Kondrašev reflects to Neržin:

In a human being, from birth, there is instilled a certain Essence! And no one knows which forms what: life may shape man or man with his strong spirit may shape life! Because ... man has something with which to compare himself. Something to *look to*. For there is in him an image of Perfection, which in rare moments suddenly emerges. Before the spiritual gaze. [VKP, 228]

And Dr. Oreščenkov muses that the meaning of existence lies in the extent to which men

succeed in preserving—undimmed, uncongealed and undistorted—that image of eternity which is given to every person.
Like a silver moon in a peaceful pond. [RK, 361]

Pierre tells Andrej:

We must live, we must love and we must believe ... that we live not only in the present on this patch of earth, but that we have lived and will live eternally, there, in the whole, (and he pointed to the sky). [V, 133]

Šulubin tells Oleg:

But sometimes I feel so clearly: what is in me—that's not the whole "I." There is still something else, quite indestructible, something very lofty! Some fragment of the World Spirit. [RK, 405]

Tolstoj explains Pierre's decision to set out against Napoleon:

It was the feeling ... which impels a man to perform actions which are (from a commonplace point of view) insane, as if he were measuring his personal power and strength and affirming the existence of a higher, nonhuman judgment of life. [VI, 404]

And Neržin gives up the relative security of the šaraška for "death or a hard victory over death" in the camps:

You know what they say: "It's not the sea that drowns you but the puddle." [VKP, 501]

Despite such congruences, Solženicyn's philosophic relationship to Tolstoj is most interesting where he is powerfully attracted yet not entirely convinced. The life story which Neržin hears from Spiridon embodies all of Tolstoj's accumulated wisdom about the peasant—"What Spiridon loved was the land. What Spiridon had was a family." So that Neržin wonders: "Did not Spiridon's complicated life ... somehow correspond to the Tolstoyan teaching that there are no just and no guilty in the world? Was there not revealed in these almost instinctive acts ... a universal system of philosophic skepticism?" But Spiridon says no: "The wolf-hound is right but the man-eater is not" (VKP, 352, 355, 356), and in this rejection of the Tolstoyan view one hears Solženicyn's voice also.

However deep his response to the idea that "God Sees the Truth" but men cannot judge, Solženicyn has experienced (and his conscience has compelled him to depict) too much injustice to himself and others to assume so lofty and in some ways comforting a detachment. And yet he remains aware of the "circle of wrongs" which can issue from righteous judgment, and of how easily consciousness of just intentions can muffle the conscience. With painful irony he ascribes his own doubts about the Tolstoyan position to Rusanov, Rusanov whose whole life has been a history of non-resistance to evil and active compromise with it: "He's a namby-pamby, your Tolstoj!... Evil must be resisted, my boy, evil must be fought!" [RK, 99].

These words end the chapter of *Cancer Ward* called "What Men Live By" but the question reverberates throughout the novel. Just as Solženicyn introduced the vital theme of man's soul into *First Circle* in a humorously deprecatory Tolstoyan citation ("It is well known"), so the problem which dominates *Cancer Ward* first appears with a concealed Tolstoyan joke, for Demka, who has brought the book into the ward has dismissed it as useless in the words of Tolstoj's famous disdainment of historians in *War and Peace*: "It completely missed the point, like a deaf interlocutor who answers questions you have not asked" (RK, 97 and see VII, 335). When men begin to ask what people live by, they have rejected the traditional formulations of state, church, and "common sense," and so it is with Tolstoj and Solženicyn. In his youth Tolstoj experimented with rational epicureanism and through Innokentij, Solženicyn pursues this answer to its hollow ending. Love of the most immediate neighbor, one's family, was for a time the answer which satisfied Tolstoj, and it is a solution to which Solženicyn gives serious consideration and shattering refutation through the Makarygins, the Rusanovs, and above all through Šulubin. Solženicyn's extraordinary accomplishments as a moral philosopher-artist, however, are to be found not in his rejections nor even in his affirmations but in the delicately sustained subtlety and profundity of his explorations.

Thus in *Cancer Ward* the question, What do men live by? inheres in the separate stories of a dozen patients and doctors, provides a silent accompaniment to Oleg's encounters with Zoja and Vega, pinpoints his dilemmas—to accept hope with its risk of pain? to survive at the expense of manhood?—and skeins through the whole novel in speculations on how far the physician has the right to preserve life at any price, how far any man has the right to decide for others when at stake is that great unknown, the thing by which men should live. Thus in *First Circle*, the fabric of the novel interweaves a multitude of stories of past revelation and dawning insight, while embroidered on this fabric are the present dramatizations of men and women at moments of moral decision. Three of these protagonists are women, and so delicate is Solženicyn's treatment that one cannot say which path each will ultimately elect. Nor, even if some Belinskij ex machina could reveal that Serafima would show Neržin's notes to a future husband, that Klara will become a suitable mate for Lanskij, that Nadja will divorce Gleb, has Solženicyn prepared the way for their condemnation. The six men make their choices, at least this day's choices. The reader admires Ruska and Innokentij for the courage with which they arrive at an initial commitment and rejoices at the more long-fought and hard-won spiritual victories of Neržin and Gerasimovič. What is astonishing, however, is that Solženicyn has so arranged matters that while the reader deplores the choices made by Rubin and Sologdin, he does so with the judgment which hates the sin but loves the sinner.

Solženicyn has said that "the task of the writer is to select . . . universal and eternal questions, the secrets of the human heart and conscience."[9] In turning his teacher's answers into eternal questions, Solženicyn is at once most truly Tolstoyan and most uniquely himself.

---

[9] See "Appendix" to *Cancer Ward* (Bantam Books edition), p. 555.

GENERAL STUDIES

TOWARD A NORMATIVE DEFINITION OF RUSSIAN REALISM

BY

JOHN MERSEREAU, Jr.

I

PERHAPS NO word in literary criticism has meant so many things for so many people as "realism," unless it be "romanticism." Yet even the latter term, in spite of attempted defenestration on the part of some critics, has remained in the critical vocabulary as a point of reference, albeit loosely defined. The problem with realism is that it has served too many movements, as Jacques Barzun, following Proust, implies: "Strictly speaking, every school of art pretends to capture reality and every successful school does it."[1] Boris Ejxenbaum posited the same idea in somewhat more formal terms:

"Realism" is merely a conventional and constantly repeated slogan by which a new literary school fights against the devices of an old school which have become outworn and stereotyped and therefore too conventional.[2]

The denotative essence of realism is further obscured by the circumstance that critics have so often used the term without any indication, and sometimes even no awareness, as to whether their discussions pertain to the particular author's intention or self-evaluation, the distinctive elements in his text, or an effect experienced by those who read this text. Clearly, the first problem that must be faced is to determine at least within general limits what it is we are talking about when we use the term realism; only then can we seek a definition which will enable us to employ the word productively in literary history and criticism.

A systematic analysis of this very matter was undertaken by Roman Jakobson in his "On Realism in Art,"[3] in which he illuminated the many points of view that may condition, or drastically alter, the meaning of realism. Jakobson initially posits two preliminary meanings, the first imposed by the author who conceives his work to be realistic (Meaning A), and the second imposed by the reader, who accepts this work as realistic (Meaning B). Although all literary movements from classicism onwards

---

[1] *Classic, Romantic and Modern* (Garden City, N.Y.: Doubleday Anchor Books, 1961), p. 112.
[2] B. Ejxenbaum, *Molodoj Tolstoj* (Peterburg-Berlin: Izdat. Gržebina, 1922), p. 99.
[3] "O xudožestvennom realizme," *Michigan Slavic Materials*, No. 2. *Readings in Russian Poetics* (Ann Arbor, Mich., 1962), pp. 30–36.

have declared fidelity to reality as their guiding principle, in the nineteenth century a particular movement laid claim to maximum verisimilitude and appropriated the term realism; thus arises Meaning C, the sum of the characteristic features of a particular nineteenth-century artistic current. Now, if an author feels that deformation of prevailing norms leads to greater verisimilitude, we arrive at Meaning A_1: deformation of prevailing artistic canons, conceived as approximation of reality. Meaning A_2 is the converse, for here the author is conservative and seeks fidelity to reality through maintenance of the established canons of his tradition. Meaning B_1 assumes a "revolutionary" consumer, who finds an approximation of actuality in deformation of given norms, whereas for Meaning B_2 we have a reader who finds that reality is distorted by deformation of given artistic norms. In the second half of the nineteenth century the first phase of C occurs, a manifestation of A_1, in which a group of artists fights for realism. In itself, C is approximate, and certain of its characteristics will also occur outside it. Jakobson then goes on to discuss various more subtle distinctions, and he concludes with an admonition to historians of literature to distinguish the diverse concepts which take refuge under the term realism.[4]

If one decides to pursue a definition of realism, even in the face of Jakobson's evidence of the complexity of such a pursuit, one must still appropriate and maintain the basic structure of his analysis. That is, we must distinguish between author (and intentions), text (and devices), and reader (illusions). The following simple model will serve to maintain these distinctions:

| author | text | reader |

As was mentioned before, many critics or commentators in attempting to discuss realism simply confuse the issue by failing to indicate—and in some cases failing to decide themselves—what it is they are talking about, the attitudes of the writer, the characteristics of his text, or the impressions experienced by readers.

Such unawareness is not the case with either Erich Auerbach or Harry Levin, both of whom have concerned themselves with realism in literature. Their discussions do provide, however, a good example of quite different

---

[4] Jakobson's cautions regarding the use of the term realism are repeated in "The Kernel of Comparative Slavic Literature," where he says: "Furthermore, since the revisionistic essays on Gogol', the alleged founder of the Russian Realist School, justifiable doubts have arisen whether the label 'realist' may be applied unreservedly even to the Russian nineteenth century." Cf. *Harvard Slavic Studies* (Cambridge, Mass.: Harvard University Press, 1953), I, 70.

orientations to the problem. In *Mimesis*[5] Auerbach was occupied with the question of realism as it apparently manifested itself in diverse literatures going back even to the Old Testament or Petronius' *Satyricon*. In these and other works he discovered passages or scenes which have striking verisimilitude and seem to provide windows into the reality of past ages. But what Auerbach is saying is that for himself, a twentieth-century reader, these particular selections generate persuasive illusions of reality.[6] His focus of concern, therefore, is on the relationship reader-to-text. On the other hand, Harry Levin, in his sensitive and informative *The Gates of Horn, a Study of Five French Realists*, deals with the relationship author-to-text, seeking to demonstrate that the frustration of idealism, brought about by socio-political circumstances, conditioned the literary product of the authors he investigates: "every realist is a reformed idealist, whose commentary is to be deduced from the ideals that he has lived down."[7]

With Auerbach and Levin we have, therefore, two different approaches to realism, the former focusing upon the reader's reaction to certain texts and the latter concerning himself with psychological states which condition the choice and treatment of the themes and types which we find in various texts. Both are discussing realism, but from different ends of our model.[8]

In 1963, the same year that *The Gates of Horn* appeared, René Wellek published his *Concepts of Criticism*, and in this work, in a chapter entitled "Realism in Literary Scholarship," he courageously defended the term realism and called for reinstatement of its rights in the vocabulary of criticism. In Wellek's view there is ample evidence regarding the appearance of a new and distinct literary current in European literature around 1830 and of the continuation of this current until the end of the century. In his opinion it is feasible and useful to designate this as realism, bearing

---

[5] *Mimesis* (Berne, 1946).

[6] There is good reason why this should be so, since the selections he has chosen involve utilization of devices which are typically normative for 19th- and 20th-century literary realism, such as, for example, the reproduction of individual speech characteristics.

[7] *The Gates of Horn* (New York: Oxford University Press, 1963), p. 85. Levin provides a compelling case for his thesis that disillusionment was a common denominator affecting the works of Stendhal, Balzac, Flaubert, Zola, and Proust, but one may also say the same about most romantics. In fact, disillusionment, broadly conceived, may be a stimulus for all serious literature, including comedy.

[8] One might note in passing that Levin, in certain remarks, deals simultaneously with author-text and text-reader relationships: "Every novel is realistic in some respects and unrealistic in others. Criticism can but try to estimate the proportions by comparing what the writer endeavors to show and what the reader is able to see." *The Gates*, p. 65.

in mind that this is a regulative concept, referring to a system of norms dominating a specific time. Wellek adds an additional criterion that the system of norms called realism must be distinguished from the norms of the periods that precede and follow it.[9]

It would seem that here we are finally getting down to the heart of the matter: not authors' intentions, of which they may not even be consciously aware, not readers' reactions, which are enormously diverse, but the text itself, the one stable and verifiable element in the model, becomes the source from which our definition is to be extracted. Further, in the interest of clarity, let us agree to distinguish between realism, a general manifestation common to many literatures in the nineteenth century, from Realism, which in the capitalized form will henceforth refer specifically to Russian Realism, a school or movement embodied in an aggregate of literary norms prevailing in Russian literature from approximately 1830 to 1890.

Wellek does not provide us with the system of norms which his study suggests should serve as the basis for our definition of Realism.[10] Rather, he is concerned with justifying his period concept by abstracting some general features characteristic of the literature produced during the span he designates, roughly from 1830 to 1890. Starting with the statement that realism is "the objective representation of contemporary social reality,"[11] he discusses the kinds of subject matter that realism does without (the fantastic, the world of dreams), the extension of its content (to include sex and dying), and its emphasis (on types). At the same time he finds it difficult to decide whether such features as absence of the author or historicism, features often suggested as criteria for realism, are in fact indispensable.[12] Wellek's discussion points up one of the major problems confronted by anyone trying to find a formula for realism: authors commonly accepted as realists simply will not conform to every generalization. Thus, as Wellek notes, the criterion of absence of the author would exclude Thackeray and Tolstoj, whereas the demand for historicism would exclude Jane Austen, who seems unaware of the Napoleonic wars, and possibly even Tolstoj, whose view of man is anti-historical.

There is a solution to this dilemma, which is to be found in treating Realism (or any other literary "-ism" as well) just as we treat language, where we distinguish between the language as a theoretical system and

---

[9] *Concepts of Criticism* (New Haven and London: Yale University Press, 1963), pp. 222-225.
[10] It was not his purpose to do so.
[11] *Concepts*, pp. 240-241.
[12] *Concepts*, pp. 241-253.

speech as its actual manifestation. We may do the same with Realism, positing a theoretical system of norms, the grammar of Realism, and the implementation of that system, which are the works of individual authors. Just as no speaker utilizes all of the provisions, whether grammatical or lexical, of a language, no Realist can be expected to implement the total underlying system of Realism. And just as speakers may intentionally strain the norms of a linguistic system to achieve picturesqueness or novelty of expression, so the best Realists never adhere slavishly to the grammar of their system. In fact, it is just such deviations from the norms of Realism that make Turgenev, Tolstoj, and Dostoevskij more interesting than authors who follow the conventions of Realism more consistently, such as Pisemskij or Kuprin.

Once we have decided that we cannot expect, and perhaps would not want, all Realists to satisfy completely a system of norms, we can approach the reconstruction, or abstraction, of this system. But first we should comment upon another problem which has caused difficulty, namely, what to do with those elements in our system of Realism which quite obviously appeared *before* the nineteenth century but which, because of the frequency of their appearance, must be considered normative for nineteenth-century Realism? For example, a number of features of Realism are also found in the works of earlier generations of writers, even those of medieval times. In virtually all periods of literature one can discover examples of description, dialogue, or exposition of action which would fulfill a norm of Realism. They occur owing to satisfaction, accidentally or otherwise, of some criteria for the generation of illusions of reality, among them such qualities as expository objectivity, local color details, individualization of speech characteristics, and so forth.[13] Soviet scholars have been particularly assiduous in seeking such "elements of realism" or "tendencies toward realism" in the literary monuments of Russian literature. On the pages of *Problems of Literature* (*Voprosy Literatury*) in 1957 and 1958 a number of scholars sought to determine realism's heritage from writers of earlier eras.[14] "Elements of realism" were found in the

---

[13] In my study "Orest Somov and the Illusion of Reality" I termed these apparently timeless elements of realism "invariants," thus distinguishing them from the "variants," that is, those elements peculiar to nineteenth-century Realism and not appearing before its advent. See *American Contributions to the Sixth International Congress of Slavists* (The Hague: Mouton, 1968), pp. 130-154. I have since come to believe that such a distribution is not really possible, or in any case of little utility.

[14] The quest for realism's "genealogy" was for them a serious undertaking, because the canonization of Socialist Realism as the furthest, and final, level to which art may aspire makes it imperative to link the important authors of the past with this ultimate blossoming of literary art.

twelfth-century *Lay of the Host of Igor*, but the scholars of *Problems of Literature* reached no consensus as to the definite direction or depth of the taproot of realism. Some found it in folklore (dialectically, this is a most desirable source, since folklore is the product of the people), others in works representing "anti-feudal" or "anti-church" attitudes, and some confined their search to eighteenth-century authors. V. Vinogradov has since rejected all such "element" or "tendency" seeking as pointless, since in his opinion realism as such could not exist before the establishment of a national literary language, a development which did not take place until the thirties and forties of the nineteenth century.[15]

The presence of these "elements" of realism in works prior to the appearance of the "movement" in the nineteenth century is well documented, but even were it not one might assume the inevitability of their occurrence: literature has always been in some respects an attempt to imitate life, and literature's evolutionary dynamism has been provided by the quest for more adequate ways to achieve this imitation. But the random appearance of "tendencies" or devices typical of nineteenth-century Realism prior to that "movement" does not mean that they were normative. Therefore, will disregard their earlier manifestations in seeking a description or definition of Realism based on norms prevailing from 1830 to 1890.

II

The definition of Realism which is the aim of this study will follow René Wellek's proposition for a period concept based on a system of norms, the period covering roughly 1830–1890, with its norms to be distinguished from those of the periods which precede and follow it.[16] The material for investigation will be exclusively textual, that is, authorial intentions and reader responses will be specifically excluded. The latter, which are connected with the illusion of reality, are the proper subject for psychological investigation but irrelevant to this study. Authorial intentions are also irrelevant, because, as has already been stressed, each new literary movement marches under the banner of realism.[17]

The popular idea that realistic literature is like a mirror being carried

---

[15] V. Vinogradov, *O jazyke xudožestvennoj literatury* (Moscow, 1959), p. 466.
[16] *Concepts*, p. 225.
[17] To the authority of Èjxenbaum, Jakobson, and Barzun, previously quoted, we may add Proust: "From age to age a certain realism is reborn, by way of reaction against the art that has been theretofore admired." Quoted by Levin, *The Gates of Horn*, p. 73.

down the road is inaccurate: no writer reflects reality nor, in the view of D. Čiževskij, is it within a writer's power even to describe it. To the skeptical he suggests that they seek to *describe* a typewriter. Rather, Čiževskij declares, writers *represent* objects and events, and for this end they have two available means, one metaphoric and the other metonymic. The metaphoric approach seeks to represent things by comparison with other things, often from a different plane of existence. The metonymic approach operates on the principle of contiguity, representation being realized either through indication of individual features which make up the whole of an object or indication of its "circumstances," its environment, its past, or even its future.[18] Earlier Jakobson had investigated the problem of what he termed "the metaphoric and metonymic poles," and he arrived at some very interesting theoretical conclusions. First, he concluded that poetry tends to orient towards metaphor (implying representation based on revelation of similarities), whereas prose is oriented towards metonomy (implying representation through utilization of contiguous or proximate features and elements). He proceeds, however, to a further formulation, one which is particularly appropriate for the present investigation: Romantic and Symbolist prose orient towards metaphor, whereas Realist prose orients towards metonomy:

> The primacy of the metaphoric process in the literary schools of romanticism and symbolism has been repeatedly acknowledged, but it is still insufficiently realized that it is the predominance of metonymy which underlies and actually predetermines the so-called "realistic" trend, which belongs to an intermediary stage between the decline of romanticism and the rise of symbolism and is opposed to both. Following the path of contiguous relationships, the realistic author metonymically digresses from the plot to the atmosphere and from the characters to the setting in space and time.[19]

Here we have what must be considered one of the basic normative features of Realism. Taking just one aspect of contiguity as it relates to character, we see the principle of metonymic digression applied to bring in details of a protagonist's genealogy (often to the third or fourth generation), his upbringing and education, his associations with and relationship to relatives, colleagues, superiors, and so forth. Servants also appear as another variation of this means, since domestics so often reflect their masters' virtues, and especially their vices.

The problem of "objectivity" has been widely discussed in connection with realism in art, and on this matter Wellek has this to say:

---

[18] D. Čiževskij, "Čto takoe realizm?", *Novyj Žurnal*, no. 75 (1964), pp. 130-148.
[19] R. Jakobson, "The Metaphoric and Metonymic Poles," *Fundamentals of Language* ('S Gravenhage: Mouton, 1956), pp. 77-78.

> "Objectivity" is certainly another main watchword of realism [the other watchword is "type"]. Objectivity means again something negative, a distrust of subjectivism, of the romantic exaltation of the ego: in practice often a rejection of lyricism, of the personal mood.[20]

Wellek is essentially correct, yet his discussion really concerns an authorial attitude ("distrust," "rejection") which may somehow influence the text. In seeking norms based on texts rather than intentions, it is better to characterize this objectivity as an apparent absence of an author from his work. One may quibble that any author is immanent in his work, but it is characteristic of Realism that he not appear directly. Therefore in Realist prose we do not expect to encounter evidence of authorial control of story material or chatty comments which call attention to author-reader relationships.

Closely related to the absence-of-author norm is a very significant characteristic noted by Boris Tomaševskij, namely, the non-obtrusiveness of devices in Realist works:

> Two literary styles may be distinguished in terms of the perceptibility of the devices. The first, characteristic of the writers of the nineteenth century, is distinguished by its attempt to conceal the device; all of its motivation systems are designed to make the literary devices seem imperceptible, to make them seem as natural as possible —that is, to develop the literary material so that its development is unperceived.[21]

Although for the most part Russian Realists did not overtly call attention either to themselves or to their devices, they did not eschew the privilege of didacticism, and, in fact, they were at least as didactic as any other school. However, they hid their own voices behind those of first-person narrators or utilized so-called "objective material," such as letters, diaries, and journals purporting to be the composition of a character or characters within a work and thus "independent" of the author. A popular device used in the developmental stage of Realism was the framed story, where the exterior narrator of the frame reports his own reactions (and sometimes those of fellow auditors) to events related by an interior narrator.[22] Another means for the conveyance of a message was the utilization of a porte parole from among the dramatis personae, but one whose role was not crudely manifest, as in the case of the *raisonneur* of Classical literature. Whatever the means, the non-presence of the author is normative for Realism, Tolstoj's overt didacticism notwithstanding.

---

[20] *Concepts.*, p. 247.

[21] B. Tomaševskij, *Tematika*, quoted from *Russian Formalist Criticism. Four Essays*, Translated and with an Introduction by Lee T. Lemon and Marion J. Reis (Lincoln: University of Nebraska Press, 1965), p. 94.

[22] Lermontov, in creating the first novel of psychological Realism, employed all the means discussed above.

In Realist prose the omniscient narrative voice is semantically homogeneous, with the communicative function of language collaborating with its artistic function. Thus, although exposition is never "neutral" or "non-artistic," it may appear to the casual reader that it serves primarily to provide information. Characteristically there is an absence of ornamentalism, grandiloquence, neologisms, or stylistic affectation which might impede the transmission of information or introduce ambiguity. In the case of first-person narration, the discourse of the "I" narrator may be completely individualized or may appear to tend towards a "neutral," simply referential language, but in either case semantic homogeneity is observed.

Whatever the mode of narration, omniscient or first-person, a distinction between exposition and characters' speech is established and preserved. Further, each character embodies his own means of expression, conditioned by class origin, education, social status, and personality.

Russian Realist literature discloses a normative predilection for structuring setting and delineating character through an agglomerating of details. This feature is, of course, connected with the orientation toward contiguity, for the details which become part of the agglomeration are in a general sense synecdochic or proximate. Physical features are represented with apparent thoroughness, including not only petty details but even so-called "dirty details," such as yellowed teeth, black fingernails, pimples, or body-odor.[23]

Setting is established through presentation of sufficient details to enable the reader to create a mental image of the scene. Often the details are apparently random, such as a description of a room which would mention the floral design of the wallpaper, the peeling gold paint on a chair, a table lamp with a green shade on a marble base; but more basic information, such as the number of windows, the kind of floor and floor covering, presence or absence of fireplace, height of the ceiling, may not appear.

Details of setting may often function primarily as a means of characterization or psychologization. Thus, a protagonist's study, or bedroom, or other private quarters provide keys to personality: books (if opened) reveal intellectual interests, choice of rugs, drapes, bronzes, pictures tell

---

[23] Tolstoj utilizes synecdochic details as a sort of telegraphic means of stimulating the reestablishment in the reader's mind's eye of a visual image of his characters, as for example recurrent references to Hélène Kuragina's bare shoulders, Pierre Bezuxov's glasses, or Napoleon's effeminate hands. For Tolstoj this device also has symbolistic overtones, since the reiterated details suggest Hélène's wantonness, Pierre's blindness to others' motives, and Napoleon's feminine vanity.

us about taste and concern for comfort.[24] A different aspect of contiguity is employed in the detailization of a protagonist's clothes, their condition, manner of wearing. Eating habits and food preferences are important, for the man who prefers oysters is not the same man who prefers bread and cheese. The list of such personal contiguities is almost endless.

Roman Jakobson has identified another technique of Realism which is similar to the device of petty details but more inclusive, namely the device of the inessential detail. Thus protagonists frequently meet or encounter persons who, though described, are to play no role in the further development of the story.[25] Such peripheral types wander through Realist literature in goodly numbers, so much so that it was almost a violation of the code of Realism if an author did not provide some superfluous figures.

In Romantic literatures events range from the probable or simply possible to the implausible and even fantastic. It is characteristic of western European realist works that events transpire in accordance with probability. In this respect, Russian Realism seems to present a somewhat special case, since probability does not play the dominant role one would expect: too much happens in the Russian novel of Realism that belongs to the realm of the possible rather than to that of the probable. This extension of Romanticism's quality of possibility into Russian Realism is a special feature of the latter movement which distinguishes it from the realisms of western European literature.

Connected with the matter of probability and possibility is the question of motivation (*motivirovka*) or justification, which plays a vital role in the establishment of verisimilitude. Russian fiction of the Realist canon does reveal a normative tendency for the provision of motivation for all elements of a story or novel. This applies not only to major plot elements, such as duels, journeys, amorous relationships, but even to such minor items as names: the given and surname correlate to the character's class or origin.[26] In addition, the requirements of motivation necessitate the establishment of a causal relationship between behavior and circumstances.

---

[24] The device of "revelatory quarters" may be extended to include a preferred place of habitation, such as Petersburg, Moscow, a provincial estate, or a Caucasian spa.

[25] Jakobson sees the development of literature as a progressive evolution of inessential details: the suicide scene of *Anna Karenina* includes references to her handbag, a feature which would not have been understood by Karamzin. However, Karamzin's *Poor Liza* would have seemed a chain of inessential details to writers of the mid-eighteenth century. "O xudožestvennom realizme," p. 35.

[26] Naturally, I am not referring to the grotesque motivation provided by the absurd rigmarole connected with the naming of Gogol''s clerk-cipher, Akakij Akakievič Bašmačkin, which is a travesty of the Realist concern for justification of story material.

Characters in Realist prose are therefore not as "free" to act as their Romanticist forebears, whose behavior was not required to be logically justifiable.[27]

Classicist authors were concerned with universal types; Romanticists sought to create individuals, but they tended to depict them as psychologically uncomplex and static, perhaps governed by some dominating emotion or attitude. Realists developed characters with involved and individualized psychologies, and the history of Realism's evolution reveals a progression towards greater intricacy in this area. Thus I would disagree, at least in so far as Russian Realism is concerned, with Wellek's statement that "The emphasis on type is almost universal in realist theory...."[28] The creation of types is not normative for Russian Realism, notwithstanding the continual reference to the hero of nineteenth-century novels as typically a "superfluous man." This formula has been applied ex post facto to a group of protagonists, and it tells us only that Russian authors more often created characters who failed than ones who succeeded. Pečorin, Oblomov, Bazarov, Olenin, Stavrogin, Vronskij, or any of the other so-called "superfluous men" are set strictly apart by the uncommon denominators which underscore their individuality. Nor are they types. One quickly apprehends the inappropriateness of typological classifications when faced with the diversity of the "Nihilist types" in works of Gončarov, Turgenev, Dostoevskij, Pisemskij, and Leskov. Rather, it is individualization which is the law of Russian Realism, with particular emphasis on complex psychological portraits. The imperative of "psychologization" (*psixologizacija*) is a governing element in Realism, to which intrigue, structure, setting, and even theme are subordinated.

Henry James in *The Art of Fiction* correctly states that character is but the determination of incident and incident but the illustration of character, but in Russian Realism the equilibrium between incident and character which James' statement suggests is not maintained: more weight is given to character, and devices are utilized for characterization which do not involve incident, such as interior monologue. This device, widely employed during Realism's ascendancy, takes the form of a direct expression of the flux and flow of a character's thoughts as they reach the level of consciousness. The particular advantage or utility of the device of interior monologue is that it provides the reader with direct access to

---

[27] Note how the requirement of motivation is observed in the case of Dostoevskij's characters, whose déclassé nature justifies their falling prey to radical philosophical ideas; on the other hand, Tolstoj's aristocrats are restricted by the weight of class tradition and thus are faced with problems of a different sort.

[28] *Concepts*, p. 245.

inner workings of a protagonist's mind, thus deepening the psychological portrait.

A period concept of a literary school or movement may legitimately concern itself with dominant themes, but there seems little justification in becoming involved in questions of theme in this present effort at a normative description. Theme is a Pandora's box, and it is unlikely that any really inclusive catalogue of Realism's themes could be created. Thematic frequency would be another aspect of the problem that would defy statistical results. We can, however, generalize that Russian Realists, like their western European counterparts, were concerned with contemporary economic, social, and political problems. Realist literature chronicles and examines these problems, and characters are enlisted to dramatize them. Nonetheless, one must emphasize that it was the existential problems of the characters themselves which provided the primary center of focus. So-called "ultimate" themes concerned with moral behavior and faith played an enormous role in Realist literature, and irrespective of the extent to which topical, contemporary problems were treated, ethics and religion were key themes. Thus, in *Crime and Punishment* we see sociological features of life in a Petersburg slum, and poverty does have an effect upon Raskol'nikov's manner of living, but his basic problem is connected with his attempt at supermanhood. *Fathers and Children* treats a wide variety of contemporary problems, with particular attention to the theme of Nihilism, but Bazarov's Nihilism, which remains unfractured by the attacks of others, proves impotent to assuage the cosmic anguish he suffers at the realization of his insignificance in the context of time and the universe.

III

In attempting to provide a normative definition of Realism, the foregoing study has proceeded through two steps. The first step sought to establish and justify an approach to the problem which is based upon tangible invariants, that is, the literary texts themselves. Authorial intentions of representing "reality" and readers' perceptions of "reality" from contact with the literary material were excluded as irrelevant to this investigation owing to their illusive and idiosyncratic nature. On the basis of good evidence presented by René Wellek, a period, roughly 1830–1890, was assigned as the temporal span of Realism. The search for normative common denominators in the prose fiction of this period proceeded from Jakobson's postulation concerning the orientation of realistic prose toward representation through contiguity, a basic quality

A Definition of Russian Realism

of Realism. The main normative features discussed included absence of author, imperceptibility of devices, homogeneity of narrative voice, individualization of characters' speech, density of details, possibility (rather than probability) as the determinant in the relationship of events, motivation of all story material, and most important, psychologization, to which all the foregoing were subjected and to which theme itself was subordinated. The discussion included mention of certain devices commonly employed in the realization of specific norms.

It should be understood that this study has in no way been projected as a final word.[29] On the contrary, it is a preliminary and general statement which, it is hoped, will encourage others to the isolation of additional and more specific norms of Russian Realism.

---

[29] Other studies of realism, which may prove helpful in understanding the problem, include: Harry Levin, "What is Realism?" *Comparative Literature* (Summer, 1951), III, no. 3, 193-199; Renato Poggioli, "Realism in Russia," ibid., pp. 253-267; Robert Scholes and Robert Kellogg, "The Problem of Reality. Illustration and Representation," *The Theory of the Novel* (New York: The Free Press, 1967), pp. 371-387, reprinted from *The Nature of Narrative* by these same authors; also articles by Auerbach, Watt, Levin, and Trilling in *Approaches to the Novel*, ed. Robert Scholes (San Francisco: Chandler Publishing Co., 1961), reprinted from various sources.

EXPRESSIONISM IN RUSSIA

BY

VLADIMIR MARKOV

WESTERN EUROPEAN poetic expressionism did not attract the attention of Russian poets, critics, and scholars until after the revolution of 1917; however, this statement may be slightly modified by future research. Interest in this movement, both in its literary and artistic manifestations, became noticeable only at the very beginning of the 1920's; then suddenly it produced a minor flood of essays and books which either discussed expressionism from a variety of viewpoints or attempted to inform the reader of its scope, content, aims, and essence.[1]

But was there a Russian expressionism? This question can be answered in two different ways. First, there have been attempts to reinterpret some well-known figures of modern Russian literature, or simply to label them, as expressionist, whether they considered themselves so or not. Such attempts actually belong to the history of Russian literary criticism, and they may still be a topic for discussion.[2]

---

[1] Some examples are the translation of chapter 4 from the 2nd edition of Oskar Walzel's *Die deutsche Literatur seit Goethes Tod*, which appeared in Russian as a book under the title *Impressionizm i èkspressionizm v sovremennoj Germanii* (Petersburg: Academia, 1922); Vsemirnaja Literatura's collection of essays on expressionism, translated from German, edited by E. M. Braudo and N. È. Radlov, entitled *Èkspressionizm* (Petrograd–Moscow, 1923), which, as stated in the preface, was published to fight confusion in the Soviet interpretation of the term; A. Lunačarskij's "Neskol'ko slov o nemeckom èkspressionizme," *Žizn'*, no. 1 (1922); E. Boričevskij, "Filosofija èkspressionizma," *Šipovnik*, no. 1 (1922); B. Arvatov, "Èkspressionizm kak social'noe javlenie," *Kniga i Revoljucija*, no. 6 (18) (1922). After a long silence on the subject, *Èkspressionizm: Sbornik statej* (Moscow: Nauka, 1966) appeared recently and was immediately sold out; in this book, many pre-revolutionary and Soviet artists and theater men are called expressionists and even in Majakovskij's work expressionist features are found (p. 12).

[2] A. Lunačarskij considers Majakovskij, Vasilij Kamenskij, Aseev, Tret'jakov, and, "partially," Pasternak expressionists ("Georg Kajzer," *Sobranie sočinenij v vos'mi tomax*, V [Moscow, 1965], 420). È. Gollerbax in *Poèzija Davida Burljuka* (New York, 1931), pp. 22–23, sees in his subject "some affinity" with expressionism; he also calls the late work of Mixail Kuzmin expressionistic and adds that expressionism touched, more or less, all "progressive phenomena in art," but he admits that the idea of expressionism is "vague." In his ambitious study *Èkspressionizm v Rossii* (*Trudy Vjatskogo Pedagogičeskogo Instituta imeni V. I. Lenina*, tom 1, vypusk 4, 1928), K. V. Drjagin tries to prove that Leonid Andreev's drama is expressionistic rather than symbolist. He also considers Majakovskij an expressionist, though not a pure one. The unjustly forgotten book by I. I. Ioffe, *Sintetičeskaja istorija iskusstv: Vvedenie v istoriju xudožestvennogo myšlenija* (Leningrad, 1933) chooses Pasternak to represent expressionism ("psychic functionalism") in poetry and sees its essence in the "deformation of the visible."

There was, however, at the beginning of the 1920's, in Moscow, a group (or perhaps two) of poets which called itself expressionist. It was, to be sure, a small group, easily dwarfed by the celebrated imagists of that time, but it had an interesting and by no means short history by avant-garde standards—at least three and a half years and more than a dozen publications. Moreover, the group had ties, both expected and unexpected, with Russian as well as European literature. In addition to this, expressionism was part of the colorful literary background of those years when (at one point, namely in March, 1922) there were 143 private publishing enterprises in Moscow,[3] and when a critic complained that the time may be near when he will have to write reviews about those who do not write poetry, rather than about those who do.[4] At no other time was there such a large number of poetic groups and organizations. In addition to the familiar symbolists, acmeists, and futurists (with or without the prefix "neo-"), there were centrifugists, biocosmists, luminists, presentists, neoclassicists, nonsensists, kthematicists, nothingists, fuists, antitaxidermists, and probably many others. Even granted that the creative efforts of some of these poets produced, to borrow a Zoščenko phrase, *malovysokoxudožestvennaja literatura*, it is one-sided, to put it mildly, to reduce the literary history of this period to monochromatic descriptions of the activities of proletarian groups.

The history of Russian expressionism begins with one man—Ippolit Vasil'evič Sokolov. In 1919 he considered himself a "euphuist" and was active in and around the All-Russian Union of Poets. On July 11, 1919, as he himself reports it, the idea of "expressionism" as a synthesis of futurism dawned on him.[5] There was nothing special in such an idea; any group with avant-garde claims at that time felt obliged to do some-

---

Among the recent applications of the term to Russian literature, see William E. Harkins' Freudian analysis of Jurij Oleša in "The Theme of Sterility in Olesha's *Envy*" (*Slavic Review*, XXV, no. 3, 1966) in which the author also undertakes a definition of expressionism; Aleksis Rannit's introductory essay ("Zabolotskij—A Visionary at the Crossroads of Expressionism") to Nikolaj Žabolockij's *Stixotvorenija*, (Washington, D.C.-New York: Inter-Language Literary Associates, 1965); and the rather indiscriminate use of the term by Johannes von Guenther in his *Die Literatur Russlands* (Stuttgart: Union Verlag, 1964). Von Guenther calls Remizov "the first Russian expressionist prose writer" (p. 186) and, in contradiction to this, Zamjatin "the first Russian expressionist" (p. 197). He also considers Prišvin "an expressionist-naturalist" (p. 187), Zabolockij "an expressionist with a predilection for surrealism" (p. 213), and says that Vasilij Kazin "wrote in a concentrated expressionist language" (p. 197).

[3] *Istorija russkoj sovetskoj literatury v trex tomax*, I (Moscow: Izdatel'stvo Akademii Nauk SSSR, 1958), 595.

[4] È. Bik (Sergej Bobrov), review in *Pečat'* i *Revoljucija*, no. 1 (1922), p. 299.

[5] Ippolit Sokolov, *Bunt èkspressionista* (Moscow, 1919), p. 6.

thing with futurism: either to reject it, wholly or partially, or in some way to "overcome" it; and either attempt invariably remained just a statement on paper. In Moscow in 1919 the only real futurist poet in sight was Majakovskij (since all his friends were scattered across Russia by the Civil War), and such a situation was probably felt by the young poets to be a poetic vacuum. Sokolov shared his idea with the world at one of the numerous public appearances sponsored by the above-mentioned Union of Poets, and the prominent Marxist critic V. L'vov-Rogačevskij mentioned him later in one of his public talks, sponsored by the same union; and this was enough to set his hopes soaring.[6]

Ippolit Sokolov was, however, no greenhorn in literature. Only a month before his discovery of expressionism, he published a slim, "M"-page[7] booklet which contained only six poems but was entitled *Polnoe sobranie sočinenij. Izdanie ne posmertnoe. Ne stixi.*, which he later described as being "without the author's portrait and without a critical-biographical essay by V. Brjusov."[8] The only manifesto-like element of the book was the sentence preceding the poems: "Well, I am hurling [at you?] my new, polymetrical principles." Sokolov's "polymetry" turned out to be simply free verse which, in imagery, combined the "Mezzanine of Poetry," which, at that time, had been dead for five years, with imagism (*imažinizm*), a movement beginning just then. The former is evident in Sokolov's poetic landscapes in which nature is consistently "translated" into the terms of the beauty salon and of women's (and occasionally men's) wardrobe (manteau, face powder, curlers, fabrics, make-up, tuxedoes) with an admixture of theatrical and "cultural" imagery (such as "a ravine with Voltaire's sarcastic smile"). Sokolov is, however, interested in unusual metaphor as such, and occasionally he abandons the atmosphere of the drawing-room, dressing-table, and dance-hall, or, rather he eclectically combines it with "unaesthetical" tropes like "pockmarked sky." Finally, in the poem "Madonna" he comes close to the combination of blasphemy and sex one is accustomed to expect from Russian imagists: the poem ends with the poet going to bed with the Madonna—only in his dream, however. In addition, one finds urbanist imagery of restaurants and streets of definitely futurist character, reminiscent of Majakovskij. *Polnoe sobranie sočinenij* was to remain Sokolov's only book of verse. From then on, he published theoretical writings and his poetry appeared only in joint collections (or as an appendix to his own theories).

A more ambitious book by Sokolov came out in the fall of the same year

---

[6] Ippolit Sokolov, *Ėkspressionizm* (Moscow, 1920), p. 3.
[7] In this book the pages are lettered alphabetically, instead of being numbered.
[8] *Bunt ėkspressionista*, p. 17.

with the title *Bunt èkspressionista* on its cover (and further down the page "published, of course, by the author himself"). The first pages in the book contain a manifesto of expressionism, "Xartija èkspressionista," which begins with a quotation from Gogol's madman, Popriščin, and ends with a quotation from St. Luke. The manifesto cheerfully launches what it calls expressionism and contains practically everything a good manifesto should contain: a historical perspective, polemics, and a constructive program. The two "-isms" Sokolov argues against are imagism and futurism, but his interpretation of these two familiar terms is not quite customary. Sokolov claims that imagism (which he spells *imažizm*, and not *imažinizm*) is just a device and not a school, that its representatives are Majakovskij, Vadim Šeršenevič, Konstantin Bol'šakov, and Sergej Tret'jakov; and that its flowering took place in 1913–1915. As to the contemporary imagism of 1919, Sokolov dismisses it as pseudo-imagism that vulgarizes its own principles, is newspaper-oriented, and amounts to nothing more than poor futurism. He suggests that a better name for it is "hyperbolism."

Futurism, on the other hand (which for Sokolov includes Marinetti, Ezra Pound, Apollinaire, and, again, Majakovskij), however great it might have been, belongs to the past: during its nine-year history it became fragmented, with each part cultivating only one aspect of the futurist creed. Expressionism does not reject any of these predecessors, but it claims to be a synthesis of all facets of futurism. A "revolutionary," constructive part follows, which lists: (1) abolition of the old versification from Homer to Majakovskij as well as introduction of a new, "chromatic" verse based on musical pitch; (2) "polystanzaics"; and (3) "higher euphony." All that Sokolov offers in the way of definition is that his expressionism aims at a "maximum of expression" and a "dynamism of perception and thinking."

Sokolov's poetry which follows the "charter" is a very questionable illustration of his tenets. The ambitious, five-page "Fešenebel'naja noč'," offered as an "essay in chromatic versification," is nothing more than free verse, reminiscent of Xlebnikov's "Zverinec," otherwise differing very little from Sokolov's earlier verse. He merely tries to shock the reader more (*veter-onanist, tverdoe kak posle zapora kalo ljudej, anal'noe otverstie doma*), but, as before, he combines this anti-aesthetic imagery with the salon dandyism of the "Mezzanine." Too often he slavishly follows the imagism he castigates so much in the polemical part of the book, and he himself indulges in "hyperbolism" ("A woman's foot with an instep as steep as the peak of the Himalayas"). In other poems he experiments, and not very originally, with rhyme.

There was no poetry in Sokolov's *Èkspressionizm*, which appeared in the summer of 1920 and contained little that was not already in *Bunt èkspressionista*: the phrases about "maximum of expression" and "dynamism of perception" appear again, and so does the expressed desire to create a synthesis of "amorphous Russian futurism," the latter being subdivided by Sokolov into imagism, rhythmism, cubism, and euphonism. In fact, he visualizes a new era of "high futurism" (i.e., expressionism) which will replace "early futurism," just as was the case with the Italian Renaissance—or so he says.

The immodesty of the last remark is explained elsewhere in the essay: Sokolov writes that some time during the spring of 1920 he learned about the existence of expressionism in Europe and rejoiced at being able to show L'vov-Rogačevskij that he, Sokolov, was not a curio and an ephemeron, but part of a strong, European-wide movement which had already touched Germany, Austria, Czechoslovakia, Latvia, and Finland. The unexpected perspective obviously made Sokolov slightly dizzy, and, as a result, this work of his is more fanfare than substance; accordingly, his predilection for making syntheses went to extremes: he not only generously labels as "geniuses" some of his contemporaries (and, by implication, himself), but claims in a rather Xlestakovian way to have created the theory of expressionism in the theater, which combines the Meiningen theater, the Moscow Art Theater, Serge Diaghilev, Vsevolod Mejerxol'd, Aleksej Kručenyx, Nikolaj Evreinov, Vjačeslav Ivanov, Max Reinhardt, the communist cultural commissar Keržencev, Aleksandr Tairov, and Marinetti.

Sokolov also names his source of information about western European expressionism—Teodor Markovič Levit (b. 1904), a shadowy, marginal figure in the literature of that time, who, like Majakovskij, wrote texts for "Rosta" propaganda posters, was briefly listed as a futurist in a Poets' Union publication, published little poetry, was a member of a later, expressionist-oriented group "Moskovskij Parnas," and soon faded out of literature. It was evidently he who also acquainted Sokolov with Kasimir Edschmidt's well known book *Über den Expressionismus in der Literatur und die neue Dichtung*, after which Sokolov decided that Edschmidt's and his main tenets "coincide" technically, philosophically, and historically. However, the only examples he gives of this coincidence are the desire to know the essence of things and the presence of expressionism in all nations and times.[9]

---

[9] The edition of Edschmidt's book referred to by Sokolov is Berlin, 1919. Sokolov does not show, however, any firsthand knowledge of Edschmidt's essay (originally

Sokolov wrote this time as the leader of a group, and he named, in addition to himself, three Russian expressionists: Boris Zemenkov, Gurij Sidorov, and Sergej Reksin.[10]

Boris Sergeevič Zemenkov (b. 1902) joined the group, like Sokolov, both as a theoretician and a poet. His only book of verse, *Steorin* [sic] *s prosed'ju: Voennye stixi èkspressionista* (1920), consists of poetical impressions, based on his own Civil War experience and is bursting with catachrestic imagery strongly reminiscent of Šeršenevič, who clearly also influenced Zemenkov's metrics and rhyme. Of slightly later origin is his treatise *Koryto umozaključenij* (1920), written at the end of 1919 and the beginning of 1920, in which Zemenkov tries to lay foundations for expressionism in the pictorial arts. This abstruse essay, filled with foreign words whose meanings, one suspects, are not quite clear to the author, is, nevertheless, on the whole, closer to the idea of Western expressionism than the theoretical writings of Sokolov. Zemenkov postulates the final aim of the world as "dematerialization" and demands from art persuasiveness rather than truth, a persuasiveness which is equal to that of incantation.

Gurij Sidorov was, by that time, not only the author of two books of verse, but a veteran of the young Soviet movie industry as well: he had appeared in Majakovskij's film version of Jack London's *Martin Eden* (called *Ne dlja deneg rodivšijsja*). Both of his books, *Raskolotoe solnce* (a *poèma*) and *Vedro ognja*, were rather inarticulate imitations of Majakovskij (especially of *Oblako v štanax*), Šeršenevič (rhyme), and Bol'šakov (occasional agrammaticality). In spite of this imitativeness, his poetry is not devoid of some wild originality of its own. His joining the expressionists probably resulted in his third publication, *Xoduli* (1920), for which Zemenkov designed the cover. This and the next slim collection, *Jalik* (also published in 1920, but including much of his earlier poetry), contain strongly emotional love poems and hyperbolic cityscapes, written in rhymed or rhymeless verse and using most available metrical possibilities —from traditional meters to free verse. There is much self-affirmation in this poetry as well as the "cosmic" quality, fashionable at that time, occasionally approaching the apocalyptic. Sidorov's nervous, chaotic, and ecstatic quality was to disappear in his last known book of verse *Stebli*

---

a speech of 1917), and it is safe to assume that he knew it only from Levit's oral report. Many of Edschmidt's points are, in fact, in direct contradiction to what Sokolov said in his theoretical writings.

[10] Otherwise, Reksin published only one "Majakovskian" imagist-oriented poem in the miscellany *Jav'* (Moscow, 1919). He never published anything with the expressionists.

(1922), a poetic account of his affair with a married woman, slightly reminiscent of Vasilij Kamenskij's poetry.

In the meantime, Sokolov continued to publish theoretical writings, and his most ambitious undertaking in this genre was *Bedeker po èkspressionizmu* (1920), the "climax" of Russian expressionism just before its sudden demise. It was a naïve attempt to "deepen" his earlier theories by using impressive sounding "-ism" terms and by filling his sentences with as many names as possible. Sokolov kept his old slogan about "the maximum of expression," but found his previous synthesis of futurism too narrow. He declared his expressionism not only a "new vision," but a "synthesis of all achievements in all arts." In addition to this "synthesism," as he calls it, Sokolov added two more essential features: "Europeanism" and "transcendentalism-noumenalism." All this develops into a paean to Henri Bergson, whose philosophy is declared to be the successor to outdated Christianity. In addition to this, Sokolov scatters throughout the essay undeveloped ideas and statements like "perhaps there are 20 or 30 dimensions and 20 or 30 sensations," or "We have a feeling of the end." He also alludes to the broadest possible spiritual basis for his expressionism including occultism, anthroposophy, etc. Anticipating well deserved criticism, Sokolov hastens to add at the end that his expressionism "is not a moronic desire on the part of a few young poetasters to attach to themselves, at any price, a sonorous label with an 'ism' in it in order to conceal, somehow, the mediocrity of their doggerel."

At the same time or, most likely, a little earlier, Sokolov also published his "propaganda leaflet," *Renessans XX veka*, in which he announced the existence of "pan-futurism." The list of those scientists, writers, and scholars who belong to the movement (among them, Bergson, Einstein, Losskij, Roman Jakobson, Vasilij Rozanov) as well as artists, poets (of which only four Russians are named: Majakovskij, Sokolov, Šeršenevič, and Xlebnikov), et al. is endless and makes the leaflet a veritable orgy of names, to which Sokolov adds another list—that of outstanding "passeists." At the end of his catalogue, the author calls himself the "Russian Marinetti" and proclaims the arrival of the "Renaissance of the twentieth century" from his "Mount Sinai."

Despite all his efforts, the days of Sokolov's expressionism were numbered, and all his attempts to inflate it were in vain. One reason he failed was that in Sokolov's (or in his fellow expressionists') poetic practice he could never separate himself from Russian imagism, then the dernier cri in poetry. Sokolov not only imitated some aspects of Mariengof's rhyme or much of Šeršenevič's imagery, but often aped and caricatured the early, pre-imagist poems of the latter, which probably both flattered and amused Šeršenevič. At any rate, Šeršenevič later wrote, "The most murderous criticism of my poetry is to be found not in the witchdoctor-like babbling of the Fričes and the Kogans [the Marxist critics of the day] but in Sokolov's book of verse."[11]

There is reason to believe that all three expressionists tried to join imagism but, perhaps, were eventually given a cold shoulder. The second edition of Sidorov's *Jalik* was published by the "Imažinisty" publishing enterprise. Zemenkov managed to attract two imagists, including Šeršenevič himself, to the miscellany *Ot mamy na pjat' minut* (1920), which he published under the imprint "Farširovannye manžety" and in which he also printed his poetry—still labeled expressionist. As for Ippolit Sokolov, in 1921 he published his next essay, *Imažinistika*, which was, for the most part on a higher level than all his expressionist theory and makes one suspect that the author seriously considered becoming a leader and a theoretician in the imagist movement. In his book Sokolov applies a statistical method to the study of tropes and tries to trace a quantitative and qualitative evolution of tropes in Russian poetry, beginning with Kantemir. Imagism (which, he again insists, ought to be called in Russian *imažizm*, and not *imažinizm*) is considered a logical, and crowning, stage in this evolution. Sokolov even points to the ways in which the image has to develop in the future, and here he touches on some tenets of future constructivism.

All three expressionists of the "first period" were preparing new books of verse, and Sokolov intended to investigate expressionism in painting and in the theater and also announced a book with the title "Opyt postroenija programm nemeckogo, francuzskogo, ital'janskogo i anglijskogo ėkspressionizma." Edschmidt's book mentioned above was announced for publication in Teodor Levit's translation and with his preface and commentaries.[12]

In 1921 the original expressionists, after the disintegration of their group, tried alliances with some of the mushrooming and short-lived grouplets of the period. Zemenkov went over to the *ničevoki* ("nothingists"); Sokolov's peregrinations were more complex. Zemenkov applied for membership in the *ničevoki* group on April 15, 1921; and only two days later he was a cosignatory of one of their "decrees." Then he wrote

---

[11] Vadim Šeršenevič, *2 × 2 = 5: Listy imažinista* (Moscow: Imažinisty, 1920), p. 16; Ivan Gruzinov also treated Sokolov contemptuously in *Gostinica dlja putešestvujuščix v prekrasnom*, no. 4 (1924), p. 13.

[12] See p. 8 of *Ėkspressionizm*. Levit was mentioned by Veniamin Kaverin as his co-member in the group "Zelenoe Kol'co" in 1919 and "junoša neobyčajnyx sposobnostej i poznanij" (V. Kaverin, *Avtobiografičeskie rasskazy*, Moscow: Biblioteka "Ogonek," 1961, p. 52).

his own "decree" on painting, became a part of the *ničevoki* "tribunal," and planned the publication of a book of his own verse in their publishing enterprise called Xobo (Hobo) which they defined as "a refined, revolutionary tramp." Much of this activity was in direct contradiction to their much-quoted slogan which read in part, "Don't write anything, don't publish anything."[13]

The *ničevoki*, whose history has many fascinating details and deserves closer scrutiny, originated in Rostov-on-the-Don in August, 1920, and had a rather unpromising start with the slim collection *Vam*. This book contained a militant and incoherent manifesto which "buried" both imagism and expressionism and some poetry which was nothing but a poor imitation of imagism. It is to the *ničevoki*'s credit, though, that later, when the "movement" moved to Moscow, they openly recognized imagism.[14] "Anyone can be a *ničevok*" was declared in one of their decrees,[15] and they divided themselves into "*ničevoki* of creativity" and "*ničevoki* of life." Only one of them developed into a poet worthy of attention—Rjurik Rok, whose best poetry can be found in the *poèma*, *Ot Rjurika Roka čtenie* (1921), but even in this work with apocalyptical overtones he remained essentially an imagist (with an admixture of the "Scythian" Esenin and of Majakovskij). The ideology of the *ničevoki* consisted not only of revolutionary nihilism with the professed aim "to disintegrate and to demoralize belles-lettres," but of anti-materialism and a sort of neo-idealism. Minor points of their aesthetics echoed expressionism. The *ničevoki* were active until the beginning of 1923, and in January and February, 1922, they confronted Majakovskij and denied him the right to purge Soviet poetry, as he had attempted to do at that time. Some reports say that the *ničevoki* were unsuccessful in this attempt and were finally condemned, sharing this "honor" with such unlikely bedfellows as Axmatova and Vjačeslav Ivanov.[16] The climax of the *ničevoki* movement can be found in the two editions of *Sobačij jaščik* (1921 and 1923), in which they practically admitted their desire to be a Russian version of Dada and which, this time in better agreement with their slogans, contained no poetry. Within this framework, it is of interest to note that Rjurik Rok was preparing a book on both Dada and expressionism and that he published a translation of Ivan Goll's *Die Chapliniade*.[17]

[13] *Ničevoki: Sobačij jaščik* (Moscow: Xobo, 1923), p. 8.
[14] Ibid., p. 8.
[15] Ibid., p. 6.
[16] See V. Majakovskij, *Polnoe sobranie sočinenij v trinadcati tomax*, XII (Moscow, 1919), 461.
[17] Rjurik Rok, *Sorok sorokov: Dialektičeskie poèmy ničevokom sodejannye* (Moscow: Xobo, 1923), p. 4.

In Xobo's last publication, there was an announcement of three books by the "fuist" poets, and this is an interesting piece of evidence not only of ties between the two groups of that period but also of the transition from the "imagist" expressionism to the "centrifugist" expressionism, as we shall see later.

Actually, the fuists began their activities much earlier, at the beginning of 1921, when they published a collection under the laconic title *A*. One of the three co-authors was Ippolit Sokolov, who contributed four poems containing apocalyptic (cf. "feeling of the end" in his *Bedeker po èxpressionizmu*) and macabre imagery. There is urbanism and the familiar desire to shock in these poems, but there is also the appearance of Lenin, radio, and "the victory of new forces." Sokolov did not continue his association with the fuists, but one of the original three remained a fuist to the very end. He was Boris Perelëšin, and he was joined in the next collection (*Mozgovoj ražžiž*, 1922) by Nikolaj Lepok in advocating the destruction of imagery. Finally, their ranks were increased in April, 1923, when Boris Nesmelov became a part of the group, and they published the three books mentioned above.[18] However, this seeming climax was also the end of fuism. Their theory, as presented in the prefaces to each of the three publications, though complicated by the inclusion of the Asiatic element, obviously entered the stage of stagnation and vagueness, while looking ambitious and super-polemical on the surface. Nesmelov and Perelëšin were later associated with Kručenyx.[19] Despite their theoretical shortcomings, some of the fuists' poetry would reward the attention not only of the scholar, but of the general reader as well. Their rhyme and some of their poetical syntax definitely deserve study. Sergej Bobrov, the most important of *Centrifuga's* leaders, was benevolent towards Lepok and Perelëšin and wrote about their deriving from the poetic practice of his group.[20]

The fuists were, however, only a transitional group, leading to "centrifugist" expressionism. The beginnings of this second phase of Russian expressionism are to be found in the 16-page joint collection *Èkspressionisty*, published in 1921, again in Moscow. The participants, in addition to the ubiquitous Ippolit Sokolov, were Sergej Spasskij, Evgenij Gabrilovič, and Boris Lapin. Sokolov was generously represented in what was apparently his farewell to poetry. These poems add little to what he wrote

---

[18] *Bel'ma Salara* by Perelëšin, *Dialektika segodnja* by Perelëšin and Lepok, and *Rodit' mužčinam* by Nesmelov—all three in April, 1923.

[19] For example, Nesmelov wrote a preface to Kručenyx's *Četyre fonetičeskix romana* (Moscow, 1927).

[20] *Pečat' i Revoljucija*, no. 1 (1922), p. 301.

before: the same preoccupation with tropes based on remote associations or on shocking contrasts, this time with an occasional "baring the device" (*obnaženie priema*), and the same free verse (occasionally rhymed). His themes here are mostly erotic, but there are also theosophical and the familiar apocalyptical poems. Sergej Dmitrievič Spasskij (1898–1956) had many avant-garde affiliations throughout his varied, but peripheral, literary career; but he remained essentially a neo-symbolist poet (a fact especially noticeable in the poems printed in *Ėkspressionisty*). Occasionally he reminds one of Pasternak, which, of course, does not contradict his neo-symbolist quality.[21]

The same Pasternakian (or rather "Centrifugist") features can be discerned in the bold, though obscure, imagery of Boris Matveevič Lapin (1905–1941), who, together with Evgenij Iosifovič Gabrilovič (b. 1899), soon became a central figure of this late, non-imagist, "Centrifuge"-oriented phase in Russian expressionism. Gabrilovič's prose in *Ėkspressionisty* is highly elaborate in its use of punctuation, typographical effects, and contrasting syntactic structures as well as in its fragmentation, mixing of planes, repetitions, and pauses. It is movie-script-like prose with an admixture of lyrical poetry and bears resemblance to both Andrej Belyj and Viktor Šklovskij.

Similar traits can be seen in Gabrilovič's other expressionist prose, "Lamentacija," printed in *Molnijanin* (Moscow, 1922), where fragmentation again reigns supreme and where minimal description is combined with stream of consciousness. Gabrilovič shares the pages of this book with Lapin, who contributes fourteen poems. Lapin's poetry is definitely immature, but intriguing, being a strange melange of metrical and metaphorical restraint (especially if compared with imagists and their followers) and show-off erudition. Noticeable is a strong German orientation, particularly in epigraphs and dedications; and it extends from expres-

---

[21] Spasskij was a prolific poet and probably had his work printed in more cities than any other Russian man of letters. His literary debut took place in Tiflis, then he published poetry not only in Moscow and Petrograd (Leningrad), but in Penza, Nižnij Novgorod, Rjazan', and Samarkand as well. Before expressionism, he was close to futurism: K. Bol'šakov wrote a preface to his collection of verse *Kak sneg* (Moscow, 1917), he knew Xlebnikov well, participated in the *Gazeta futuristov*, and recited his poetry in "Kafe Poètov." In 1930 he joined "Pereval." In addition to several collections of his own poems, much of his poetry can be found in miscellanies of different origin and affiliations (e.g., *Bez muz*, *Jav'*, *Sopo*, and even in the antifuturist *Čet i nečet*). More interesting than his books of poems are his autobiographical *povest'* in verse *Neudačniki* (Moscow, 1929) and his short novel *Parad osuždennyx* (Leningrad, 1931), which has Velimir Xlebnikov among the characters and depicts scenes of life in the anarchist colonies in Moscow soon after the Revolution. Also noteworthy is his book of memoirs, *Majakovskij i ego sputniki* (Leningrad, 1940).

sionism (Ehrenstein) to the romantic (E. T. A. Hoffmann) and the preromantic times (Jacob Lenz); there are even German titles to poems. Also noticeable is a tribute to the "Centrifuge": an epigraph from Bobrov, a dedication to Ivan Aksënov, and some influence of Pasternak. The distinguishing characteristic of Lapin's poetry is, however, a certain strangeness which touches on the absurd and makes him a predecessor of Russian *oberiuty*. *Molnijanin* aimed, however, at more than showing samples of expressionist prose and poetry. It begins with a mannered manifesto, full of topical allusions, which makes one thing clear: Lapin and Gabrilovič consider themselves expressionists; they reject Russian futurism as a passé thing, and they show respect for the "Moskovskij Parnas" group (which, incidentally, published *Molnijanin*). This expressionism is not defined, except that they "re-tune (their) iron lyres to a lyrical tonality" and thus say good-bye (*au*) to their futurism, which, nevertheless, means "no return to the *Casta diva*." Highly interesting is the list of writers' ancestors, "the indestructible names of our uncles"; and they make it clear that "the shining world of expressionism" has practically no other names to its credit besides Aseev, Aksënov, Johannes Becher, Bobrov, Albert Ehrenstein, Pasternak, and Xlebnikov.

"The Parnassus of Moscow," whose branch the second-wave expressionists considered themselves to be, was actually nothing but the last stage in the evolution of the "Centrifuge" group, in which prerevolutionary neosymbolism is to be found merged with futurism. To be sure, the "Centrifuge" proper still existed by that time, and "The Parnassus of Moscow" included poets who did not belong to the "Centrifuge," namely, Benar, Adalis, Šišov, V. Kovalevskij, et al. Nevertheless, Sergej Bobrov and Ivan Aksënov, the two "Centrifuge" leaders who were very influential in the Muscovite literary circles at the beginning of the 1920's, clearly dominated "The Parnassus of Moscow." The group published two issues of the miscellany with the same name, but No. 1 never went on sale. It was announced, however, that Bobrov, Aksënov, Aseev, Spasskij, and Gabrilovič were to be among the contributors. The second issue did appear, containing, among other things, poetry, prose, and criticism by Bobrov, poetry by Aksënov (who, in the prefatory essay to the book, emphasized the unconscious element in art and considered the latter an attempt to remember a dream) and by another Centrifugist, Evgenij Šilling, a story written jointly by Lapin (whose poetry was also included) and Gabrilovič and a critical review by Levit on a book about E. T. A. Hoffmann. What makes the issue especially interesting for us, however, is the abundance of translations from German expressionists, nearly all of them done by Lapin and many of them accompanied by brief notes about the author and/or biographical data as well as by announcements of plans to publish books of translations of their work. Among this material there is an essay by Wieland Herzfelde on the funeral of another expressionist, Alfred Lichtenstein, poems by Lichtenstein himself (who is presented as "the greatest poet of early expressionism"), as well as by Jakob van Hoddis, and Georg Heym. There are references (epigraphs, etc.) to, and translations from, other European poets and writers from Angelus Silesius to the obscure Dadaist Teophil Müller, and from Jules Romains to the Communist poet and Comintern functionary, Henri Guilbeaux.

It was "The Parnassus of Moscow," too, that published the only book of verse by Boris Lapin in October, 1922 (1923 on the cover). The book was entitled 1922-*ja kniga stixov* and was the most promising publication of Russian expressionism as well as, ironically, its finale. In the highly allusive preface to the book, Lapin both rejects in advance the possible accusation that the collection is "non-futurist" and attacks the futurists.[22] Surprisingly, the antidote to harmful futurism and an ideal ("life in poetry" as opposed to the contemporary futurist "tours de force and pretensions" [*fokusničestvo i akterstvo*]) are found in Russian and German romanticism of the early nineteenth century. Žukovskij, Novalis,[23] and Schelling are mentioned (or quoted) and further, in a poem, Lapin calls Tieck, Brentano, and Eichendorff "my forefathers." The forty-seven poems comprising the collection are not, however, a reconstruction of that professed romanticism, though names, motives, and echoes from German romantic poetry can be found in abundance on its pages: in addition to those named above, there are E. T. A. Hoffmann, Kleist, Friedrich Schlegel, and La Motte-Fouqué. This does not exhaust the German, and Western, element: one can add Schiller and even Klopstock as well as Kipling and the English ballad (there is also American *couleur locale* in the mention of Chicago and the word "boss"). On the Russian side, Žukovskij is joined by Lermontov, Marlinskij, and Fet. There had hardly been such wholesale embracing of German romanticism in Russian literature since Žukovskij, and the themes of Lapin's poetry conform to, or, at least, do not contradict it: poetry, death, the motives of the "last romantic," alchemy, astrology. Part of this derives, of course, from Sergej Bobrov and the early "Centrifuge" cult of Hoffmann. The Bobrovian display of erudition, references to Bobrov's works, his very tone of voice can be found in these poems; and the introductory poem resembles the

---

[22] It is difficult to say whom he calls "futurists." My guess is that these futurists might be the budding constructivists, who might have caused the disintegration of the postrevolutionary "Centrifuge."

[23] Cf. Petnikov's preoccupation with Novalis.

verse manifesto of the "Centrifuge" of 1914. However, there is a definite parodic element, perhaps a version of German romantic irony for the Russian 1920's, which, nevertheless, touches on the absurd and clearly anticipates the poetry of Xarms and other *oberiu* poets. Finally, there is the cult of Xlebnikov:[24] a poem on his death, a few neologisms in his manner, some use of his "internal declension"; and finally, in the "postscript" to the book, Xlebnikov, to the readers' surprise, is proclaimed to be the one who found the needed middle ground between futurism and neoclassical trends.

The prevalent impression of Lapin's book is that of strangeness, which originates mainly from the fact that the romantic "content" is presented in an avant-garde garb. There are irrelevant epithets as well as a general predilection for the absurd, the reverse and the oxymora (*tixo i šumno; severojug; a dol opuščen vzoru*) and a tendency for mixing everything. There are also many irregularities, used, however, with restraint, especially the "agrammatical" and "asyntactical" structures (*ub'ja; ulybaja; očen' ljubov', očen' krov'*). Being a "Centrifuge" apprentice, Lapin indulges in metrical adventures; he is attracted by unusual kinds of the *udarnik* verse and even produces a *dol'nik* version of the Sapphic stanza. At least some of Lapin's metrical rarities might represent an attempt to reproduce jazz rhythms in verse (see the postscript to the book). Lexically, Lapin's poetry is a curious cocktail of various names, coarse words, technical terms, foreign words, and neologisms; and the sonic aspect is characterized by the use of paronomasia and of many kinds of and devices in the area of rhyme, such as assonances, split rhymes, placing rhyming clausulas far from each other, etc.

The book ends with an envoy in prose addressed to Gabrilovič which contains some expressionist ideas, though the word "expressionism" is never used. Lapin speaks about the "elusive reality of objects," juxtaposes the futurist "word-material" and the expressionist "word-revelation" and says: "Turning into a word, reality becomes a new world on this earth, the world of wild reflex and relativity."

Lapin's book, though not a masterpiece, was interesting and highly promising; but it was hardly noticed. Brjusov, in a review,[25] condescendingly admitted that Lapin was gifted, but chided him for affectation, tortuous imagery, "desperate" metaphors, childish distortion of language, and obscurity (which, Brjusov hastens to add, any reader of Mallarmé, the decadents, and the futurists could decipher).

---

[24] See also Lapin's "Xlebnikovu" in *Molnijanin*. Also see V. Kovalevskij's poem "Na smert' Xlebnikova" in no. 2 of *Moskovskij Parnas*.

[25] *Pečat' i Revoljucija*, no. 4 (1923), p. 136.

But this book was also the end of Russian expressionism. When, in November, 1924, the Brjusov Institute (from which Lapin graduated) organized an Evening of Contemporary Poetry, such poetry was represented by *Lef, Oktjabr', Molodaja Gvardija, Pereval*, and the imagists, but it boasted no expressionists, fuists or *ničevoki*. Ippolit Sokolov became active in the Soviet movie industry;[26] Zemenkov illustrated books and wrote books on the arts, and later became associated with art museums;[27] Gabrilovič first joined the constructivists, then achieved prominence in journalism and especially in film script writing. His recent memoirs[28] ignore the expressionist episode in his life. Lapin, too, was close to the constructivists. He came to neglect poetry and soon was known in Soviet literature mainly as a journalist who specialized in the frontier areas of Russia. He traveled abroad a good deal and wrote, individually and jointly, numerous books about his experiences. He faithfully followed all the twists and turns of Soviet literary policies and published his essays in a collection on the construction of the White Sea canal or in a miscellany entitled *I žizn' xoroša i žit' xorošo*, among other things. He also translated. Some time before World War II he became a war correspondent. He continued to write verse, but seldom published it, except that he used it occasionally in his books of essays. Some of his unpublished poetry, taken from the archive of his friend Il'ja Èrenburg's widow, appeared in the anthology, *Sovetskie poèty pavšie na Velikoj Otečestvennoj Vojne* (Biblioteka poèta, Bol'šaja serija, M.-L., 1965). No avant-garde features can be seen in it, even in the poems dated 1923.

Such was the "external" history of Russian expressionism. An analysis of its poetry for the establishment of its precise ties with the West and contemporary Russian poetry is a task for the future; here it could only be suggested. Even without such analysis, however, a few things can be summed up at the end of this survey. Expressionism was born in Russia

---

[26] His first book on the subject was *Kinoscenarij: Teorija i texnika* (Moscow, 1926). Later he wrote a monograph on Chaplin, *Čarli Čaplin: Žizn' i tvorčestvo* (Moscow, 1938) and compiled *Istorija sovetskogo kinoiskusstva zvukovogo perioda* (Moscow, 1940). The switch of Russian avant-garde poets to cinematography is a subject worth investigating. Rjurik Rok and his brother, Marian Goring, became movie directors (they published jointly the book on art in the United States, *Xèp, xèp, mister* [Moscow: Proletkul't, 1926]); one day they did not come back from a European trip and they continued to be active in films abroad. Seršenevič switched from imagist poems to writing books about film actors. Kručenyx wrote a book *Govorjaščee kino* (Moscow, 1928). Especially interesting is the impact of German expressionist film evident in Kuzmin's last book of verse, *Forel' razbivaet led* (Leningrad, 1929).

[27] *Udarnoe iskusstvo okon satiry* (1930), *Grafika v bytu* (1930); *Gogol' v Moskve* (1954), *Pamjatnye mesta Moskvy* (1959); *Očerki moskovskoj žizni* (1962).

[28] Evg. Gabrilovič, *O tom čto prošlo* (Moscow: Iskusstvo, 1967).

in 1919 as one of numerous groups which, at that time, tried to build a new avant-garde poetry on the ruins of pre-revolutionary Russian futurism; it lasted until 1923. Its pioneer was Ippolit Sokolov, who aspired to create a synthesis of Russian futurism in his theory, but in his poetry continued the traditions of the "Mezzanine of Poetry," resulting only in another version of imagism. When news about "genuine" expressionism in the West reached Sokolov, he was forced partly to change and to broaden considerably his theoretical tenets; and this led to overextension: Sokolov's expressionism burst like a soap bubble. Participants in this early, imagist phase of expressionism had contact with some other avant-garde groups of the period, such as the *ničevoki* and the fuists who, in their turn, displayed occasional interest in Western expressionism. The second phase was connected with the names of Lapin and Gabrilovič, and for them expressionism meant an amalgam of "Centrifuge," German expressionism, Xlebnikov, and German romanticism. The "Centrifuge" itself during this last period of its existence came close to German expressionism—closer, in fact, than any variety of Russian expressionism proper.

An unmistakable achievement of Russian expressionism was the poetry of Boris Lapin which, though lacking maturity, showed originality and great potentialities. His poetry, whether in its real or potential qualities, was a part of an unnoticed flowering which included the late verse of Benedikt Livšic, Mixail Kuzmin, Ivan Aksënov, and Sergej Bobrov and which would be an interesting subject for future study and appreciation. This poetry was overshadowed by the publicity accompanying other avant-garde groups, not to mention the groups encouraged by the government; and an investigation of this poetry has yet to be made. So far, out of all this poetry, only the genius of Mandel'štam begins to break through the crust of neglect accumulated for decades.

NIEBORÓW, THE *KUŹNICA* PROGRAM, AND THE ROLE OF THE YOUNG IN THE STALINIZATION OF POLISH LITERATURE

BY

LAWRENCE L. THOMAS

ON JANUARY 11, 1948, under the auspices of the Department of Books and Literature of the Ministry of Culture and Art, there began a seven-day (or ten-day?—accounts differ) seminar for young writers at Nieborów, an estate formerly belonging to a member of the Radziwiłł family, near Łowicz. The ministry provided stipends for forty-four young writers to attend the seminar; seven more came at their own expense.[1] The seminar was not a leisurely affair; reports of it speak of days filled with lectures by older writers,[2] discussions, and evenings devoted to showings of modern films. Intellectual exchanges at the seminar seem to have been intense; conversations and debates between the young writers continued late into the night; for four days of the seminar, a bulletin-board newspaper was published which contained lampoons of the young writers' mentors.[3]

The seminar was supposed to contribute to the young writers' artistic, and political, maturation. Whether it did either is a debatable point, but it did produce two notable results—a sense of generational solidarity among the young writers, and a feeling that literature and politics could not be kept separate; it also produced a confrontation between the young writers and their elders, but more of that later. In the words of one of the youthful participants:[4]

In the private conversations of the literary "Warsaw group" . . . a project for making literature conform more to the party line was developing. "Conforming to the party line," of course, in the sense of a political determination of one's ideological attitude. It followed from the long discussions that many of the young people had become

---

[1] Published accounts of the seminar differ in their estimate of the number of youthful participants. The figures I have given come from St. Wygodzki, "List do redaktora," *Odrodzenie* (1948), no. 7, p. 4. Since he and H. Michalski organized the seminar, it is likely that his figures are correct.

[2] The older writers were St. Wygodzki, H. Michalski, J. Iwaszkiewicz, M. Jastrun, J. Kott, W. Kubacki, S. Pollak, A. Stawar, A. Wat, K. Wyka, J. Zawiejski, and St. Żółkiewski. See A. Włodek, "To więcej niż 'Obiady czwartkowe' (Studium młodych pisarzy w Nieborowie)," *Dziennik literacki* (1948), no. 6, pp. 1–2.

[3] Cf., e.g., L. Bartelski, "Na studium w Nieborowie," *Nowiny literackie* (1948), no. 7, p. 2.

[4] Both quotations are taken from T. Konwicki, "Studium nieborowskie," *Twórczość* (1948), no. 2, p. 123.

tired of a martyr-like perch astraddle the barricade. The difficult situation in literature does not allow a writer to fence himself off with apoliticalness—which, under present conditions, is quite clearly political.

Young writers from all the literary centers of Poland had the possibility of meeting each other, of speaking frankly and in a comradely fashion about many problems that lay close to their hearts. From these public and private discussions they acquired many new experiences and new problems.

Both the sense of fellowship among the young and their attitude toward literature and its tasks were to have an important effect on the development of Polish literature in the years immediately following, but, before turning to these matters, we must arrive at some definition of what constituted a "young writer" in the sense in which that term will be used in this article.

The "young writers" or, as they were soon to be derisively called, the "pimply ones," were by and large born between 1920 and 1930. But a purely chronological definition of them would be highly inadequate. Some of the writers who did not join the ranks of the young and had no sense of solidarity with them were scarcely any older. A definition which corresponds to the realities must rest upon a description of life experiences. The vast majority of the young writers were people whose education had not attained the university level before the German occupation of Poland. They were then forced to get an education either by their own wits or, if they were fortunate enough to be in one of the larger centers, by attending an underground university. The atmosphere was abnormal, lectures were sporadic, and there was no easy access to well-stocked libraries. Furthermore, many of them had to work for a living and, in addition, most of them took part in the underground resistance movement. If they were very young, they participated in petty sabotage; others were either among the guerrilla units in the countryside or were regular members of the underground army.[5] Very few of them were in the People's Army (under Communist direction)—most were in the National Army (under the direction of the Polish Government in Exile, in London). A surprisingly large number of the most influential ones participated in the Warsaw Uprising (in which two of Poland's most promising young poets, Krzysztof Baczyński and Tadeusz Gajcy, lost their lives). The loss of Warsaw, the

---

[5] As one of the young writers put it: "Most hurt by the war were ... those whose university studies occurred during the occupation. For us [those studies] were replaced—we know this very well—by guerrilla warfare and sabotage. And when we lacked even these possibilities we got our experiences where we could ... We were workers, prisoners, and conspirators. For us, studies were something secondary, and it was an unusual coincidence when one of us had the possibility of studying in the secret university classes." L. Bartelski, loc. cit., n. 3.

loss of the country to the Communists, and the fact that they were greeted, immediately after the close of hostilities, as the "bespitted dwarves of reaction"[6] produced in them a sense of despair, disillusion, and bitterness. They had spent five years under extremely trying conditions (in some instances, in concentration camps); they had lived within a cult of patriotism, individual and collective heroism, and loyalty. All their hopes had come to nothing. They were, however, still very young, and there was yet time to seek other gods.[7]

The authorities sought ways to harness the energies of the young and to provide them with new gods. For the youth at large they utilized the League of Fighting Youth, a conspiratorial organization organized by the Communists in 1942. Within its framework, in 1945, was formed the Academic League of Fighting Youth. In 1948, these and other youth organizations were merged into the all-embracing League of Polish Youth (which was to last until Gomułka returned to power, in 1956). University youth engaged in Polonistics were approached in another manner: "The gradual winning-over of teachers and students took place within an organized format—through yearly, problem-oriented scholarly meetings of students of Polish literature, beginning with 1946."[8] Quite a number of the young writers belonged to such organized endeavors, but they still presented a special problem. They had to be won over in their capacity as writers and they, in turn, had to win over their peers. To achieve this end, several short-lived periodicals were started, which catered to, and were edited by, young writers.[9] These periodicals had an ephemeral existence because the young were simply too frank and blunt—they had not yet learned a sufficiently Aesopic language. A good example is that of R. Bratny, the editor of *Pokolenie* (Generation).[10] In the sixth number of his journal, he wrote[11]

---

[6] See R. Bratny, "Próba rachunku," *Pokolenie* (1946), no. 1, p. 1.

[7] R. Bratny wrote a fictional account of members of his generation and the Warsaw Uprising in his novel *Kolumbowie-rocznik 20* (Warsaw, 1957). A fine non-fiction account of wartime experiences in Warsaw was written by L. Bartelski: *Genealogia ocalonych. Szkice o latach 1939-1944* (Cracow, 1963).

[8] St. Żółkiewski, in St. Żółkiewski and J. Stradecki, *Rozwój badań literatury polskiej w latach 1944-1954* (Warsaw, 1955), p. 15. The themes of the meetings, and a bibliography, are given on pp. 96-97. The theme of the first meeting was "The Political Attitude of the Youth in View of the Transformations Taking Place in Contemporary Life."

[9] See A. Lisiecka, *Pokolenie "pryszczatych"* (Warsaw, 1964), pp. 8, 16. See also W. Woroszylski's introduction to T. Borowski, *Utwory zebrane* (Warsaw, 1954), I, 48-52. Woroszylski was later to complain bitterly about the suppression of some of these periodicals; see his "Notes for a Biography," in P. Mayewski, ed., *The Broken Mirror* (New York, 1958), pp. 117-118.

[10] This biweekly, which had a short existence from the end of 1946 to the beginning

On what is a "recalcitrant" to base the conviction that the USSR's *raison d'état* is our *raison d'état*? Probably on the following material premises: A Poland friendly toward Russia is a Poland useful to Russia. A Poland inimical toward Russia is—then there is no Poland. The period of the *General Gouvernement* proved at least that. A Poland without an alliance with Russia is always a potential victim of Germany.

And now—it seems to me, that one can do something for Poland only by simply *doing* something for her, by working. Isn't that so?

Bratny received his answer in the very next issue of his own journal. Wł. Sokorski pointed out that there could hardly be any talk of an "ideological turning point when the current policy of the People's Government is being explained in terms of topical political realism," and when "the youngest literary generation comes forward with a slogan of neopositivism and practical rationalism." He also warned against "loyalism," "accommodation," and an "apotheosis of the philosophy of Švejk."[12]

The path to Communism was, therefore, not an easy one for the young. But they were gradually educated and indoctrinated, particularly those who were living in the intellectual centers of that time, Łódź and Warsaw. Their disillusion gradually gave way to a new enthusiasm. By the time the Nieborów seminar was convened, they were ready to launch a frontal attack against the older writers and react seriously to H. Michalski's opening statements: "The generation of older writers is a slave in its relationship to tradition. The new generation is in a better position at least in that it can achieve an indifferent attitude toward past literature."[13]

At Nieborów, the wrath of the young was not directed at older writers in general, but specifically against those who were connected, in one way or another, with the literary newspaper *Kuźnica* (The Smithy).[14] The

---

of 1947, is not to be confused with the periodical of the same name which began publishing early in 1948 under the auspices of the League of Polish Youth.

[11] "List," *Pokolenie*, no. 6, p. 1.

[12] "O istotę przełomu," *Pokolenie* (1947), no. 1, p. 1. Woroszylski, in his introduction to Borowski's collected works (cf. supra n. 9), was later to defend the periodical: "The completely negative view of the periodical is wrong. Its task was to break down the attitudes of the post-AK [National Army. L.L.T.] youth—attitudes which were hostile toward the People's Government. The task was fulfilled as far as large segments of the youth are concerned. The editorial board of *Pokolenie* was composed exclusively of former AK people, and it knew how to find a common language with its colleagues from the underground."

[13] Reported by Włodek, op. cit. (supra n. 2), p. 1.

[14] *Kuźnica* began to appear in Łódź, in June, 1945. Until October of that year it appeared in monthly issues, after that it became a weekly. It was moved to Warsaw in June, 1949. In March, 1950, it ceased publication. Its chief editor was St. Żółkiewski until June, 1949, when he was replaced by P. Hoffman.

reason the *Kuźnica* group bore the brunt of the assault is not hard to find. In some instances, there were personal scores to settle, since some writers in the group had taken part in the effort to restructure the thinking of the younger generation, but the real reason lay, rather, in the fact that the *Kuźnica* group represented, as a whole, a *liberal* Marxist view. The members of the group shared an eighteenth-century rationalism (hence the name of the newspaper—a reference to Hugo Kołłątaj's circle) anticlericalism (note the reference to Boy-Żeleński in the appendix to this paper), a belief in social justice, and a firm conviction that Polish economic and social conditions had to be reformed. That is why their journal carried so many articles having to do with land reform, expropriation, book publishing, coal production, the lot of the peasant, the reform of the school system, and any number of other social, economic, or humanitarian subjects. They were not proponents of a Soviet-style revolution, but rather, believed in Poland's ability to find its own road to socialism.[15] In the years 1945–1948 there were countless debates about realism on the pages of *Kuźnica*—but one will look in vain for a serious reference to Socialist Realism. Russian (and Soviet Russian) literature was discussed, and translations from it were published, but much more space was devoted to West European and American literature. An anthology of Russian poetry in translation published by M. Jastrun and S. Pollak in 1947 was later attacked for presenting a distorted picture of Soviet poetry because it emphasized such poets as Pasternak and Mandel'štam while completely ignoring such poets as D. Bednyj, Surkov, and Isakovskij.[16] *Kuźnica*'s literary policy, for all the polemics which were constantly raging on its pages, was quite liberal.[17] It is, in retrospect, amusing to see what K. Brandys was writing in 1946:[18]

We often hear alarums from the opposite side to the effect that the cultural activity of the Left is leading to the imposition of foreign models on Polish literature—in short, models from Soviet literature.

---

[15] In this, they were following the ideas sketched out during the war by A. Lampe. See his "Z projektu tez programowych, Sierpień, 1943 r.", in *Myśli o nowej Polsce* (Warsaw, 1948), pp. 16–17.

[16] W. Woroszylski, "W walce o literaturę Polski Ludowej," *Twórczość* (1951), no. 5, p. 115. For an attempt at rehabilitation of the *Kuźnica* group's attitude toward Soviet literature, see St. Żółkiewski, *Przepowiednie i wspomnienia* (Warsaw, 1963), p. 341.

[17] For a discussion of these policies see M. Stępień, "Program literacki *Kuźnicy*," *Ruch literacki* (1964), no. 4, pp. 169–186; Z. Żabicki, "Spór o realizm w publicystyce *Kuźnicy* 1945–1948," in *Z problemów literatury polskiej XX wieku* (Warsaw, 1965), III, 106–130; and especially Z. Żabicki, *Kuźnica i jej program literacki* (Cracow, 1966).

[18] Both quotations are taken from his article "Do pisarzy," *Kuźnica* (1946), no. 42, p. 1.

There can be no thought today of borrowing recipes for Polish literature from anywhere whatever. We can open our artistic door only with our own Open, Sesame! Soviet literature arose under conditions peculiar to it, amidst difficulties and storms which are far removed from us. It continues to be formed by imperatives which are foreign to us. The socio-economic structure from which it springs is different from ours. It may be that poems and novels which have arisen in a land of kolkhozes have to be different from those which arise where there are no kolkhozes.

There is every reason to believe that the imposition of Soviet models on Polish literature—which is probably to be dated from a speech given by President Bierut on the occasion of the opening of a radio station in Wrocław on November 16, 1947, on the eve of a congress of the Union of Polish Writers in the same city—was viewed with consternation by the majority of the writers of the *Kuźnica* group. There was a period of marking-time and watchful waiting for political events from 1947 to 1949.[19] Later surveys of the history of literary events of those years all complain that the *Kuźnica* group had lost its militancy.[20] The militancy of the youth, however, was just beginning, and they were quite willing to anticipate political events rather than wait for them. It was of special interest to the Party that the revolt of the youth be directed specifically against the *Kuźnica* group. As the only body of consistently radical, progressive literary figures in the country, they represented a special danger in their reluctance to accept Stalinism.

The majority (29) of the young writers at Nieborów were poets and the most violent misunderstanding, if it may be called that, took place concerning poetics. The young poets accused older ones of being formalistic, hermetic, classical, and isolated from contemporary events. When Jastrun assured them that excessive formalism should be replaced by a revolutionary content, they immediately pointed out the discrepancy between his statement and his own poetic practice. They demanded that poetry serve the working class, that it be immediately communicative, and that its content be enlarged to include current events, reportage, and Party slogans. T. Borowski summarized their stand: "It seems to me that a writer who would accept the principles of Marxist humanism, would have to rethink his esthetic concepts, transform the technical devices of

---

[19] A consideration of these political events is outside the scope of this paper. Suffice it to say that the evolution of Polish literature always followed upon them, never out-distanced them.

[20] See, for example, St. Żółkiewski and J. Stradecki, op. cit. (supra n. 8), pp. 18–19; W. Woroszylski, op. cit. (supra n. 16), pp. 106, 112 ff.; H. Markiewicz, "Krytyka literacka w latach 1945–1951," *Twórczość* (1952), no. 3, pp. 128 ff.; G. Lasota, "Czas przełomu," in *Kierunek natarcia* (Warsaw, 1953), pp. 30 ff.; J. Andrzejewski, *Partia i twórczość pisarza* (Warsaw, 1952), pp. 136, 137.

his workshop, and make a conscious selection of the reader for whom he is writing."[21] They were very well aware of their position and their (largely future) role: as A. Kamieńska, who wrote perhaps the fullest account of the Nieborów seminar, put it,[22]

> In the main, the young writers know that their role is that of social ideologists—hence, perhaps, the publicistic tone of their experiments, a tone which is still, often, too easy and simplistic. They feel the necessity of breaking through the existing caste structure of the intellectuals by means of broader social ties. There is talk of a second career for the writer, of positions of social and cultural activity which are opening up.

The discussion of poetry, which of course had implications for literary craftsmanship in general, initiated in 1948 was to rage on well into 1950, and we need not dwell on it for the purposes of this article. What we need to do is establish the Party's role in the whole process. Contemporary accounts are, of course, silent on the subject. It was not until much later that these matters came to be discussed openly. The frankest statements I have been able to locate were made by A. Lisiecka.[23]

> The spontaneous sectarianism of the "young" was headed in the same direction as the official road-sign of cultural policy after the routing of the "rightist deviation." It is also no accident that they (Bratny, Woroszylski, Konwicki) joined in with the general current of criticism of the so-called "opportunism" in the policy of our party before 1948. And it is also no accident that *Kuźnica* was condemned precisely for opportunism and rightist deviation at the same time.

> The "pimply ones" did not operate in a vacuum. They were a literary grouping of a generation of young workers, engineers, and members of the intelligentsia. They were also—as writers—a salient ideological vanguard whose actions and words radiated over a whole generation. They had the fullest, most affirmative, to some degree "model" consciousness of the programs of the time .... Earlier and with more self-assurance than Ważyk or even Kierczyńska they launched into a conquest of literature under the banner of Ždanovism .... It was a revolt only in name—in fact, it was headed in the direction of blind obedience.

To draw an analogy with the history of Soviet literature, it is as if the

---

[21] "Początek niełatwej roboty," *Odrodzenie* (1948), no. 7, p. 5. See also A. Włodek, op. cit. (supra n. 2), and A. Kamieńska, "Czterdziestu najmłodszych pisarzy," *Wieś* (1948), no. 5, pp. 1-2.

[22] Op. cit. (supra n. 21), p. 2.

[23] Op. cit. (supra n. 9). The quotations are taken from pp. 18 and 178-179. In a much milder and, of course, much more guarded fashion, St. Żółkiewski makes the same kind of statements with regard to the work of T. Borowski (who, until his suicide in 1951, was the most ideologically prolific of the young writers), op. cit. (supra n. 16), p. 349. W. Woroszylski, in his introduction to T. Borowski, *Utwory zebrane* (Warsaw, 1954) I, 64, states that Borowski became a Party member immediately after the Nieborów seminar.

Polish communists had deliberately participated in the formation of a RAPP, whose subsequent activities it would direct and control. For the next few years moderate Polish writers were to find themselves hemmed in by Party directives on the one hand and a howling pack of young political activists on the other.

APPENDIX
THE *KUŹNICA* PROGRAM

Published on the first page of the first number of the newspaper, June 1, 1945, and signed by the *Kuźnica* group. On p. 4 the editorial committee is defined as consisting of Z. Nałkowska, A. B. Dobrowolski, M. Jastrun, J. Kott, A. Rudnicki, and St. Żółkiewski. In issue no. 51/2 of 1947, on p. 16, there are caricatures of the *Kuźnica* group. There are drawings of P. Hertz, K. Brandys, R. Matuszewski, M. Jastrun, J. Kott, A. Ważyk, St. Żółkiewski, A. Rudnicki, and J. Żuławski.

We are on the threshold of a long-lasting peace. Fascism has been crushed. The Polish State is being rebuilt within new boundaries pushed to the West, with a unified national composition. It is capable of overcoming its economic backwardness and entering into new ways of developing its industry. Social reforms which the progressive faction of society has been striving for for decades have become fact. Hence follow a number of inevitable consequences such as profound changes in the internal structure of the state and a reversal of our relations with our Slavic neighbors.

Can the creators of national culture—starting with the village teacher, the engineer, the doctor, the architect, and the university professor, and ending with the actor, the literary figure, and the composer—remain, in the face of the events taking place, in an atmosphere of eclectic flaccidness, mystic, pessimistic, elite flights from reality, a cowardly avoidance of taking up a clear and unmistakable position?

Our group represents that wing of creators of Polish culture (and, therefore, of the national future), whose attitude is defined by the radicalism of progressive Polish thought. We spring from the same soil from which, 150 years ago, arose the Enlightenment and the Polish Jacobinism of Kołłątaj and Staszic, Jezierski and Jasiński. Hence, taking our cue from native sources, we are bringing the *Smithy* back to life. For us, the landmarks of the development of Polish radical thought are the debunked, living Adam Mickiewicz and Juliusz Słowacki, Edward Dembowski, Ludwik Waryński, Montwiłł-Mirecki and Julian Marchlewski, Narcyza Żmichowska, and Eliza Orzeszkowa, Aleksander Świętochowski, Ludwig Krzywicki, Wacław Nałkowski, and Boy-Żeleński. Since we are an independent organ, we reject no one who, in the years of great national diaster, comprehended the stern lesson of history. We have no intention either of encompassing all possible viewpoints or of publishing, in our columns, any amnesty for every indecision or covert or overt obscurantism We will not yield an inch to the shadows of the past.

We also reject all conceptions of isolation, or opposition, or elevation of the Polish intelligentsia above or outside of radical peasant and worker movements. We welcome the inevitable process of the rise of a new worker and peasant intelligentsia, which will bring its own contribution to the building of Polish culture. Our task is to aid in the process of the grafting of new strata of intelligentsia onto the progressive and radical achievements of our ancient culture.

In the actions and the program of the Provisional Government we see a consistent policy for the establishment of social justice in Poland. Within this democratic reality we recognize the necessity of a sober criticism which will assist in the unification of national forces in the task of re-building and development of the nation. We reject the rampant, snobbish dependence on everything which has already become old-fashioned abroad. However, taking our stand on the Polish tradition, we nonetheless feel a sense of union with those values which the achievements of European creativity, the contemporary great Soviet culture, and the radical thought of the West have contributed to realistic humanism. As professors of a lay ethic, we will combat divisive post-war symptoms beginning with harmful pacifism and ending with all sorts of attempts to return to mystical and irrational slogans which have been so compromised.

In the radical smithy of the intelligentsia we wish to forge the foundations of a progressive Polish ideology and culture in the broadest sense.

ON MODERN RUSSIAN LITERATURE AND THE WEST

BY

CZESŁAW MIŁOSZ

IT HAS BEEN said long ago that amazement is the mother of philosophy and this is undoubtedly true. Yet in our approach to literature we often tend to be ashamed of our most naïve reactions. The few words which follow are an attempt to be as uninhibited and simple as possible.

One thing is absolutely incomprehensible to me in all the success of such Russian writers as Pasternak or Solženicyn with the Western public and especially Western literary critics. If we assume that critics and reviewers who praise these writers so highly are sincere, a question arises, which it is perhaps tactless to ask—but in matters of human spirit tact is an ally of hypocrisy. The question I am unable to answer is, are these critics, and readers too, aware that they are maintaining double standards?

For it is obvious that a literary critic who writes on those Russian authors is compelled, by the very nature of his profession, to look at them in conjunction with their contemporaries in other countries—their rivals for fame. He must compare, juxtapose, draw parallels, establish contrasts. And any normal human being who reads these Russian writers in America, for instance, must have one dominant feeling—that of shame. Not because he himself is privileged, lives in an affluent society, and is not endangered by whims of those in power, while the Russian writers tell of suffering imposed upon millions of their fellow-men. The shame should come from the realization that freedom of choice is being misused today by Western writers for the purpose of creating dehumanized literature —true, perhaps, under the pretext of rebelling against a dehumanized world. But are the Western writers themselves conscious of the difference between a genuine concern and what is just subservience to fashion or a market device?

To put it briefly, Pasternak's and Solženicyn's works, in a sense, "judge" all contemporary literature, by reintroducing a hierarchy of values, the renunciation of which threatens mankind with madness. Or, to put it another way, they reestablish a clear distinction between what is serious in human life and what is considered serious by people who *s žiru besjatsja.*

And let me note a formidable paradox: in the countries where Christian churches thrive there are practically no genuinely Christian novels. Truly Christian writing has had to come from Russia where Christians have been persecuted for several decades. Then how can a critic, if he is a hot-blooded creature and not a frog, placidly bypass such a challenge and not shout on the rooftops his protest against the use made of freedom by Western literati?

I have my reservations as to Pasternak's poetics and Solženicyn's novelistic technique. Yet poetics and techniques should be appraised not as abstract notions but according to the function they perform in given circumstances. Pasternak's high regard for the poet as a passive receptacle, as a shaman in touch with ineffable forces of life, stems from a premise common to the all-European artistic movement prior to World War I, namely, that Art is the highest ritual, replacing religion. A peculiar logic of development led then in the West to a gradual estrangement of the poet from ordinary mortals, and to a break in communication. An analogous transformation, behind which there is a desire to make Art completely autonomous, may be observed in painting: after all, modern painting may be considered to be the result of the destruction of the human figure, which was accomplished by cubists prior to World War I. But Pasternak's belief in the surpreme poetic wisdom, achieved by the poet through passivity, proved to be his best defense. It protected him from ratiocinations. Under circumstances where anyone who engaged in discourse was lost, he succeeded in safeguarding his integrity and dignity. Moreover, what in the West favored a priestly hauteur of the poet and thus contributed to his isolation, became for Pasternak an encouragement to listen and to convey innumerable voices of human despair, with love and compassion. As for Solženicyn, he is often weighed down by the technique which bears a strong imprint of socialist realism. Yet in his effort to convert socialist realism into realism he achieves a directness which has been lost by the post-Joycean novel.

I am preparing for print the memoirs of my late friend Aleksander Wat. Since many chapters deal with his odyssey through Soviet prisons including Lubjanka, and are, in fact, a gallery of portraits from various strata of Soviet society, I live very much in the Russia depicted by Pasternak and Solženicyn. Instead of hammering upon the contrast between the meaning of the written word in Russia and in the West, I take the liberty of translating two fragments of those memoirs, for they tell more than I would be able to say.

Wat found himself in October of 1940 in a transfer prison (*peresyl'naya tjur'ma*) in Kiev and he relates his readings of graffiti in the prison toilet:

> Inscriptions by Russians: if not for underworld communications (*blatnye*) and not for practical purposes, they are philosophic. Many poems, *častuškas*. Mostly obscene,

but not without a wild energy, by members of the authentic underworld, by pseudo-underworld, and by the intelligentsia. Some words still linger in my memory:

> Ot Vorkuty idut katoržane,
> Vory, bljadi, millionaja rat'.
> (From Vorkuta prisoners are walking,
> Thieves, whores, an army million-strong.)

—a lyrical poem, a work of a true poet, poignant.

I was most impressed by the meditative sentences I was to find later on, the same in every provincial prison.

> Bud' prokljat kto vydumal nazvanie
> Ispravitel'no-trudovye lagerja.
> (Be cursed whoever invented the name:
> Corrective-labor camps):

this is the beginning of a poem.

The most beautiful was an age-old maxim:

> Ot sumy i tjur'my ne otkazyvajsja.
> Vyxodjaščij ne sumis',
> Vyxodjaščij ne radujsja.
> (Do not refuse the beggar's bag and prison.
> Entering, be not disturbed,
> Leaving, do not rejoice.)

—like an antiphon of a chorus, in the ancient tragedy of the Russian people. In the old maxim of run-away serfs and pilgrims the fate of all the nation expressed itself now, the most fully, the most truthfully, and with the greatest dignity. I was spellbound by the solemn tone of that sentence, by its severe truth. But I, a newcomer from another world, defended myself against such spells: "The terror of bolsheviks could not maintain itself without a national acquiescence to the beggar's bag and to prison; *les idées-forces*—conceived in the West by a monstrous tangle of oppression and rebellion— found in Russia their land of election," I thought scornfully. But when I returned to my plank-bed and, among the quarrels of my miserable co-prisoners so Occidental a short time ago, repeated those words in their solemn anapestic cadence, I knew: here was a sacred thing. I closed my eyes and I tried to visualize the face of an unknown prisoner who on a dirty wall of a prison toilet, instead of a cry "Help, help!" wrote those solemnly humble words. A man from the people? One of millions? In senselessness and in aimlessness, in the spontaneous accidental nature of his own agony, he found the meaning for the fate of his nation. After twenty-five years, when I read *One Day in the Life of Ivan Denisovič* and "Matrëna's Home," those words return and with them the face, as I imagined it, of a Christian and, at the same time, of a stoic sage of the Russia of concentration camps.

Here is another fragment—Wat's reflections upon the behavior of his cell-mate at Lubjanka, a young sailor, and upon Soviet youth in general:

> I observed innumerable times, later, already out of prison, that in the young people's minds there was an iron barrier between large and small prohibitions. The big prohibitions were taboos and were surrounded by an appropriate halo as in a

primeval era. But by breaking small prohibitions one was proving his toughness and defied good manners which in his opinion had been condemned by history; it was a compensation for obeying taboos. In 1944, in Ili (Kazakhstan), a convalescent soldier of my acquaintance raved about the riches and distractions to be found in small Bulgarian towns, where he had been during the campaign. "Would you like to stay there for good ?," I asked. "Never in the world! No freedom there." I established without difficulty that he had in mind freedom, for instance, to get dead drunk in a public place, to spit and blow his nose on the floor, to push old men and women in a streetcar, to curse without inhibition, etc. Other freedoms not only were of no use to him but encumbered him like Nessos' net, and, what is worse, they would enforce upon him free decisions as to his fate, while he had been taught to abandon them forever. In this sense, Stalin's terroristic paternalism reduced a few Soviet generations to the level of the Guarani Indians in the eighteenth-century Jesuit communistic republic. The barrier in the minds I am speaking of, was, however, movable: that brought an element of diversity into the routine of the Stalinist epoch. For instance, the word *žid* was in 1942 under the rigors of a taboo, but already two years later, in Ili, the deported Polish Jews were showered with a hail of that insult as well as—sporadically—with stones by children and teenagers from the local highschool. Today, in 1965, those pioneers from Ili are young engineers, literary critics, apparatchiks. Whoever in the West does not realize that there is such an "iron barrier" in the minds and is unable to understand the answer of the soldier, will not comprehend very much of psycho-ideology and of the young people's rebellion in the USSR.

In order to liberate themselves from Stalin's heritage in *their souls*, they must first "detach themselves from the enemy"; like a snake sheds its skin in the springtime, they must throw off not only any concern with Stalinism, Communism, revisionism, but those ugly words themselves. In this sense, the free men are not Andrej Voznesenskij, Evtušenko, or Tarsis but such people as the poet Iosif Brodskij, as Solženicyn of "Matrëna's Home," as Terc-Sinjavskij of his last (apolitical!) works. For political thinking has become so distorted and so depraved during the long, long half-century, that one has to begin with tearing it out, together with its roots, from one's soul, so that the ground be prepared for a political thing, healthy, humane, which makes for the *virtu* of a free citizen. Anticommunists in the West do not understand this. Of course, acts of political rebellion and, even more, a political rebellion of the mind, are useful, for they squeeze concessions from the rulers, but nevertheless in the Russian Empire they will remain—for many years to come—abortive, powerless to touch off a movement of the masses; personally I see the hope of Russia not in them but in life itself, in existing (*Sein*) in an utterly different spiritual space.

With what delight the adolescent Brodskij discovered John Donne and how beautifully his discovery bore fruit! How effectively Sinjavskij (in his aphorisms), liberated himself from the nightmares of anti-Stalinist neurosis and renewed himself at the sources of ancient Russian folk religiosity! What great internal beauty emanates from the folkish-Christian *caritas* of Solženicyn! How movingly Pasternak identified himself with the misfortune of the whole, immense *mnogostradal'nyj* Russian people! With what depth of suffering Axmatova set herself and the world aflame, when standing at her son's prison. No other such values have been created by Russian literature since Blok's "The Twelve," in nearly fifty years. Thinking young Soviet men and women know incomparably more about the miseries and monstrosities of Communism than do Western Sovietologists; every word of authentic religion, of idealistic thought and of disinterested beauty in poetry and in ethics falls there upon fertile ground. Could I repeat here my recent conversations with representatives of that thinking youth! Beckett, Gombrowicz, Genêt, Sartre, various strip teases (personally, I esteem them) may only blight young seedlings there . . . . "

This is what Wat said. I, too, have a considerable amount of esteem for literary "strip teases." Yet I think of them with sadness. Perhaps in the crazy, careening rush of artistic revolutions succeeding each other in Western literature and art there is a sort of inevitability. But we live in one world. If thinking Russians are ready to pay dearly, with their careers, their lives, for their attempts to restore moral and artistic values, while their Western colleagues engage in sheer destruction for destruction's sake, what can we expect from a true, and not official, meeting of the East and the West? And how can literary critics writing on Pasternak or Solženicyn so easily shirk their duty, which calls them to point out this ominous disparity?

www.ingramcontent.com/pod-product-compliance
Lightning Source LLC
Chambersburg PA
CBHW021709230426
43668CB00008B/779